Philobiblon
Ricardi de Bury

PHILOBIBLON

RICARDI DE BURY

TEXTUM EDITUM

ET ANGLICE REDDITUM

AB ERNESTO THOMAS

QUONDAM SCHOLARI COLLEGII SANCTAE

ET INDIVIDUAE TRINITATIS

NUNC RECENSUIT MICHAEL MACLAGAN

EIUSDEM COLLEGII SOCIUS

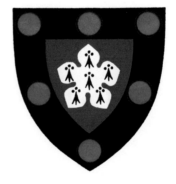

OXONII

APUD PRELUM SHAKESPEARE HEAD NUNCUPATUM

BASILIUS BLACKWELL

PHILOBIBLON

RICHARD DE BURY

THE TEXT

AND TRANSLATION OF

E. C. THOMAS

SOMETIME SCHOLAR OF TRINITY COLLEGE

EDITED WITH A FOREWORD BY

MICHAEL MACLAGAN

FELLOW OF TRINITY COLLEGE

OXFORD

PUBLISHED FOR THE SHAKESPEARE HEAD PRESS BY

BASIL BLACKWELL

Reprinted in Great Britain by offset from the edition of 1960
by Alden & Mowbray Ltd., Oxford
and bound by the Kemp Hall Bindery, Oxford

CONTENTS

℃ This edition of the *Philobiblon* of Richard de Bury was prepared in honour of the seventieth birthday, on 29 May 1959, of Sir Basil Blackwell by his sons and colleagues. The book was designed by Ruari McLean and printed by Vivian Ridler at the University Press, Oxford. The type is 'Monotype' Centaur. The lettering and coats of arms on the title-pages were drawn by John Woodcock.

INTRODUCTION

BIOGRAPHICAL[1]

THOUGH the account[2] given of himself by Richard de Bury in the *Philobiblon* is far from satisfying our curiosity, it must be reckoned a fortunate circumstance that he has told us so much as he has of his career and of his pursuits. Apart from the autobiographical particulars which he has there set down, we should have had but scanty materials from which to present his portrait. The chief authority for his life is William de Chambre, one of the Durham historians, whose sketch,[3] however, is so slight that, although he tells us of the Bishop's great affection for books, and his wonderful collection of them, he says nothing of his project of founding a library at Oxford, and makes no mention of the *Philobiblon*.

℩ Richard de Bury was born on 24 January 1287 in a little hamlet near Bury St. Edmund's, in Suffolk, which was famed

[1] The text of the Introduction is by Thomas: the notes are by the present editor though they often incorporate material from Thomas's edition.

[2] A fuller account of the career of Bishop de Bury has since been given by Dr. N. Denholm-Young in the *Transactions of the Royal Historical Society*, 4th series, vol. xx (1937), and reprinted as the first item in his 'Collected Papers on Mediaeval Subjects' (Blackwell, 1946). Cited as Denholm-Young with

page references to the latter version.

[3] First printed in Wharton's *Anglia Sacra*, but more accurately by Raine in the Surtees Society edition of the *Scriptores Tres*. The section on de Bury is probably partly from a tablet in the Cathedral and partly from Chambre's reminiscences retailed in 1380 or later. See 'The Birth of a Chronicle' in *Bodleian Quarterly Record*, vol. vii, no. 80, pp. 325–8, and Denholm-Young, p. 2.

Introduction

for its monastery.[1] His father was Sir Richard Aungervile, a knight, whose ancestor had come over with the Conqueror, and settled in Leicestershire, where the family held the manor of Willoughby. The charge of his education was undertaken by a rector-uncle, John de Willoughby, who in the fashion of the times had assumed the name of his birth-place. From the grammar-school he was sent to Oxford,[2] where he is said to have distinguished himself in philosophy and theology. It is sometimes said that he then became a Benedictine monk in the Convent at Durham; but if this is so, it is curious that none of the Durham authorities refer to the circumstance, and it seems more likely that the story rests upon a blunder in the chronicle of Adam de Murimuth. His university distinction appears to have attracted the attention of the Court, and he was called from his studies to become governor of Prince Edward of Windsor, afterwards Edward III, who was born in 1312. Dibdin gives de Bury credit for having communicated to his royal pupil some share of his own affection for books.

❡ In the year 1322[3] he was appointed Chamberlain of Chester, having apparently already held the office of clerk to the justices of Chester, though the identity of the Ricardus de Sancto Edmundo of the Chester records with our Richard de Bury had been obscured until Mr. J. E. Bailey recently called

---

[1] The *Dictionary of National Biography*, following the *Encyclopaedia Britannica* and the *Biographia Britannica* says 1281, but this date rests upon an entirely mistaken reading of the final note in the Cottonian copy.

[2] He was probably at Oxford about the years 1302–12 and may be presumed to have taken in this time a M.A. and also a B.D.—Denholm-Young, p. 2.

[3] Rather fuller information is now available on his career, and he can be traced as a clerk at Chester as early as Oct. 1316.—Ibid. 3.

Biographical

attention to it.[1] He was next appointed the King's principal receiver in Gascony,[2] which was then an English province. In this position he became mixed up with the wretched intrigues and disturbances which ended in the deposition of Edward II. When Prince Edward and his mother Isabella were at Paris, in 1325, Richard furnished them with a large sum of money which he had received in his office. The King's lieutenant in Gascony pursued Richard with four-and-twenty lancers to Paris, where, in fear of his life, Richard had to hide himself for seven days in the Campanile of the Friars Minor.

❡ The accession to the throne, on 14 January 1327, of the prince, to whom he had had such opportunities of endearing himself, was a decisive event for the fortunes of de Bury. He was appointed, in quick succession, Cofferer to the King, then Treasurer of the Wardrobe,[3] and afterwards Clerk of the Privy Seal.[4] The King, moreover, repeatedly wrote to the

---

[1] See *Papers of the Manchester Literary Club*, 1880, pp. 283–8; *Academy*, 20 Mar. 1880, p. 214. In the Wells register he is called 'Ricardus de Bury, alias de S. Edmundo'. Wharton, *Angl. Sacra*, i. 589.

[2] In fact de Bury had held other offices, including that of clerk to Sir Robert Holland, Justice of Chester, before he became Constable (that is, the chief financial officer) in Gascony for three months in 1326. It was at this phase of his life that he compiled, probably in 1324–5, his *Liber Epistolaris* which has been nobly edited for the Roxburghe Club by Denholm-Young (1950) from Lord Harlech's manuscript at Brogyntyn.

[3] His inventory of the Crown jewels on resigning their charge is printed in *Archaeologia*, vol. x, pp. 241 ff.

[4] On his later career in detail see Denholm-Young, pp. 8–16; also T. F. Tout, *Chapters in Mediaeval Administrative History*, vol. iii, esp. pp. 54–55, 175–6. Tout has shown in his *Chapters* the part played by de Bury in developing the importance of the Privy Seal. It is not clear what part de Bury played in the events leading to the accession of Edward III. A famous letter of September 1329 or 1330, written in his holograph, in the Vatican Archives begins a secret correspondence with the Pope and has on it the first royal autograph in English history. See C. G. Crump in *English Historical Review*, vol. xxvi(1911), pp. 331–2. Also Pantin, *English Church in XIV Century*, pp. 77–78. The letter has been reproduced in C. Johnson and H. Jenkinson, *English Court Hand* (1915).

Introduction

Pope, with his own hand, recommending his 'beloved clerk and secretary' for ecclesiastical promotion.

In 1330, and again in 1333, de Bury was sent as ambassador to the Papal Court, which was then in 'Babylonian captivity' at Avignon. It was an age of splendour and display, and Richard fully maintained the dignity of his office and of his master. Whenever he visited the Pope, or any of the cardinals, he was accompanied by twenty clerks uniformly attired, and by thirty-six esquires, all wearing his livery. It is of more interest to note that during his stay at Avignon, he made the acquaintance of Petrarch, who has left upon record a brief account of his intercourse with him, the extent of which has been somewhat exaggerated. So far from a literary correspondence having been established between them, Petrarch complains that he could get no answer to his letters: 'quamvis saepe litteris interpellatus exspectationi meae non aliter quam obstinato silentio satisfecit.'[1] He so commended himself to the Pope, John XXII, that he was made his principal chaplain; and, besides other privileges, received a rochet in place of a bull for the next vacant bishopric in England. His ecclesiastical preferments[2] were already so numerous and valuable, that he was master of an income of 5,000 marks. The most considerable of them was the deanery of Wells, to which he was appointed in 1333—'a goodly preferment in those daies, better I think than the Bishoprick is now', as Bishop Godwin says.[3] Nor had he long to wait for the promised bishopric.

 ¶ On 25 September in the same year, the See of Durham

---

[1] *Ep. Fam.* iii. 1. De Sade, i. 165–9, points out that their friendship must have been formed during de Bury's first visit, as Petrarch was absent from Avignon in 1333.

[2] For a full list see Denholm-Young, pp. 24–26.

[3] *Bishops of England, 1601,* p. 524.

Biographical

became vacant by the death of Bishop Louis de Beaumont. The vacancy led to an unfortunate conflict of interests, in which, however, the King appears to have been more to blame than de Bury. On 7 October Edward issued his license to the Prior and Convent of Durham to elect a new bishop, and the choice of the electors fell upon their learned sub-prior, Robert de Graystanes. Having received letters proclamatory from the Archbishop of York, Graystanes proceeded to the King at Ludgershall, to ask for the temporalities. Meantime the King had written to the Prior and Convent and also to the Pope to secure the appointment of Richard de Bury; and his answer to Graystanes on his arrival was, that he did not wish to offend the Pope,[1] who had already provided de Bury to the See, and could not, therefore, consent to his election. Graystanes returned to York, and after taking advice, was consecrated by the Archbishop of York, and duly installed at Durham, after which he made another ineffectual attempt to see the King. It was impossible for Graystanes and the Convent to withstand the King further, and Graystanes returned to his cloister—'sine episcopatu episcopus'. He has left upon record a temperate statement of his case, in which he refrains from throwing any of the blame upon de Bury.[2]

❡ Richard was on his return from Avignon while these things were happening, and the temporalities were only restored to him on 7 December. On the 19th of the same

[1] This was on 14 October, and apparently cost de Bury 9,000 florins. See *Richard d'Aungerville of Bury* (Surtees Society, vol. 119, 1910), p. 9. This volume is an important source of documents connected with de Bury, includ-ing fragments of his register. There is a useful preface, unsigned but in fact from the hand of Dean Kitchin of Durham.

[2] In *Scriptores Tres*, pp. 120 ff.

Introduction

month, the Sunday before Christmas Day, he was consecrated by the Archbishop of Canterbury, in the Abbey of the
Black Friars of Chertsey, the Bishop of Lincoln paying all the
expenses at the King's direction. Richard was installed by
proxy on 10 January following, but was not enthroned in person until 5 June, amid great festivities, attended by the King
and Queen, the Queen Mother, the King of Scots, two arch-
bishops, five bishops, seven earls with their countesses, and
all the magnates north of the Trent, together with numbers
of knights and esquires, and still more abbots, priors, and
religious persons, and an innumerable multitude of common
folk. The Bishop was present at Newcastle, on 19 June, when
Edward of Balliol did homage to the King.

The Bishop had already on 3 February in the same year
been appointed Lord Treasurer, and on 28 September following he exchanged the Golden Keys for the Great Seal. A few
days before his appointment as Lord Chancellor he was made
a commissioner, with the Bishops of Coventry and Norwich,
to visit Oxford[1] to inquire into the grave disturbances which
had led to a secession of a large number of the students to
Stamford. In 1332 Bury had visited the sister university of
Cambridge as one of the commissioners to inquire into the
state of the King's scholars there; and it was perhaps upon
this occasion that he became a member of the Gild of St.
Mary—one of the two gilds which founded Corpus Christi
College.

℆ De Bury did not long occupy the Marble Chair of the

---

[1] Where he probably stayed at   *MSS. Comm.*: 6th Report, App., p. 548
Merton College, with which, as will be   (Merton Archives).
seen, he had other associations. *Hist.*

Biographical

Chancellor, whether because its duties were not very congenial to one who has spoken so disparagingly of the law, or perhaps more probably because his services were even more urgently required elsewhere. At all events, on 6 June 1335 at York he restored the Great Seal to the King, who transferred it to John Stratford, the Archbishop of Canterbury. The attention of the King and nation was at this time chiefly concentrated upon foreign politics and the claim put forward by Edward to the French Crown. The keenest and coolest intellects of the age were required for the tasks of diplomacy, and the choice of the sovereign again fell upon de Bury. The next few years of the Bishop's life were mainly devoted to this service, in the course of which he thrice visited Paris and spent some time in Flanders, Hainault, and Germany.

℃ Before proceeding abroad, however, the Bishop was called upon to put his Palatinate into a condition to resist a threatened attack from the Scottish border. The King spent great part of the year 1335–6 in the north, and appears to have been at Auckland from 12 to 21 December 1335, where he was no doubt the guest of the man whom he delighted to honour. A truce having been made with the Scotch, Richard de Bury was appointed a special ambassador with the Bishop of Winchester and two others to the King of France with full powers to treat as to a proposed crusade, and as to all questions in dispute between Edward and Philip, and also to treat for peace with David Bruce. Their appointment was on 6 July 1336, and they returned on 29 September, the result of the mission being unfavourable. In October the King appears to have been again at Auckland. During the year 1337 Richard de Bury was three times put at the head of commissioners

xvii

Introduction

nominated to lay the King's intentions before assemblies of magnates at York and Newcastle, as to an invasion of Scotland.[1]

℟ All the energies of the King were engaged in pushing forward preparations for the struggle with the French King. But in deference to the Pope he consented to make another attempt to agree with his adversary; and on 21 June 1338 full powers were given to John Stratford, Archbishop of Canterbury, Richard de Bury and others, to treat of all causes of difference. On 16 July the King himself sailed for Antwerp, where he landed on the 22nd, and on the same day revoked the powers conferred upon his ambassadors, and they were not renewed until 15 November. Edward was busily engaged in procuring allies and engaging assistance in the Low Countries and Germany. De Bury accompanied his master on his magnificent progress up the Rhine in August and September to that stately meeting between Edward and the Emperor Lewis at Coblentz, which must have rivalled in the splendour of its pageantry the more famous meeting on the Field of the Cloth of Gold.[2] Edward and Lewis sat on thrones surrounded by more than 17,000 barons and knights, and Edward was appointed Vicar-General of the Empire. The task of negotiating with Edward's allies proceeded slowly, and we find Richard named as one of the hostages for the observance of a treaty made with the Duke of Brabant on 22 June 1339.

[1] Authority for de Bury's various diplomatic appointments can be traced in Rymer's *Foedera* and details of his expenses and entourage can be discovered in the Calendars of Patent and Close Rolls. There are fuller references in Thomas's own notes.

[2] See Pauli, *Bilder aus Alt-England* (1860), pp. 118 ff., for an account of this mission drawn from the Wardrobe Accounts.

Biographical

Edward was so pressed for money that he was obliged to pledge his crowns. In September a commission was issued to the Prince, the Archbishop of Canterbury, and de Bury, to lay the King's pecuniary difficulties before his people, and Richard seems to have returned to England on 10 October[1] in that year, and by December was again in his bishopric. His dread and dislike to the war which had now begun is clearly visible in his letter to the Prior of Durham, ordering thanksgiving for the naval victory of Sluys in 1340. Though he was appointed with others to treat of peace with Philip on 10 April 1341, there seems to be no record of his expenses; and, as a fresh commission was issued for the same purpose to other ambassadors on 24 July, it is probable that de Bury did not proceed upon the embassy: at all events we find him attending parliament at Easter, and appointed with others to consider the charges of treason preferred by the King against the Archbishop of Canterbury[2] and other ministers of the Crown.

❡ This appears, accordingly, to have been de Bury's last visit to the Continent. Henceforward, save for his attendances in Parliament, he seems to have spent his time in the care of his diocese and in communion with his books, a communion less uninterrupted, doubtless, than the peace-loving Bishop would have wished, by the more military duties imposed upon him in the protection of the Palatinate.

[1] His accounts for the period 12 July 1338 to 10 October 1339 are in the Record Office (Var. Acct. 311–36) and show that in these fifteen months he spent over £1,500. He only received £1,341 odd back: see *Cal. Close Rolls* (*1339–41*), pp. 582, 597.

[2] As Denholm-Young points out, de Bury was one of the few people who survived the ministerial crisis of 1340–1 without even temporary disgrace. He had, however, no official position to lose.

Introduction

On 28 April 1340 he was appointed a commissioner with others to treat with the Scotch for peace, and a truce was concluded in September. But in the following July, de Bury and others were directed to take measures for the defence of the realm against the Scotch, and in September a commission of array was directed to de Bury. In December Edward was again at Newcastle to invade Scotland, and granted an indemnity to de Bury, who had furnished forty men-at-arms at his own personal expense. The expedition effected little, and in April 1342 de Bury was again appointed to treat for peace or a truce with Bruce.[1] In the following years we find de Bury enjoining the Prior of Durham not to absent himself from the Convent, in anticipation of an inroad of the Scotch.

Meantime Edward was devoting all his efforts to the preparations for the great conflict with France, which was to exhaust the energies of both peoples during the next hundred years. In 1344 the peers called upon the King to cross the sea and appeal to the judgement of God by battle, and the representatives of the clergy eagerly voted him three years' supplies.

De Bury therefore saw and heard quite enough of the temper and circumstance of war to sharpen the pen with which—probably about this very time—he was describing the injuries inflicted upon literature, in the *Querimonia Librorum contra Bella*. He does not present to us, however, that curious combination of the soldier and the bishop which was familiar to the age of chivalry; and we are not called upon to picture him, like his predecessor Anthony Bec, leading

---

[1] This was the last active appointment given to de Bury: nor does he appear after 1342 in Parliament. At this time he was making provision for life for those who had served him well: Denholm-Young, p. 15.

Biographical

a host of '140 knights, 500 horsemen and 1000 foot' to war under the sacred banner of St. Cuthbert. On the contrary, Chambre tells us not only that the Palatinate enjoyed reasonable tranquillity during his pontificate, but that his maintenance as Lord Palatine of the rights of the liberty of Durham despite his frequent absences caused the lot of his subjects to contrast favourably with the burdens and exactions imposed upon the rest of the country.

❡ How soon de Bury felt the attack of the disease from which he died we do not know, but Chambre tells us that he died *longa infirmitate decoctus*, and it appears that he was not in parliament in 1344. To this period we are to assign the writing of the *Philobiblon*, which was completed, according to the concluding note, on the Bishop's fifty-eighth birthday, 24 January 1345. The latest documents in his Register are dated 5 April of the same year at Durham Castle, and on 14 April, at his manor of Auckland, in the words of the memorandum entered on the rolls of his Chancery: 'Dominus Ricardus de Bury migravit ad Dominum'. He was buried on 21 April, honourably indeed, but in the judgement of his warm admirer Chambre, not with all the honour he deserved —'quodammodo honorifice non tamen cum honore satis congruo'—before the altar of St. Mary Magdalene in the western angle of his Cathedral. The place of his sepulture was marked by 'a faire marble stone,[1] whereon his owne

---

[1] This quotation comes from a 'Description of all the ancient monuments, etc., in the church of Durham' (Surtees Society, vol. xv, *Rites of Durham*, p. 2). This tomb appears to have been destroyed in the Civil War. Early in this century a monument was erected to him at the same place and at the expense of the Grolier Club of New York; it embodies in the inscription two extracts from the *Philobiblon*. Cf. H. Hensley Henson, Surtees Soc., vol. cxix, pp. xlii–xliv.

ymage was most curiously and artificially ingraven in brass, with the pictures of the twelve Apostles of either side of him, and other fine imagery work about it, much adorninge the marble stone'. Chambre records that after his death one of his chests which was supposed to contain treasure was found full of linen, shirts, and hair breeches: so that his abundant charities and his expenditure upon books had left him but little. His benefactions to the Cathedral during his lifetime had been considerable. The horses which bore his body to the grave and his ecclesiastical vestments were the admitted per-quisites of the sacrist, who, however, had some difficulty in obtaining them. Other rich vestments which de Bury in-tended for the Cathedral, he had been obliged to pledge to Lord Neville, who ultimately presented them to the Church. In accordance with ancient usage, his four seals of silver were broken up and dedicated to St. Cuthbert; a silver-gilt cup was made of them with the inscription:

> Hic ciphus insignis fit presulis ex tetra signis
> Ri: Dunelmensis quarti, natu Byriensis.[1]

❡ De Bury's passion for the collection of books was not selfish, and he intended to bestow them so as to promote the

[1] The seals of Richard de Bury were reproduced in Surtees's *History of Dur-ham*, vol. i, pl. iv. The most beautiful of them is also shown in *Archaeologia*, vol. xxvii, pp. 401–2: it is one of the masterpieces of the medieval seal-maker's art. See also Hunter-Blair, *Durham Seals*, p. 456. In this distich Thomas, following Surtees Soc. edi-tion, p. ccclxxxviii, reads 'signis' for 'sigillis'.

The shield which appears on the title-page opposite to that of Blackwell can only be claimed with caution as the arms of the Bishop. No coat of arms appears on his seals (save that of England) but the blazon: 'Gules, a cinquefoil ermine, and a bordure sable, bezanty' was to be seen (according to Burton, *Leicestershire*, p. 288) in the church of Willoughby, and occurs in the Parliamentary Roll of Edward II. The charge of a cinquefoil would reflect a Leicestershire origin. Hunter-Blair (*Durham Seals*, p. 456 n.) is satisfied that these were the arms of the Bishop.

Biographical

advancement of learning and the interests of the students of his old University. It has been assumed that this intention was duly carried out and it may appear unreasonable to doubt the truth of the tradition to this effect. But apart from the fact that there is little early or positive evidence that the library was really established, there are one or two circumstances which confirm rather than allay our doubts. We have seen that de Bury actually died in debt, and we know that his executors sold at least some portion of his books. It has already been noticed that de Chambre says nothing of a library at Oxford; and the language of Leland is quite consistent with the idea of a scheme that was never carried into effect. If now we look into the nineteenth chapter of the *Philobiblon*, we find that in the best manuscripts, instead of naming the Hall to which his books are to be presented, the Bishop leaves a capital letter N in the text—which was the common fashion of indicating a place left for the insertion of a proper name. In the eighteenth chapter he speaks of his long-nourished design of founding a hall, but so as clearly to imply that this intention had yet to be fulfilled—and it must be remembered that de Bury died less than four months after finishing the *Philobiblon*. That the Bishop had more than an intention to found a college we know, because he had in fact entered into an agreement with King Edward for himself and his successors under the following circumstances. The Crown and the Bishop each claimed the right of presentation to the Church of Symondburn and an action was pending in the King's Bench to decide the matter when the battle of Halidon Hill was fought. On the eve of the conflict Edward vowed that if victorious he would found a house for thirteen monks

Introduction

of St. Benedict. He won the battle and was bound to carry out his vow, and accordingly agreed with de Bury to resign the advowson in question on condition that the Bishop or his successors should found a Hall for a prior and twelve monks of Durham at Oxford, on the site of the house established by Prior Hoton in 1290.[1] The formal brief issued by the King, and dated at Walton on 25 June 1338, is one of the earliest documents appearing in de Bury's Register. It is quite evident that the Bishop in the eighteenth chapter of his book refers to this intended foundation, which was only carried into effect by his successor Bishop Hatfield, who founded Durham College, where Trinity College now stands. Unfortunately de Bury's will has not been preserved, so that we are deprived of any light which it might have afforded us upon this question.

The traditional account of the library is that the Bishop's books were sent in his life-time or after his death to the house of the Durham Benedictines at Oxford, and there remained until the dissolution of the College by Henry VIII, when they were dispersed, some going into Duke Humphrey's (the University) Library, others to Balliol College, and the remainder passing into the hands of Dr. George Owen, who purchased the site of the dissolved college. That a library belonging to the college was then dispersed is probable enough, but it is far from clear that it contained any of de Bury's books.[2]

[1] Maxwell Lyte, *History of the University of Oxford*, p. 105.

[2] Cf. Gutch's Wood, ii. 911, or 'Some Account of Durham College, Oxford' (Durham, 1840). Unconvincing attempts have been made to suggest that de Bury's Library really did come to Oxford (see *Notes and Queries*, 11th series, vol. viii, pp. 341, 397, 435; 12th series, vol. ix, p. 17, and 13th series, vol. ii, p. 355 and vol. xi, p. 435).

Biographical

It has been assumed by Cocheris, who has been followed by more recent writers, that the regulations laid down by de Bury for the management of his intended library were taken directly from the regulations made for the library of the Sorbonne in 1321. The cardinal points of the Sorbonne rules are, according to Cocheris, the system of pledges, and the election of keepers by the *socii*. It is true that we find these two points in de Bury's regulations, but it is not necessary to suppose that he borrowed them from the Sorbonne. The practice of taking a pledge for the loan of a book had long been exceedingly common; and the appointment of keepers by the *scholares* was but a natural extension to the case of books of the general system of government in the colleges of Oxford and Cambridge. The regulations of the Sorbonne, which are only partly quoted by Cocheris, have since been printed by M. Alfred Franklin,[1] and the rules prescribed by de Bury will be found to be more minute and complete than those of the Sorbonne. Among other important variations, de Bury does not direct that any of his books are to be chained, which is a main feature of the system of the Sorbonne.

The 'special catalogue' of his collection, which de Bury tells us he had prepared, has unfortunately not survived. No doubt from his own book and from the books cited in the works of his friends and housemates, who may reasonably be supposed to have drawn largely from the Bishop's collections, it would be possible to restore a hypothetical but not improbable *Bibliotheca Ricardi de Bury*. The difficulty would be with that contemporary literature, which they would think below the dignity of quotation, but which we know the

[1] *La Sorbonne*, 2nd ed. 1875, p. 45.

Introduction

Bishop collected. How considerable the contemporary literature was in point of quantity, we may learn from Le Clerc,
who has registered no less than 10,000 productions for the
fourteenth century.[1]

❡ Chambre's account of de Bury exhibits him as an excellent bishop, and an amiable and warmhearted man. He was
discreet in the government of his household, hospitable to
strangers, and zealous in dispensing charity. Every week he
distributed to the poor eight quarters of wheat, besides the
fragments that were left, and any who were too late for this
distribution received a halfpenny. On his journeys from place
to place in his diocese, he would bestow in alms between
Newcastle and Durham, twelve marks; between Durham and
Stockton, eight marks; between Durham and Auckland, five
marks, and between Durham and Middleham, a hundred
shillings—all which sums must of course be multiplied many
times to represent the difference in the value of money then
and now.

He was quick of temper, but easily appeased, and he delighted to have about him, besides his chaplains and friends,
the sons of the gentlefolk in his diocese, so that he was much
beloved by his people, and he always showed great regard for
the monks of his Cathedral church. Chambre tells a couple of
anecdotes which illustrate the Bishop's character. He was at
Paris when the news reached him of the death of his predecessor, Beaumont, and one of his clerks, William de Tykall,

[1] J. de Ghellinck in his three extremely important articles on Richard
de Bury, 'Un bibliophile au XIV
siècle' (*Revue d'Histoire Ecclésiastique*, vol.
xviii (1922), pp. 271–312 and 402–
508, and vol. xix (1923), pp. 157–200,
suggests (p. 175) that a total of about
1,500 books might be plausible for
Richard de Bury's library.

Biographical

rector of Stanhope, urged him to write to the cardinals and other friends at the Curia, urging his claim to the bishopric, but he answered that he would not ask for that bishopric or any other. Again, when the news was brought to him of the death of Graystanes, his unlucky rival on that occasion, as he was sitting in company at York, he was so much affected that he could not bear the presence of the messenger. And when his companions asked why he grieved so greatly, he answered: 'If you had known his worth as I do, I believe that you would grieve as much as I; for he was fitter for the Papacy than I or any of my fellows for the smallest dignity in Holy Church'.

❡ Chambre's account of his book-loving propensities adds something to the Bishop's own account of them in his book. 'Iste summe delectabatur in multitudine librorum'; he had more books, as was commonly reported, than all the other English bishops put together. He had a separate library in each of his residences, and wherever he was residing so many books lay about his bedchamber, that it was hardly possible to stand or move without treading upon them. All the time he could spare from business was devoted either to religious offices or to his books. Every day while at table he would have a book read to him, unless some special guest were present, and afterwards would engage in discussion on the subject of the reading. The haughty Anthony Bec delighted in the appendages of royalty—to be addressed by nobles kneeling, and to be waited on in his presence-chamber and at his table by knights bare-headed and standing; but de Bury loved to surround himself with learned men. Among these were such men as Thomas Bradwardine, afterwards Archbishop of Canterbury, and author of the *De Causa Dei*, Richard

Introduction

Fitzralph, afterwards Archbishop of Armagh, and famous for his hostility to the mendicant orders, Walter Burley, the 'Plain and Perspicuous Doctor', who dedicated to him a translation of the *Politics* of Aristotle made at his suggestion,[1] John Mauduit the astronomer, Robert Holkot, author of many books, Richard de Kilvington, Richard Benworth, afterwards Bishop of London, and Walter Seagrave, who became Dean of Chichester.[2]

The *Philobiblon* may be supposed to represent the fruit of the Bishop's intellectual converse with these and other learned men, as well as of his own reading and experience. It is unnecessary to present any summary or analysis of a treatise which is so short, and which every reader will prefer to peruse for himself. De Bury tells us that he designed it to justify his all-absorbing devotion to books in the eyes of those who had condemned it as excessive, by indicating their supreme value, and the disinterestedness of his own love for them, as shown by his ultimate purpose in their collection. But he felt that it was not enough to provide the books, unless he could kindle in the hearts of those for whom they were intended the love that burned so warmly in his own. And so he gives his treatise a name which expresses the central theme of his discourse—the love of books.[3]

[1] Brit. Mus. MS. Burney, 304.

[2] For a list of some of de Bury's clerks see Denholm-Young, pp. 23–24. Bradwardine, Burley, Mauduit, and Kilvington were all Fellows of Merton College, cf. p. xvi, n.

[3] The word Philobiblon seems to be of de Bury's own minting and should be so written. As Thomas points out: 'Even Fabricius uses the unauthorized form *Philobiblion*, which is of course quite impossible, while τὸ φιλόβιβλον is at least defensible. It is, perhaps, just possible that it was suggested to him by the article in Suidas (whose book is said to have been translated by Grosteste) on Philo Biblios the grammarian, who wrote a treatise Περὶ κτήσεως καὶ ἐκλογῆς βιβλίων. The adjective φιλόβιβλος, of course, occurs

Biographical

❦ Widely varying judgements have been passed upon the intellectual position of de Bury. It was long the fashion to speak of him with Sir Henry Savile as the learnedest man of his age. More recent critics have regarded him as not a scholar himself, but a patron and encourager of scholarship. The truth lies perhaps midway between these different verdicts. There is no reason to suppose that he was a sustained or original thinker like Occam or Bradwardine; nor did he share the literary productiveness of Burley or Holkot. He has left us nothing of his own but what may be described in his own phrase as a 'panfletus exiguus'. But we must bear in mind that de Bury was essentially a man of affairs, and that his official preoccupations left him comparatively scanty intervals of time to devote to literature. The judgement of Petrarch may be sufficient to satisfy us as to the extent of his knowledge and the width of his literary interests.

We must not indeed look in de Bury for cultivated taste or historical criticism. The age in which he lived was, in the phrase of Savile, 'aetas minime omnium critica', and he shares its defects. Not to speak of his faith in books and sciences 'before the Flood', he cites, in common with Holkot and Bradwardine, Hermes Trismegistus and the Pseudo-Dionysius, quotes the *De Pomo* as Aristotle's and seems to have no suspicion that the miserable verses of the *De Vetula* are not Ovid's own. His knowledge of Greek was probably slender enough, but is unduly depreciated by Hallam. He was anxious to see the study of Greek, Hebrew, and Arabic more zealously prosecuted, and prepared grammars of the two

in Strabo, xiii, 609, who says of Apellikon, the purchaser of Aristotle's library, that he was φιλόβιβλος μᾶλλον ἢ φιλόσοφος.'

Introduction

former languages, as well as glossaries of grammatical terms and 'exotic' words. On the other hand, I find nothing in de Bury to justify the view of one of his recent critics, that he was 'penetrated with the principles of humanism', and I fear that he would have felt little sympathy with Petrarch's enthusiasm for the 'new learning', or at least with his continual invectives against the aims and methods of scholasticism. This is evident enough from his complaint that the dialecticians of Paris produced no new authors. It was in his days that the University of Oxford was the scene of the last effort of scholasticism, before the revival of classical culture which was to revolutionize the studies of Europe. Again, he does not rise above the view that the liberal arts and the writings of the poets are to be studied only in order to assist the understanding of the Scriptures and of the Fathers. He is not free from a certain ecclesiastical narrowness, which leads him to forbid even the handling of books by the laity; and there is nothing in his book to show that he felt any interest in the vernacular literatures which were springing up in France, in Italy, and in his own country.

The style of de Bury is exactly what the foregoing considerations would lead us to expect. There is no attempt, as in the case of Petrarch, to return to a classical standard, which he had not learned to appreciate. His models are not the purest writers of the purest age of Latinity, but the late grammarians and the Fathers of the Church. His style is stiff with a heavy embroidery of scriptural quotation and allusion; like that of many among the medieval writers, it is 'made of the Scriptures'. Though he affects to write 'in the lightest style of the moderns', he has none of the ease and fluency of

Biographical

such writers as John of Salisbury, and his rhetoric, genuine as no doubt it is, is too often clumsy and overlaboured. Although his book can scarcely claim to rank as a masterpiece of literature, the text now printed will show that his style is much more correct than has been hitherto supposed.

The special interest to us of Richard de Bury is that he is, if not the prototype, at least the most conspicuous example of a class of men who have been more numerous in modern than in ancient or medieval times. No man has ever carried to a higher pitch of enthusiasm the passion for collecting books. On this point, at least, de Bury and Petrarch were truly kindred spirits, and their community of feeling finds expression in a striking similarity of language. The letter in which Petrarch seeks the co-operation of his brother Gerard presents close resemblance to a well-known passage in the *Philobiblon*. Petrarch writes:[1]

Aurum, argentum, gemmae, purpurea vestis, marmorea domus, cultus ager, pictae tabulae, phaleratus sonipes, caeteraque id genus, mutam habent et superficiariam voluptatem: libri medullitus delectant.

One might think that the writer had had before him the very words of de Bury in his eighth chapter.

Again, Petrarch bids his brother employ trusty and learned men to search for books for him:

Etruriam perquirant, religiosorum armaria evolvant caeterorumque studiosorum hominum. . . . Scias me easdem preces amicis aliis in Britanniam, Galliasque et Hispanias destinasse.

The words seem but an echo of de Bury's account, in the same chapter, of his own procedure.

[1] *Ep. Fam.* iii. 18.

Introduction

There is one other point of similarity between Petrarch and de Bury: that each of them intended to bestow his books for public uses. In each case, moreover, this pious intention appears to have been frustrated by the carelessness of their successors.

ℂ De Bury has told us in his book a good deal of his principles and practice as a collector. He collected everything, and he spared no cost; a book in his opinion could never be too dear—unless one might reasonably hope for an opportunity of purchasing at a cheaper rate. Besides maintaining a staff of copyists and illuminators in his own household, he was on excellent terms with 'the trade'—limited as it then was—not only in England, but in France and Germany. He pressed into his service the members of the religious orders, who supplied him with books from the monastic libraries, and used in his behalf the opportunities of picking up rare volumes, which their wandering life abundantly afforded. He made use of his various offices in Church and State to gain access to every quarter whence he might expect some accession to his treasures. The gifts which were then the recognized perquisites of such exalted officers came to him in the shape of books. Let us hope that he speaks no more than the truth when he declares that meantime 'justice suffered no detriment'. One or two anecdotes have survived which throw a curious light on this aspect of the matter. It is recorded in the history of the Abbots of the great monastery of St. Albans, that one of its abbots, a man himself distinguished for his literary and scientific zeal, presented to de Bury, then Clerk of the Privy Seal, four volumes, viz. Terence, Virgil, Quintilian, and Hieronymus against Rufinus, in the hope of

Biographical

securing his favourable influence in forwarding the interests of that house. Besides this, the abbot sold him thirty-two other books for fifty pounds of silver. The pious chronicler expresses his horror at this transaction, and records that after he had become Bishop, de Bury, conscience-smitten, restored several of the books, and that others were bought from the Bishop's executors by the next abbot, Michael de Mentmore, at a price below their real value. Richard faithfully carried out his compact; for it is recorded that by his aid the abbot obtained the right, which ordinarily appertained only to bishops, to imprison excommunicated persons as a matter of course, and not by a special writ.[1]

It appears that later Richard's interference in the business of the convent brought him into trouble. It happened that the abbot suffered from leprosy, and there was a cabal within the convent to have him removed. Representations were made to the Papal Court, and Richard appears to have put the Privy Seal to the letter sent to the Pope. The matter was brought before Parliament, and de Bury was censured for this use of the seal without authority. The only excuse he could offer was that pressure had been put upon him by men who were too powerful to be withstood.[2]

There is now preserved in the British Museum a large folio manuscript of the works of John of Salisbury, which was one of the books bought back from the Bishop's executors. It bears upon it a note to the effect that it was written by Simon (who was Abbot of St. Albans, 1167–1183), and another note, which runs as follows:

Hunc librum venditum Domino Ricardo de Biry Episcopo

---

[1] *Chronica Mon. S. Albani*, ii. 200, 283.   [2] *Ibid.*, p. 288.

Introduction

Dunelmensi emit Michael Abbas Sancti Albani ab executoribus predicti episcopi anno Domini millesimo CCC° XLV^{to} circa purificationem Beate Virginis.[1]

℄ There seems no sufficient reason to suppose that de Bury wrote any other book than the *Philobiblon*. Boston and Leland mention only this book, but Bale and Pits add a volume of *Epistolae Familiares* with another of *Orationes ad Principes*. This list has been repeated by subsequent writers, and even figures to this day in the *Encyclopaedia Britannica*. Bale was not a very exact bibliographer, and there seems to have been some confusion, the source of which it is perhaps not difficult to indicate. Bale gives as the initial words of the *Philobiblon*: 'Thesaurus desiderabilis' and of the *Epistolae*: '*Ricardus miseratione divina*'. Now the former words are the beginning of the first chapter of the *Philobiblon* omitting the prologue, and the latter words are at the beginning of this prologue or introductory letter to the reader, so that Bale has merely made the one work into two. This suggestion derives support from the fact that in at least one manuscript the prologue is omitted and the *Philobiblon* begins with the *Thesaurus desiderabilis* of Chapter I.[2] This is perhaps a more probable explanation than to suppose, as Dr. Creighton suggests, that Bale had heard of the letter-book of Richard de Bury, which has recently been described for the Historical MSS. Commission, and more fully by Sir Thomas Hardy.[3] This is not a work of literary interest, but a collection of precedents, no doubt collected by the Bishop for the use of the clerks in his

[1] Royal 13 D. IV. 3.
[2] The Magdalen College MS.: cf. p. lviii *post*.
[3] These descriptions have been com-

pletely replaced by the edition prepared by Denholm-Young for the Roxburghe Club (1950).

Biographical

chancery. It is described on the first page as 'Liber Epistolaris quondam domini Ricardi de Bury, Episcopi Dunelm.'; and from another inscription, 'Liber Monachorum Sancti Edmundi Regis et Martiris', appears to have for some time belonged to the Monastery of Bury St. Edmund's. Sir Thomas Hardy suggests that it was probably bought by the monastery out of consideration for its original owner. It is now in the possession of Lord Harlech. Very few of the documents transcribed into it throw any light upon the career of de Bury. It is perhaps just possible that this book may be the foundation of fact for the supposed volume of *Orationes ad Principes*, of which Bale speaks.

I need only mention that in James's Bodleian Catalogue of 1620, and the Catalogues of 1738 and 1843 *The Contemplacyon of Sinners*, printed by de Worde in 1499, is attributed to de Bury, an error due to a confusion between Richard de Bury and Richard Fox, one of his successors in the See of Durham, at whose request this treatise appears to have been written at the end of the fifteenth century.

❡ Some reference must be made to the attempts to deprive de Bury of the authorship of the *Philobiblon* in favour of Robert Holkot. This claim, which has the support of Tanner, Hearne, and Warton, appears to have been first formally put forward by Altamura and Echard, the bibliographers of the Order of the Friars Preachers, who rely upon the authority of Laurentius Pignon and Lusitanus. These authorities are, of course, a century later than the time of de Bury and Holkot; and if this were all, there would be no difficulty in disposing of the claim. But in seven of the extant

xxxv

Introduction

manuscripts of the *Philobiblon* the book is ascribed to Holkot, as well as in a manuscript once in the possession of Fabricius, and perhaps in another which was formerly in the Royal Library at Erfurt. The Paris manuscript has simply 'Philobiblon olchoti anglici', and it does not contain the concluding note of which I have elsewhere spoken. In the other manuscripts, in which I have found the work attributed to Holkot, the concluding note is found, but they begin with some such words as 'Incipit prologus philobiblon Ricardi Dunelmens. Epī quē librum compilauit Robus Holcote de ordine predicatorum sub nomine dicti episcopi'. In the great majority of manuscripts then, including the earliest, this preliminary note is not found, and in nearly all the manuscripts where it does occur, it is accompanied by a final note, which is, to say the least, hardly consistent with it.

As evidence, therefore, that Robert Holkot wrote the *Philobiblon* it is not very satisfactory. In order to gain such light as can be thrown upon the matter from internal evidence, I have read through most of Holkot's own writings, and I have no hesitation in saying that so far as the evidence of style goes, there appears little reason to assign the *Philobiblon* to Holkot. Lord Campbell has already pointed out that the essentially autobiographical character of the book is all in favour of de Bury's authorship. Holkot, who was one of de Bury's chaplains, may indeed have acted as the Bishop's amanuensis in the preparation of the book. A traditional and perhaps exaggerated account of this may have reached the ears of some scribe or possessor of a manuscript of the *Philobiblon*, and he may have set down the note in question. But it would be unfair to deprive de Bury of the credit of having planned

Biographical

and written his own book on such shadowy evidence as can be adduced in favour of Holkot's claim.

It is the more satisfactory to think that we are not called upon to deprive de Bury of the authorship of the *Philobiblon*, as, now that his books have been dispersed, and his tomb despoiled, it is the sole abiding memorial of one who loved books so much in an age and country that loved them so little. One who has sung his praises, in his own words, 'even to raving', has truly said of Richard de Bury, that 'his fame will never die'.[1] So, too, the *Philobiblon* will ever continue to kindle the love of those silent teachers who 'instruct us without rods and stripes, without taunts or anger, without gifts or money; who are not asleep when we approach them, and do not deny us when we question them; who do not chide us if we err, or laugh at us if we are ignorant'.

BIBLIOGRAPHICAL

1. *Printed Editions*

We many infer from the corruption of the many existing manuscripts that the *Philobiblon* was frequently copied, and from their distribution that it soon found its way into the libraries not only of our own country, but of France, Germany, the Low Countries, Italy, and Spain. In 1358 long extracts from it are found embodied in a University statute at Oxford, yet, as has been already stated, the Bishop's biographer Chambre makes no mention of his book; and the

---

[1] Dibdin, *Reminiscences*, i. 87 n.

Introduction

earliest references to it that I have found are in Boston (✝ 1410) in this country, and in Trithemius (✝ 1516), the famous Abbot of Sponheim, on the Continent. It has been suggested that Thomas à Kempis made use of the *Philobiblon* in his *Doctrinale Iuvenum,* but I have shown elsewhere that the suggestion is unfounded.

The book appears to have found a wider audience abroad than at home, and it was three times printed on the Continent—at Cologne in 1473, at Spires in 1483, and at Paris in 1500—and then had to wait for another century before it found an English printer. The edition of Thomas James, Bodley's first librarian, appeared in 1598–9. It was then again printed in Germany by Melchior Goldast, apparently without any knowledge of the English edition, in 1610, and reprinted in 1614 and 1674. It was also included in 1703 by J. A. Schmidt in his supplement to the collection of treatises on libraries published by J. J. Mader. There is then no edition to record until the present century, when an anonymous English translation was published in 1832. In 1856 Cocheris issued the Latin text with a French translation at Paris; and in 1861 Cocheris's text and Inglis's translation were reprinted in the United States.

The bibliography of the *Philobiblon* long remained uncertain and obscure, and indeed is hardly yet well understood. Trithemius says of the book in his *De scriptoribus ecclesiasticis* (begun in 1487 and printed 1494) 'iam impressus est', but there is nothing to show whether he was acquainted with the Cologne or Spires edition, or with both. Leland, Bale, and Pits do not mention a printed text. The Paris printer must have known that the book was in print, for he prefixes to his edition

the account of de Bury from Trithemius, but carefully omits the statement that the book had been already printed. When James came to print it, he described his own impression as 'editio iam secunda', and Goldast intimates on his title-page that his issue of the book was a first impression. When the incunabulists set to work to register the early productions of the press, they ignored one or other of the Cologne and Spires impressions, or, worse still, confounded them together. Thus Maittaire, Panzer, and Denis mention only the Spires edition, and Hain is the first to record the two impressions, assigning both, however, to 1483. Other bibliographers were no less at fault: Fabricius and Clement know nothing of the Cologne impression; Peignot dates both editions 1473. Our own Dibdin believed that the supposed Cologne edition was a myth; and it was with surprise as well as delight that he found it 'fall to his good fortune' in the *Bibliotheca Spenceriana* 'to describe the present rare and inestimable impression', meaning this very edition of Cologne.

There has been a good deal of confusion as to the Paris edition of 1500 and a supposed reimpression of James's edition at London in 1600. I will show presently that there was in the former case only a single impression, and that in the latter case there was no impression in 1600, but that James's book was first printed in 1598 and reissued the following year. Again, none of the bibliographers has given a full list of the several impressions of Goldast's text, and a complete account of them here appears for the first time. Finally, it has been asserted by the *Dictionary of National Biography* that the edition now in the reader's hands was published 'in 1885'.

Introduction

I propose now to describe the various editions in their chronological order:

1473 *Cologne*

The *editio princeps* of the *Philobiblon* was printed at Cologne in a small quarto volume of 48 leaves, without pagination, signatures, or catchwords. Its printer is said to have been G. Gops de Euskyrchen. It contains no indication of authorship outside the text, but begins:

> Incipit plogus in librū de amore libroɣ qui
> dicitur philobiblon . . .

It ends:

> Explicit philobiblon ſci liber
> de amore librorū Colonie impreſ
> ſus anno dnī Mcccc.lxxiij. ɀc.

On ff. [5 v.] and [6 v.] there are indications in at least one copy of a rearrangement of the type during the process of printing. The text was no doubt printed from a single manuscript without any attempt at editing. It presents a very close resemblance to the Cologne manuscript described farther on. There are two copies of this impression in the British Museum, and I have had the opportunity of consulting the copies in the possession of Earl Spencer, Mr. W. Amherst T. Amherst, M.P., and Mr. Sam Timmins. Dibdin's account of the Althorp copy is not very accurate, as I found no trace of the 'copious ms. memoranda' to which he refers. According to Cocheris there are two copies in the Bibliothèque Nationale. Mr. Quaritch gave £45 for the copy in the Wodhull sale in 1886.

Bibliographical

Ten years afterwards the *Philobiblon* was printed by the
brothers John and Conrad Hiist in a small quarto volume of
39 leaves, with 31 lines to the page, without pagination, catchwords, or signatures. The *recto* of the first leaf is blank. On
the *verso* is a letter from the anonymous editor, who simply describes himself as 'minimus sacerdotum', to the brothers Hiist,
who are addressed as 'studiosissimi impressores'. The letter
is dated 'idibus Ianuarij anno xp̄i etc. lxxxiii', and the writer
speaks of the difficulty he had found in performing the edito-
rial task imposed upon him, owing to the defective state of the
copy he used. On the second leaf the title is given as follows:

> Phylobyblon difertiſſimi viri Richardi
> dilmelmeñ ep̄i. de q̄rimonijs libroꝝ om̄ib⁹
> lr̄aꝝ amatorib⁹ putil' ꝑlog⁹ Incipit.

It ends with the words, after *conspectum Amen*:

> Valete ꝫ scīaꝫ lr̄aꝝ colite.

The book, which was no doubt printed from a single manuscript, presents a somewhat better text than that of Cologne,
though both are very defective. Dibdin's suggestion that it
would 'be probably considered to be a mere reprint of the
Cologne impression' is without foundation. The Spires
editor allowed himself the liberty of altering the opening
words of the prologue to 'Universis litterarum cultoribus'
and of omitting the following clause. Other traces of editorship may also be noticed in the book.

This edition seems to be even rarer than the *editio princeps*.
Cocheris could find no copy in Paris. It is in the British
Museum; and I have had the use of the copy belonging to
Mr. Sam Timmins. A copy was sold at the Williams sale for

Introduction

£6. 10s.; and at the Fuller-Russell sale in 1886 I bid in vain for a copy against Mr. Quaritch, who secured it for £12. 15s.

1500 Paris

Seventeen years afterwards the book was printed at Paris in a small quarto of 24 unnumbered leaves (sig. a [i]-iiii, b i-iiii, c i-iv) with the following title-page:

Philobiblion Tractatus pulcher | rimus de amore librorum [Then follows the printer's mark and name JEHAN PETIT] Venundatur in leone argenteo | vici sancti Iacobi.

On the *recto* of the last leaf:

Explicitum eft philobiblion scilicet liber de amore librorum quem impreffit apud parrhifios hoc anno fecundum eofdem mille-fimo quingentefimo ad calendas martias Gaspar philippus pro Ioanne paruo Bibliopola parrhifienfi.

On the *verso* of the first leaf is an account of de Bury taken from Trithemius, from which, however, his reference to the printing of the book is significantly omitted. This is fol-lowed by a letter dated 1 March from the scholar-printer Iodocus Badius Ascensius to Laurentius Burellus, confessor of the King and Bishop of Sisteron, who appears to have sent the book to him to print. He expressly says that Jean Petit had joined him in the undertaking 'hoc munus nobiscum sus-cepit'. This I think explains and disposes of the statement of the bibliographers, which has been repeated down to Coche-ris, that there were *two* editions of 1500, one by Petit and the other by Badius Ascensius. Cocheris himself does not say that he has seen either edition, and he gives the title inaccurately. There can be no doubt that the Paris edition is simply a re-impression of that of Cologne. The spelling *Philobiblon*

was, however, altered by Ascensius to *Philobiblion*, and he extended the title by adding a part of the phrase employed by Trithemius: 'scripsit *de amore librorum* et institutione dictae Bibliothecae *pulcherrimum tractatum*'.

1598 and 1599 Oxford

It was not until the very end of the next century that the first English edition of this English book appeared, with the following title-page:

Philobiblon | Richardi | Dvnelmensis | sive | De amore librorvm, et Institvtione bibliothecae | tractatus pulcherrimus. | Ex collatione cum varijs manuscriptis edi-|tio jam secunda; | cui | Accefsit appendix de manufcriptis Oxonienfibus. | Omnia haec | Opere & Studio T. I. Novi Coll. in alma Academia | Oxonienfi Socij. | B. P. N. | Non quaero quod mihi vtile eft fed quod multis. | Oxoniae, | Excudebat Iofephus Barnesius. 1598. |

The book is in quarto and consists of 62 pages, with 4 un-numbered pages of preliminary matter and 8 unnumbered pages of appendix. So far as I know, the copy in the Bodleian Library is the only copy extant bearing the date 1598, and Fabricius, Oudinus, and Tanner the only bibliographers who mention this date. The other extant copies bear the date 1599 and appear to be a mere reissue with a fresh title-page. To this reissue the editor prefixes a Latin *Epistola dedicatoria* of four pages addressed to Thomas Bodley, in which he compares him with de Bury for his devotion to literature and his bene-faction to the University. He explains how he had found his author 'in membranis inter blattas et tineas semivivum, semiesum, pallentem expirantemque', and how far he was from being satisfied with his efforts to restore his author. He

Introduction

begs the reader to condone the 'barbarisms and solecisms' in the Bishop's style and his slight lapses in matters of faith and religion, both the faults of his age. He concludes by congratulating Bodley on the success of his plans for restoring the University library. The letter is dated 'Ex Muſaeo meo in Collegio Novo. Julij. 6. 1599', and is signed 'Thomas James'.

James was evidently under the impression that the book had been only once printed. It is not improbable that he had before him the Paris edition. His title-page at all events reproduces the title of that edition as borrowed from Trithemius; though he uses the phrase in a fuller form and may of course have taken it from Trithemius only. He reprints Bale's account of de Bury, together with a manuscript note of T[homas] A[llen's] in his copy of Bale, taken from Chambre's life of the Bishop, then still in manuscript.

Fabricius says that the text of James was again printed at London in the following year in the *Ecloga Oxonio-Cantabrigiensis*; but this statement appears to rest upon a misunderstanding. The *Ecloga* is an account of the manuscripts at Oxford and Cambridge, and was to have been published, as James tells us, with the *Philobiblon*. As it was not finished and the printer grew impatient, James decided not to wait for it, but instead gave the appendix which is affixed to the *Philobiblon*, and which is merely an index of authors represented in the Oxford manuscripts. But the *Philobiblon* was *not* reprinted with the *Ecloga* issued in 1600, as Fabricius must have supposed.

The *Ecloga* enables us to say what manuscripts James had at his disposal for the purposes of his edition. The manuscripts enumerated in the *Ecloga* are: At Oxford four, viz. at All

Bibliographical

Souls, Lincoln, Magdalen, and Balliol; at Cambridge, at Benet's (now C.C.C.), and one in Lord Lumley's library. The five college manuscripts are still where they were; Lord Lumley's should have passed into the Royal Library, and may be one of the manuscripts now in the British Museum. There can be little doubt that James relied largely upon the Magdalen and Lincoln manuscripts. James's text has been condemned by Dibdin as containing 'nothing more than the Cologne impression, being sometimes, indeed, less particular', and Inglis, who 'doubts his having looked into several manuscripts, but has no doubt of his having preferred his own words to those of the author'. This is not deserved; though Hearne's language is no doubt exaggerated when he says of him 'in libello perpurgando multum sudavit', there seems no reason to doubt that he honestly looked into several manuscripts. At the same time he left a good deal to be done for the text of his author. One of the copies of James's edition in the British Museum is a presentation copy to Lord Lumley, and contains an interesting autograph letter to Lumley written in James's exquisitely neat hand.

1610, 1614 Frankfurt, 1674 Leipzig

From this time until the present century the *Philobiblon* was not again printed by itself, but only in collectaneous works. In 1610 was published in a small octavo volume:

Philologicarum epistolarum centuria Vna diversorum a renatis literis Doctissimorum virorum . . . insuper Richardi de BVRI Episcopi Dunelmensis Philobiblion & Bessarionis Patriarchae Constantinopolitani & Cardinalis Nicaeni Epistola ad Senatum Venetum. Omnia nunc primum edita ex Bibliotheca Melchioris Haiminsfeldii Goldasti . . . Francofurti Impensis Egenolphi Emmelii, anno 1610.

xlv

Introduction

The *Philobiblon* occupies pp. 400–500 of the book, p. 400 being a fresh title-page bearing the words 'ex Bibliotheca et recensione Melchioris Haiminsfeldii Goldasti'. From these words and from the 'omnia haec *primum* edita' the natural inference would be that Goldast thought he was printing the *Philobiblon* for the first time, or at least that he was printing it from a manuscript. But the text with a few trifling variations is obviously that of the Paris impression of 1500, and indeed Goldast actually silently reprints from that edition the account of de Bury by Trithemius, and even the letter of Badius Ascensius already described. The edition of 1614 seems to be merely a reissue with a fresh title-page, and the reprint of 1674 at Leipzig by Conringius presents no variation to call for remark.

1703 Helmstadt

The edition printed by J. A. Schmidt in the 'Nova accessio' published by him in 1703 to the well-known collection of treatises *De Bibliothecis atque Archivis virorum clarissimorum libelli et commentationes* (2nd ed., Helmstadii, 1702, 4to), does not call for more than brief notice, as it is merely a reprint of the edition of Goldast with a few slight alterations. The *Philobiblion* (as it is called) occupies pp. 1–66.

1832 London (transl.)

In 1832 there appeared an anonymous English translation of the *Philobiblon*, 'London: Printed for Thomas Rodd, 2 Great Newport Street, Leicester Square' (8vo, pp. viii, 151). Lord Campbell, in the first volume of the *Lives of the*

Bibliographical

Chancellors, published in 1845, cites it anonymously. But it is known to have been translated by Mr. John Bellingham Inglis, a student and collector of early printed books. The translation is a work of more spirit than accuracy, and Inglis has too slavishly followed the edition of 1473, under the mistaken idea that it was most likely to represent the genuine text of the author. In consequence he unduly disparages the authority of James's text. He has added 'a few collations', which are, however, confined to printed editions, and thirty-seven pages of notes, devoted largely to what Dibdin describes as 'unprovoked and unjustifiable abuse of the English Church and her Ministers'. Probably only a small edition was printed, as the work has become scarce, and Cocheris was unable to secure a copy.

1856 Paris

The first edition of the book professing to furnish an adequate critical apparatus and explanatory notes was issued in 1856 by M. Hippolyte Cocheris, then engaged in the *Bibliothèque Mazarine*, of which he afterwards became *Conservateur*. The book formed part of a series called 'Le Trésor des pièces rares ou inédites', and bears the following title:

Philobiblion excellent traité sur l'amour des livres par Richard de Bury, Evêque de Durham, Grand-Chancelier d'Angleterre, traduit pour la première fois en français, précédé d'une introduction et suivi du texte latin revu sur les anciennes éditions et les manuscrits de la Bibliothèque impériale: par Hippolyte Cocheris. . . . Paris: Aubry, 1856. 8vo, pp. xlvii. 287. [500 copies printed, of which 22 were on special papers and 2 on vellum.]

The book was dedicated to the late Prince Consort.

Introduction

I have elsewhere expressed an unfavourable judgement of this edition, and a longer acquaintance with it has only confirmed that judgement. Though the text professes on the title-page to be 'revu', Cocheris has in fact left the text untouched and has only given the various readings of the three Paris manuscripts at the foot of the page. This he justifies on the curious ground that it was impossible to distinguish between the faults of the author and those of the copyists, though that is most assuredly the first business of an editor. Unfortunately his report of the readings of the manuscripts he has collated is quite untrustworthy and in many instances even wildly wrong. But this is not all: while professing to follow the text of the *editio princeps*, what he has really done is to send to the printer the text of 1703, with all the misprints, errors of punctuation, and defects of all kinds which it had accumulated in passing through the process of reproduction in 1500, 1610, and 1703. The result is that his text is in many points less genuine and even less correct than that of 1473. At the same time, Cocheris cannot fairly be denied the praise of industry, and he has brought together a great deal of matter for the illustration of his author, though he has done little or nothing to clear up the more formidable difficulties of the text.

1861 Albany

In 1861 one Samuel Hand published in the United States a volume which Allibone, 'as an American, is glad to register'; but which, as a flagrant piece of book-making, is not very creditable either to its editor or to America. Mr. Hand reprinted the text of Cocheris and the translation of Inglis,

reproducing all the errors and inaccuracies of both. He translated also the introduction and notes of Cocheris, but his own
few notes are worthless. It is an octavo of pp. x, 252, of which
230 copies were printed, 30 on large paper. I am glad to know
that Prof. Andrew F. West, of Princeton, contemplates an
edition more worthy of the book and of America.

The relation of the editions which have been now enumerated may be thus exhibited:

$$
\begin{array}{c}
1473 \ldots \underline{1483} \ldots \underline{1599} \\
| \\
1500 \\
| \\
\left\{ \begin{array}{c} 1610 \\ 1614 \\ 1674 \end{array} \right\} \\
| \\
1703 \\
| \\
1856 \\
| \\
1861
\end{array}
$$

It must be considered a surprising circumstance that a book
which has been so often printed abroad and so frequently
quoted at home should have remained so long without an
English editor; and in particular that neither the Surtees
Society nor the Philobiblon Society should have secured an
adequate edition. But in fact the idea of re-editing the book
has been several times entertained. In 1816 Surtees announced
in his *History of Durham* that 'Messrs. Taylor and David
Constable are at present employed in collating MSS. for
a new edition'. The announcement was repeated in the
Quarterly Review in 1829 and in the *Bibliographical and
Retrospective Miscellany* in 1830. In the first issue of Lowndes's

Introduction

Bibliographers' Manual in 1834, the compiler, though he does not mention the translation published two years before, announces that 'a new edition of this curious tract is preparing for publication, with an English translation, notes and various readings, by Edw. R. Poole, B.A.' But time passed on and neither of these promised editions saw the light; so that in 1845 Mr. Corser could still speak of the *Philobiblon* as 'a book of which, curious and interesting as it is, we have yet, to our national shame be it said, no edition which a reader can take up with pleasure'. In 1850 Mr. W. S. Gibson, M.A., of Lincoln's Inn, read a 'very elaborate' memoir of de Bury at the Oxford meeting of the Archaeological Institute; and in the *Gentleman's Magazine* for that year it was announced that 'Mr. Gibson's memoir of this Bishop is to be prefixed to a new translation of his *Philobiblon* which Mr. Gibson announces for publication'. This work, however, had not appeared when the British Archaeological Association met at Durham in 1865, where Mr. Gibson read a paper on a 'Seal of Richard de Bury'. But, despite the renewed promise, neither memoir nor translation has ever appeared, and it has remained for the present editor at least to remove from our country the reproach of so long leaving the task of preserving de Bury's literary legacy exclusively in foreign hands.

POSTSCRIPT

Thomas gives us a list of eleven books which had preceded his own and observes justifiably that of these only two had been printed in Richard de Bury's own country. These were the first English edition of the Latin text produced by Thomas

1

Bibliographical

James, Bodley's Librarian, in 1598/9, and the translation of
1832 which, though published anonymously, was in fact the
work of a certain John Bellingham Inglis. England's tribute
to the *Philobiblon* was thus confined to one Latin text, and
one indifferent English version of it. The following list of
printed editions since 1888 reveals once again the popularity
of de Bury abroad and his comparative neglect at home; most
of the books on the list are extremely hard to obtain and
a number were published in limited editions. Not surpris-
ingly the *Philobiblon* has always commended itself to this
form of printing; what is more remarkable is the number of
tongues in which de Bury has been presented to an interested,
if usually a select, band who love books and books on those
who love books. Since we are concerned with modern editions, which may be supposed to be reasonably uniform, I
have not followed Thomas's careful descriptions but merely
given enough information to identify the book in question.
I hope that I have not overlooked any important version
of the *Philobiblon*, but do not claim that the list which
follows is in any sense comprehensive. It is in order of publication and may properly be headed by Thomas's own
work.

1. 1888. *The Philobiblon of Richard de Bury, Bishop of Durham
   Treasurer and Chancellor of Edward III.* Edited and Trans-
   lated by Ernest C. Thomas, Barrister-at-Law, late
   Scholar of Trinity College Oxford and Librarian of the
   Oxford Union. London: Kegan Paul, Trench and Co.

   As is evident from the present edition, this work consists of an
   elaborate introduction in two parts (biographical: bibliographical),
   and a Latin text followed by an English translation. Though not

a limited edition, it must have been a small issue and is now exceedingly scarce.

2. 1889. *Ricardi de Bury Philobiblon ex optimis codicibus recensuit, versione anglica et prolegomenis adnotationibusque auxit Andreas Fleming West.*

An edition with translation produced in New York for the Grolier Club, limited to 150 copies. Vol. I: Latin text. Vol. II: English translation. Vol. III: Introduction, notes, etc.

3. 1889. This year also saw an American edition of Thomas under the imprint 'New York, Lockwood and Coombes'.

4. 1901. *The Philobiblon of Richard de Bury.* Printed at the Elston Press by Clarke Conwell. 485 copies on hand-made paper and 25 on vellum. Initial letters by H. M. O'Kane.

A depressing edition of the Inglis translation in a blunt Gothic type, which may be commended to modern producers of fine books as an example of what to eschew.

5. 1902. *The Love of Books.* Richard de Bury (The King's Classics). Alexander Moring. London [reprinted 1903].

Thomas's translation without notes or *apparatus criticus.*

6. 1912. *Philobiblon, das ist der Traktat des Richard de Bury über die Liebe zu den Büchern.* Franz Blei. Leipzig.

A German translation without Latin text. Limited to 400 copies. It has not won much praise from the critics.

7. 1914. *Il «Philobiblon» di Riccardo de Bury, Vescovo Dunelmense. Marco Besso.* Rome: Biblioteca Besso.

A handsome illustrated quarto, limited to 500 copies, with seven appendixes of relevant texts including Chambre.

Bibliographical

8. 1916. *Ricart de Bury, Bisbe de Durham (1281–1345) Lo Philo-biblon*. J. Pin y Soler. Barcelona.

Translation into Catalan: limited to 200 copies.

9. 1921. *O miłości do ksiąg to jest Philobiblon. Tractat łaciński Ryszarda de Bury*. Spolszczył. Jan Kasprowicz. Lwów.

A Polish translation.

10. 1922. *Philobiblon, eller om Kärleken till Böckerna af Richard de Bury Biskop af Durham*. Axel Nelson. Stockholm.

A very handsomely printed edition with introduction, Latin text followed by Swedish translation, and full notes. Limited to 850 copies. The author is a considerable scholar on this subject.

11. 1927. *El Philobiblon muy hermoso tratado sobre el amor a los biblos*. Padre Tomás Viñas de San Luis. Madrid.

A Spanish translation.

12. 1931. *Philobiblon. Ein Buch für die Welt der Bücherfreunde von Richard de Bury*. Herausgeber Max Joseph Husung. Weimar; Gesellschaft der Bibliophilen.

Limited to 300 copies. Latin text and German translation. A sound critical edition.

13. 1932. *Philobiblon. Das Buch von der Bücherliebe des Richard de Bury*. A German translation with an introduction and a few notes by Max Frensdorf. Eisenach.

Limited to 300 copies. Uses the text of Husung. Not noticed by Altamura.

14. 1933. *Philobiblon of Richard de Bury*. Berkeley: the Book Arts Club, University of California.

Limited to 174 copies (*plus* 50 for the Roxburghe Club of San Francisco). Designed by members of the Book Arts Club in collaboration with Samuel T. Farquhar, University Printer. Thomas's

Introduction

English translation with a short introduction by Dorothea Waley Singer.

15. 1948. *The Philobiblon*. With an introduction by Archer Taylor. University of California Press: Berkeley and Los Angeles.

English translation only, using that made by A. F. West for the Grolier Club (see No. 2). Not noticed by Altamura.

16. 1954. *Philobiblon. Riccardo de Bury*. Edizione critica a cura di Antonio Altamura. Naples.

An admirable edition, no doubt the best now in print, with an introduction, including an important list of manuscripts, Latin text with *apparatus criticus*, notes, and eight illustrations.

17. 1955. *Philobiblon, oder über die Lieber zu Büchern*. Alfred Hartmann. Berne.

Issued for the Schweizerische Bibliophilen-Gesellschaft. Latin text and German translation.

In addition to the above works, there appear to have been translations in English published in this country by Chatto and Windus in 1911 (re-issued in 1925), by Burns and Oates (with an introduction by George Burton, but no date), and in St. Louis, U.S.A., in 1907.

Chapters I, IV, VIII, XVII, XVIII, and XIX have been translated into Russian by A. Malein in *Almanach bibliofila*, Leningrad, 1929, pp. 289–314.

Other languages and editions may well have eluded my brief researches.

M. M.

Bibliographical

II. *Manuscripts*

It has been already pointed out that the three earliest editions of the *Philobiblon* appear to have been produced from a single manuscript in each case, and that James recorded the existence of six manuscripts in this country. This was in 1600; and even at the end of the next century the number enumerated in the *Catalogi librorum manuscriptorum Angliæ et Hiberniæ* was only nine. In 1843 E. G. Vogel contributed to the *Serapeum*, a German bibliographical journal, a very careful article on Richard de Bury, in which he registered nineteen manuscripts. This article appears to have dropped out of sight, and was evidently unknown to Cocheris, whose list embraces only sixteen manuscripts, including that of Fabricius, and omits therefore four manuscripts recorded by Vogel.

The inquiries made in preparing the present work have enabled me to raise the number of manuscripts known to exist to the number of thirty-five, all of which have been examined for the purposes of this edition.[1] It is only possible here to find space for a brief account of them, which it will be most convenient to arrange in geographical order. Unless the contrary is stated, the manuscripts are all upon parchment or vellum.

London: British Museum (7)

The British Museum is in possession of no less than seven manuscripts of the *Philobiblon*, of which four belong

---

[1] The number had been increased from twenty-eight, since Thomas gave an account of them in the *Library Chronicle*, 1885, vol. ii. 129 foll.

Introduction

undoubtedly to the fifteenth century. The remaining three belong in the judgement of the Keeper of the Manuscripts to the end of the fourteenth century.

Roy. 8 F. xiv (f. 70) is a folio manuscript written probably between 1380–1400 and has at the beginning the following note: 'Incipit prologus in philobiblon ricardi dūnelmensis episcopi quē librū composuit Robertus holcote de ordine predicatoᵤ sub noīe dc̄i episcopi'; and at the end the usual note as to the date on which the treatise was finished.

Roy. 15 C. xvi (59ᵛ) is a large folio manuscript written in double columns about 1400. It begins: 'Incipit philobiblon'; and has the concluding note.

Harl. 492 (f. 55) is a small 8vo manuscript, written about 1425, and begins with the preliminary note in red in the same form as that in Roy. 8 F. xiv, except that it has *philibiblon*. It has also the final note, but with the blunder of *libro* for l (= 50) and *feciliter* for *feliciter* and adding at the end the word *Quod*.

Harl. 3224 (f. 67) is also a small 8vo manuscript, written about 1400, with no note at the beginning, and at the end the abbreviated note: 'Explicit philobiblon dni Ricardi Almgeruile cognominati de Bury quondam Episcopi Dunel-men̄.'

Cott. App. iv (f. 103) is a folio manuscript written about 1425, having no note at the beginning and at the end simply: 'Explicit philibiblion etc.'

Arundel 335 (f. 58) is a small quarto manuscript of the fifteenth century, formerly belonging to the 'Soc. Reg.

Lond., ex dono Henr. Howard, Norfolciensis'. It begins 'Philobiblon Ricō de Bury Dunelm, eͬo authore', these words being in a later hand; it has no note at the end.

Add. MS. 24361 (f. 4ᵛ) is a quarto manuscript also of the fifteenth century, purchased at the Hunter sale in 1861. It ends: 'Explicit philibiblon dñi Ricī de Aungervyle cognoīati de Bury quondam epī dunelm. Cōpletus Anno Dōi 1344ᵗᵒ etatis nrē 58 Ponͭ. nrī xiᵐᵒ.'

Oxford (9)

There are altogether nine manuscripts at Oxford, of which two are in the Bodleian Library and the remaining seven in the libraries of various colleges.

The most important of them is MS. Digby 147 (f. 9), a quarto manuscript written in Mr. Macray's opinion about 1375. It has no note at the beginning, but has the usual note at the end. This manuscript also bears a note showing that it was formerly 'Liber ecclesie sancte Marie de Mertone'; it afterwards belonged to Tho. Allen, from whom it passed to his pupil Sir Kenelm Digby.

The Bodleian Add. MS. C. 108 (f. 20ᵛ) is a quarto paper manuscript in double columns, written in a German hand in the second half of the fifteenth century. It begins: 'Incipit Philobliblon id est tractatus de amore librorum venerabilis viri dñi Richardi de buri Epī Dunelmensis editus p venerabilem mgrͫ Robertum Holkot anglicani ordinis predicatorum', but has no note at the end. It was acquired by the Bodleian in 1868.

This manuscript is followed by a glossary of some interest, as it consists chiefly of the uncommon and exotic words

Introduction

found in the *Philobiblon*; of the 244 words comprised in it, no less than 212 are used in this book. If I had seen it earlier in my work, it might have been of service in suggesting clues to the explanation of some of the difficulties of the book; but as it was, I had puzzled them out for myself before I saw the glossary. It only once or twice cites any authority, and the explanations are seldom adequate and very often incorrect. It includes *asub*, *aux*, and *ellefuga*; inserts *genzahar*, but without explanation; and makes no mention of *Crato*, *Logostilios*, *comprehensor*, *invisus*, *hereos*, *lilia*, *canonium*, *viola*, *hierophilosophus*, and many other words which urgently call for explanation.

At Balliol College, there are two paper manuscripts in folio written in the fifteenth century: clxvi (A) and cclxiii, the latter written in double columns, and with the usual note at the end.

At Lincoln College, No. lxxxi (f. 79) is a folio manuscript of the early fifteenth century in double columns, with illuminated initials. It has no preliminary note and ends: 'Explicit tractatus qui vocatur Philobiblon.' There can be no doubt that it was one of the manuscripts chiefly used by James.

At Magdalen College, No. vi (f. 164) is a small quarto manuscript of the early fifteenth century. It has no title and begins with Chapter I, omitting the Prologue. At the end is a note: 'Explicit philibiblon dñi Ricardi de Aungervile cognoīati de Bury quondam Epi dimlm̄ cōpletus anno doⁱ 1344ᵗᵒ etatis nr̄e 58. pontę nr̄i undecīo.' This also was one of the manuscripts upon which James mainly relied.

At All Souls College, No. xxxi (f. 236) is a large quarto

manuscript of the fifteenth century, written in double columns. It begins: 'Incipit prologus in philobiblon Ricardi dunolmensis episcopi.' At the end is the usual note with some variations: 'Explicit tractatus qui dicitur Philobiblon id est amor librorum editus a Dño Ricardi de Buri quondam Dunolm̄ epō completus est autem in manerio nostro de Ackeland in festo conversionis sancti Pauli A°. dñi m¹ ccc^mo xliijj°. etatis nostre lviii° pont vero nr̄i Anno xi°. finiente ad laudem dei feliciter et Amen.'

At Corpus Christi College, No. ccxxii (f. 57) is a small quarto manuscript of the fifteenth century. It begins: 'Incipit prologus in Philobiblon Ricī Dunelmensis epī quē librum compilauit Roƀus holcote de ordine predicato₄ sub nomine dicti Episcopi'; and ends with the usual note.

In Mr. Coxe's catalogue of the Corpus manuscripts, he observes under no. clxvii (p. 68) that this manuscript, which contained the *Philobiblon*, has long been missing. It is, I think, apparent on comparing the entries in Bernard under nos. 167 and 222 that two volumes have been bound together, and that nothing is really 'missing'; and the entry in Coxe's catalogue should be corrected accordingly.

At St. John's College no. clxxii (f. 2) is an early fifteenth-century quarto manuscript with an illuminated initial. After the title *Philobiblon* follow the words in red: 'Hic aurum tibi non valet vbi nitet Philobiblon.' At the end is the usual note. The manuscript bears a note to the effect that it was presented to the college in 1634. By an oversight, though duly catalogued by Mr. Coxe, it is not included in his index.

Introduction

Cambridge (3)

There are three manuscripts at Cambridge, in the libraries of as many colleges.

At Trinity College is a manuscript (R. 9, 17, f. 48) in small quarto of the early fifteenth century. A preliminary note or title has unfortunately been cropped by some careless binder. At the end it has the usual note.

At Corpus Christi College, among Archbishop Parker's books is a quarto manuscript, on f. 127 of which is the *Philobiblon*, written in the fifteenth century. There is no preliminary note, and the concluding note is very inaccurately given. It is catalogued by Nasmith, Catal. librorum MS.orum, 1777, at p. 416.

At Sidney Sussex College is a manuscript partly on parchment and partly on paper, poorly written in the fifteenth century, which was presented to the college by William Pratt, Vicar of Bossel, Yorkshire. It has the concluding note.

Durham (1)

In Bishop Cosin's Library at Durham is a fifteenth-century octavo manuscript, which found its way into the Bishop's collection through the Rev. George Davenport, its first Keeper, who presented seventy manuscripts to the library. An account of Davenport is in Surtees's *History of Durham*, i. 153, 170. The manuscript is catalogued in Rud's catalogue, at p. 177 of Botfield's Durham Catalogues. Though very neatly written, the manuscript presents numerous omissions of single words. It is without preliminary note and ends:

Bibliographical

'Explicit philobiblon Dñi Ricī Almgeruile cognoīati de Buri quōd ēpi Dunelmenþ.'

It may be noted that the *Philobiblon* is not found in any of the earlier catalogues of Durham books printed by the Surtees Society.

In private hands

Two manuscripts have been lent me out of private custody. The first of them is a very small quarto Flemish manuscript of the not very early fifteenth century. It has no preliminary note, and ends: 'Explicit phylybyblon Richardi de Bury epī de amore librorum et scientiarum: Deo gratias.' It contains several interpolations, including one of about a dozen lines.

The other is an octavo fifteenth-century German manuscript in a stamped leather binding, on which the figures of the 'Three Kings', besides the half-erased entry at the beginning 'Liber domus sancte Barbare . . .', clearly point to Cologne. This would at once suggest an association with the *editio princeps*, and a close examination of its text shows that it is very nearly identical with that of the first edition. It is, however, hardly safe to say that we have here what is so rarely met with—the actual manuscript original of a fifteenth-century book. But there can be no doubt of the very close relationship. It begins: 'Incipit prologus in librū de amore librorū qui philobiblon dicitur', in red; but has no concluding note. It belonged to David Laing and I have called it L.

Paris (3)

An account was given by Cocheris of the three manuscripts in the Bibliothèque Nationale, used by him for the purposes

of his edition, which requires to be supplemented in some important particulars.

The manuscript formerly numbered 797, now 15168, forms part of the Fonds de St. Victor, and is a small quarto containing several treatises, of which the *Philobiblon* is the first. It has a note at the foot of fol. 1ʳ: 'Iste liber est sancti Victoris parisiensis—quicunque eum, etc.'; at the foot of fol. 1ᵛ: 'Ihs. m̊. S.' [A shield with the arms of Navarre] 'Victor . S Augᵍtinᵍ' in red letters; and again at the foot of fol. 4ʳ this note: 'Iste liber est sancti Victoris parisiensis. quicunque eum furatus fuerit vel celaverit vel titulum istum deleverit anathema sit amen. O.' At the end of the *Philobiblon* is a note: 'Hunc librum acquisiuit monasterio sancti victoris prope parisius frater Johannes lamasse dum esset prior eiusdem ecclesie.' Lamasse was Prior from 1448 to 1458. This manuscript, which is in a poor handwriting, begins: 'Incipit prologus Philobiblon.'

The manuscript numbered 3352 c. is a well-written folio manuscript, which formerly belonged to Colbert, whose arms are on its red morocco covers. Cocheris by an almost incredible oversight has not noted that it bears at the top of fol. 1ʳ the words in red letters: 'Philobiblon olchoti anglici.' It begins nevertheless: 'Incipit prologus in philobiblon Ricardi dunelnensis episcopi', and ends: 'Explicit Philobiblon.'

Both these manuscripts, which I have called respectively A and B, present a fairly good text. M. Léopold Delisle is of opinion that they may have been written between 1375 and 1400, but Mr. E. M. Thompson thinks that they are not earlier than the beginning of the fifteenth century.

Bibliographical

The third Paris manuscript is a folio manuscript on paper numbered 2454 of the Ancien Fonds latin. It was written pretty late in the fifteenth century and presents a very inferior text.

The concluding note as to the date and authorship of the book is not found in any of the Paris manuscripts.

Brussels (3)

In the Bibliothèque Royale de Belgique are three copies, of which the late Conservateur en chef, M. Alvin, sent me the following account: 'Notre Bibliothèque possède trois manuscrits du *Philobiblion* de Richard de Bury: le No. 738, transcription du xve siècle, provenant du prieuré du Val St. Martin à Louvain; le No. 3,725, daté de 1492 et ne se composant que du primum manuale relatif aux livres sacrés; le No. 11,465 du xve siècle, provenant de l'abbaye des Prémontrés de Parc. Ces trois transcriptions sont trop récentes pour avoir quelque valeur paléographique et ne semblent pas contenir des variantes à signaler.'

Catalogued in *Catal. des MSS. de la bibliothèque royale des ducs de Bourgogne*, Brux., 1842, tom. i, p. 15.

Munich (2)

In the Royal Library at Munich are two paper manuscripts numbered 4705 and 5829, written in the first half of the fifteenth century. No. 5829 is actually dated by the scribe 1426, and the other was written somewhat later and was indeed not improbably transcribed from the former. Both manuscripts begin in the same way: 'Incipit tractatus greco vocabulo philobiblon (No. 4705 has phylobiblon) amabiliter nuncupatus de amore valore et conseruacione librorum.'

Introduction

Bamberg (1)

In the Royal Library of Bamberg is a quarto paper manuscript entitled: 'Tractatus de amore librorum grece dictus philobiblon. Phylobylon magnifici disertissimique viri Richardi dilmelinensis episcopi de querimonijs librorum.' A letter is prefixed to it from 'Johannes Abbas in Ebrach' to Friedrich Creussner, the Nuremberg printer. From this letter, which is dated 17 September 1484, it appears that the Abbot, who was from 1456 to 1474 professor of theology at Vienna, had read the book when a student there. He complains bitterly of the corrupted text of the Spires edition, which had appeared the year before, and he had accordingly carefully corrected it, and now sends his work to Creussner to print. So far as we know, Creussner did not print it. The Abbot's letter was published by Jaeck in the *Serapeum* in 1843, Bd. iv. 191–2.

Basel (1)

In the University Library at Basel is a quarto paper manuscript of the fifteenth century beginning: 'Incipit prologus in librum de amore librorum qui dicitur philobiblon' (in red). It is without the concluding note, and belongs to the inferior group of manuscripts. It is catalogued in Haenel, *Catal. Libror. MSS.*, Lips. 1830, p. 527.

Venice (1)

In 1650 Tomasini recorded the existence of a manuscript in the library of S. Giovanni and S. Paolo at Venice, belonging to the Dominicans, adding: 'quem miror hic Gesnerum non observasse.' It was more fully catalogued in 1778

by Berardelli, the librarian, who as a good Dominican maintains that it was written by Holkot. Since the collection has passed into the Biblioteca Nazionale di S. Marco, it has been catalogued by Valentinelli, who assigned it to the fourteenth century. The present librarian, Signor Castellani, has been good enough to send me some account of the manuscript, which enables me to correct that of Valentinelli. He has also sent a tracing of the handwriting, which appears to be of the fifteenth century.

The title appearing in the manuscript must, I think, have been added after the edition of Paris: 'Philobiblon seu de amore librorum ac de institutione bibliothecarum.' The manuscript ends: 'Explicit philobiblon magistri Roberti Holkot ordinis Praedicatorum.'

Rome (1)

In May 1885 M. Delisle, on returning from Italy, was good enough to write to me: 'Le hazard m'a récemment fait passer sous les yeux le MS. 259 au fonds Ottoboni au Vatican. C'est un volume copié au xive siècle, dont la première partie est le *Philobiblon* de l'évêque de Durham.' Mr. W. Bliss has kindly sent me an account of this manuscript, which he assigns to the '*end* of the fourteenth century, or later'. From a note upon it, it appears to have belonged to 'Daniel Aurelius, 1564'. It does not give the note at the end, and has no reference to Holkot.

Escurial (1)

There is a manuscript at the Escurial (Real Biblioteca de San Lorenzo), which was catalogued by the late G. Löwe in

Introduction

the *Bibliotheca patrum latinorum Hispaniensis*, ed. by W. von Hartel, Wien, 1887, p. 86 (cf. p. 537), who attributes the volume of which it forms part to the fourteenth century. According to Denifle, *Die Universitäten im Mittelalter*, 1885, i. 797 n., the book is attributed in this manuscript to Holcot, but of this Löwe says nothing. Father Felix Rozánski, late librarian at the Escurial, has, however, kindly sent me the following account of the manuscript:

Cod. sec. xv., II. J. 25. Inter alia fol. 157 incipit: 'Incipit libellus dictus Philobiblon editus a fratre . . . [*nomen auctoris avulsum*] predicator[e] sacre pagine preclarissimo professore ad petitionem domini Ricardi dimelinensis (*sic*) episcopi in cuius persona ipse magister Robertus loquitur in libello presenti.—Incipit prologus in philobiblon Ricardi Dimelinensis episcopi. . . .'

'Continet hoc opusculum xix. capitula finitque fol. 186: faciei conspectum. Amen. Explicit philobiblon Ricardi.'

Missing manuscripts

It may be of interest to record such traces as I have met with of the existence of other manuscripts, which may perhaps some day be found.

There was a manuscript in the *Bibliotheca Amploniana* at Erfurt, as appears by the catalogue published by Dr. Schum in 1887, p. 382. In a paper manuscript (Q. 123), described as of the end of the fourteenth century, the twenty-fifth work was the *Philobiblon*. This manuscript was sent to London for my use, but I found on examination that the portion containing the *Philobiblon* had been removed, as in fact appears from Dr. Schum's catalogue.

I cannot identify the manuscript mentioned by Fabricius in the *Bibliotheca M. et Inf. Latinitatis* as being in his possession

with any extant manuscript. Cocheris suggests that it may be the Cottonian copy, but in the first place this does not correspond to the description of Fabricius, and in the next place the manuscript was in the Cottonian Library in 1696 and can never have been in the possession of Fabricius.

J. F. Reimmann, the German bibliographer, had a manuscript in his possession, which he described in his *Bibliotheca Histor.-Lit.*, ed. sec., 1743, p. 147. He declares it to contain a text very much superior to any of the printed editions. He mentions also that it was followed by a 'carmen leoninum de re bibliothecaria',[1] which was not to be found in any of the published texts. I do not know to what this refers; it is certain, however, that the poem never formed any part of the *Philobiblon*.

The most interesting, perhaps, of the missing manuscripts is that which Dr. Thomas Kay (or Caius) tells us he saw and read at Durham College, Oxford, towards the end of Henry VIII's reign, and which he supposed to be the copy given to the college by the Bishop himself—'eundem ipsum indubie, quem ipsemet bibliothecae illi vivus contulerat': see Hearne's ed. of the *Assertio Antiquitatis Oxon. Academiae*, ii. 433.

His opponent in the controversy as to the respective priority of the two universities, Dr. John Caius, boasts of the possession of a manuscript of the *Philobiblon*, which he says was accompanied by a copy of the foundation-deed of Durham College: loc. cit. i. 242.

---

[1] These leonine verses from the Reimmann MS., now at Göttingen, are printed on p. lxxii. While they have a certain charm, they certainly have nothing to do with Richard de Bury.

Introduction

A very few words must suffice to explain the use I have made of the manuscripts in forming the text of the present edition. Of the whole number of manuscripts here enumerated I have personally examined or collated *twenty-eight*. I have not indeed in the critical notes attempted to give a collation of all these manuscripts. Nor even of the four manuscripts of which I have recorded all the important variants does the printed collation profess to be absolutely complete. In an edition intended primarily for the general reader, it seemed unnecessary to burden the notes with a mass of various readings due to the errors of copyists or to unsettled orthography. A complete collation of the best manuscripts and the important variations of all the manuscripts must be reserved for a more elaborate critical edition, if there should appear to be a demand for it. That will also furnish a more suitable occasion for a discussion of the relationship of the various manuscripts.

The manuscripts which appeared to be for my present purpose the most important were the two Paris manuscripts which I have called A and B; Digby 147, which I have denoted D, and Royal 8 F. xiv, which I have called E.

I have felt myself bound in consequence of the unfavourable judgement I had formed of the critical work of Cocheris to give the variants of the two former manuscripts, because he has affected to give them, and I have also given the various readings of D and E in all important places. In a few places of special difficulty or interest I have occasionally given the readings of other manuscripts. The readings of the Cologne manuscript I have given pretty frequently, in order to exhibit

Bibliographical

its close relationship to the text of the *editio princeps*; and for a similar reason I have given the readings of the Magdalen manuscript, to indicate the extent to which James seems to have used it in forming his text.

Occasionally I have given the readings of the early printed texts, when they differ from what may be almost called the *textus receptus*. Where I have recorded this current text, as it is found in the successive editions down to Cocheris (cf. the pedigree on p. xlix), it may be assumed that except in the matter of orthography and accidental errors of the press it reproduces the readings of the *editio princeps*.

I have thought it right to reduce the orthography of the manuscripts to a classical standard. While I accept the general soundness of the view that medieval writers should be reproduced in their own orthography, I justify my deviation from this rule on two grounds: first, that the *Philobiblon* is a work of literature and not of philology, and secondly, that I feared to repel many readers who feel no interest in medieval Latinists generally, but will be led to take up the present work from the interest of its subject and its claim upon all to whom

"Books are a passion and delight."

The explanatory and illustrative notes are mainly directed to the establishment of the text. The Bishop's style is made of scriptural and liturgical quotation and allusion; and a reference to the Vulgate frequently determines the probable reading in a doubtful passage, as well as explains its meaning. I have been more sparing in references to previous or contemporary writers, a kind of illustration which it would be easy to multiply. I have tried to leave nothing really difficult

Introduction

unexplained, without burdening the reader with irrelevant or superfluous annotation, and can only hope, in the words of St. Augustine: 'quibus parum vel quibus nimium, nobis ignoscant.'

POSTSCRIPT

Any worker on the manuscripts of the *Philobiblon* should first have recourse to the very scholarly list provided by Altamura in his printed text, pp. 19–39. The following observations are designed to give the present-day researcher some indication of the additional information which has become available since Thomas's day and to make an attempt to bring his list of manuscript sources more up to date. I treat first of manuscripts now in England and then of those on the Continent.

I. ENGLAND

1. To the list of manuscripts at Oxford should be added another recently acquired by the Bodleian, namely Lyell MS. 63, which came from the Austrian abbey of Melk (fifteenth century: written at Nuremberg).

Balliol College MS. 243 is in fact on parchment and not on paper; it is of Netherlandish provenance (Altamura makes a rare slip in describing it as MS. 263).

2. The Durham manuscript is now in the University Library and is catalogued MS. Cosin V. v. 2.

*3. Of the two manuscripts listed by Thomas as in private hands, the first mentioned (which in his time belonged to a Mr. Timmins) is now in the Morgan Library at New York

* indicates a manuscript not noticed in Altamura's list.

Bibliographical

(MS. 448), while the second (owned by Mr. David Laing in 1888) is now in the Cambridge Library (Add. MS. 3145). Neither of these changes has been recorded by Altamura.

*4. In addition the manuscripts at Cambridge should include St. John's College MS. E. 12 (115). The Sidney Sussex manuscript is listed Δ 2. 16. (38).

*5. Quaritch Catalogue 502 (1941) had a late paper copy in a Netherlandish hand.

II. ABROAD

In this section I treat first of the places cited by Thomas, and in the same order, then of those which he does not mention.

6. In Munich there are four manuscripts not listed by Thomas, viz.

   (i) 3586 (fifteenth century: coming from Augsburg and written by a Viennese Carmelite named Matthias Farinatoris).

   (ii) 17292 (fifteenth century: from monastery of Scheftlarn).

   (iii) 19742 (fifteenth century: from monastery of Tegernsee).

   (iv) 23952 (fifteenth century: provenance unknown).

7. In Basel University Library is a second manuscript, namely B. VIII. 11 (fifteenth century: coming from a Dominican convent in Basel).

8. In Venice the important fifteenth-century manuscript is now catalogued MS. lat. I. 41 (2057). It actually ends: '. . . magistri rotberti holchot ordinis praedicatorum.'

Introduction

9. There is another manuscript in Spain, at Barcelona, namely MS. Dalmases n. 635, at the Central Library. It dates from the second half of the fifteenth century.

The following manuscripts occur in places not listed at all by Thomas: they are given in alphabetical order with approximate dates where possible.

(i) Berlin MS. lat. 588 fol. (moved to Tübingen after the war: present whereabouts unknown). Probably Italian, late fifteenth century. Once Philipps MS. 16416.

*(ii) Breslau MS. Rehdigeranus 130 (almost certainly destroyed in the war).

(iii) Copenhagen University Library MS. Fabr. 21 Fol. This is the manuscript mentioned by Thomas in connexion with Fabricius (see p. lxvi). It is fifteenth century and succeeds in rendering the bishop's name as 'Muiegeruile'!

*(iv) Erlangen University Library MS. 542 (no details).

(v) Göttingen University Library MS. theol. 119 fol. This is Reimmann's manuscript as described by Thomas (on p. lxvii). It is of fourteenth-century date, perhaps about 1380. As Thomas notes it concludes with a leonine verse (of sonnet length) which it may be of interest to print here:

> Hac sunt in cella doctorum grata libella,
> que stillant mella, radiant pariter quasi stella;
> huc acies mentis divertatur sapientis.
> non donans ventis, sed eis haerens documentis
> intus librorum quisquis quemquam capit horum
> versus ut iste sonat, quae cepit parte reponat;

Bibliographical

qui libros aperis, hos claudere ne pigriteris;
a fatuis sordide libri tractantur ubique,
sed noscens litteras tractat eas ut margaritas
qui sibi concedi vult librum vel bene credi.
noster hoc ordo sonat alium mox ipse reponat
qui valeat tantum vel certe plus aliquantum;
spe defraudatur alias quicumque precatur.
pro dei laude libros lege, postea claude.

*(vi) Innsbruck University Library MS. 144 (no details).
(vii) Trier, Stadtbibliothek MS. 685/247 (fifteenth century from the Carthusian house of St. Alban in Trier).
(viii) New York: see (3).

It will have been noticed that several of the manuscripts now in English collections are of foreign provenance: the reverse does not seem to be true to any noticeable extent. We thus find reflected in the incidence of surviving manuscripts what has already become clear from the printed editions, namely, that Bishop Richard de Bury's lively work was more appreciated overseas, especially perhaps in Germany, than it was in his own land. The causes of this state of affairs would need a more learned pen than mine to elucidate. At least we hope that this present edition will do something to revive his fame among his own countrymen.

M. M.

FOREWORD

E. C. Thomas

ERNEST CHESTER THOMAS, whose text and translation of the *Philobiblon* is in all essentials presented here again, was born in 1850 at Birkenhead. He was educated at Manchester Grammar School and Trinity College, Oxford, where he graduated with first-class honours and became Librarian of the Union. From Oxford he went to Gray's Inn and was ultimately called to the Bar: but although he had a practice, his interests were predominantly literary and he devoted more time to bibliography than to being a barrister. In 1875–6 he advanced his education by spending a period at the Universities of Jena and Bonn. His interest in books was manifested in his share in the article 'Libraries' for the *Encyclopædia Britannica* (9th edition), and he published a number of short productions on law and librarianship as well as translating from the German. He died, comparatively young, at Tunbridge Wells in 1892. A full biography of him may be found in *Library* for 1893, pp. 73–80.

But to write in these terms of Thomas is to ignore his main achievement. He was a one-book man, and that book was the *Philobiblon*. A large measure of his short life must have been spent on the track of Richard de Bury and of that Bishop's masterpiece. The edition which Thomas produced in 1888 was incomparably in advance of anything that had gone before, and was the fruit of a rare combination of devotion and scholarship. He succeeded in discovering and examining about twice as many manuscripts as any previous

Foreword

editor, and no one can read through his footnotes without appreciating very fully the great care and really considerable width of reading which enabled him to identify and pin down Richard de Bury's numerous quotations or allusions to the Vulgate, the Fathers, and elsewhere. Rightly has each succeeding editor of the *Philobiblon* paid tribute to the pioneer work of E. C. Thomas in this field; whatever each may have added, and some have added little enough, he was building on Thomas's foundations. If one is to criticize him, it would be on the grounds of sometimes labouring his point too far in his notes, and from time to time (though there must always be room for disagreement here) of choosing a less happy reading or emendation.

The authorship of the 'Philobiblon'

Perhaps the most curious facet of Thomas's editorship was his attitude to this question. The preface to his edition is dated October 1888, and at the end of his Introduction, as will have been seen already, he expressed doubts as to whether the Dominican Robert Holcot was not the true author and quoted a hostile passage from Murimuth which I have not included. But earlier in the same year he had published privately in an edition of only fifty copies a short pamphlet entitled 'Was Richard de Bury an Impostor?' In this he quotes the same denigratory extract from Murimuth and generally casts doubt on the good name, good fame, and scholarship of Bishop de Bury. The picture is a sombre one, that at the end of a life's work—for he died only four years later—Thomas had come less and less to believe in the achievement of his hero. How far were these fears justified?

Foreword

The suggestion that Holcot was the true author of the *Philobiblon* is based on the fact that an important group of manuscripts credits Holcot with being either the author or editor of the work. A typical example is MS. Additional C 108 in Bodley which concludes the *Incipit* with the words 'editus per uenerabilem magistrum Robertum Holkot anglicani (*sic*) ordinis predicatorum'. Opinions have varied as to the significance of these entries. Some have contended that Holcot was the true author and that de Bury simply took the credit: others have thought in various terms of collaboration, some that Holcot advised the Bishop, others that he 'devilled for him in fact'.[1] Altamura,[2] in an elaborate and stimulating discussion of the manuscripts, suggests that they can be divided into two groups of one of which Holcot was perhaps the amanuensis: in this context he attaches considerable importance to the use of the verb *edere* to describe Holcot's part in the transaction. Against this it might be argued that by this date Holcot was already a person of enough importance in his own right to leave such tasks to the Bishop's then staff: it is beyond dispute that he had been a close member of de Bury's circle. Less than a quarter of the extant manuscripts bring in Holcot's name in this manner and these might have been derived from a (now vanished) copy produced in his own hand.

It seems simpler to suppose that Richard de Bury was in fact himself the author of the work which has so long borne his name; and it is certainly more agreeable to do so. That he may well have received assistance both intellectual and practical

[1] Pantin, *English Church in the XIV Century*, p. 145.

[2] Altamura, op. cit., pp. 47–66. See p. liv.

Foreword

from Holcot (or other members of his scholarly circle) does not detract from his achievement. There are indeed mistakes in the *Philobiblon*, e.g. the attribution to Ovid of the *De Vetula* in Chapter IX, which there are grounds for supposing Holcot would not have made,[1] for as a scholar he had a wider equipment than the busy Bishop of Durham.

The style of the 'Philobiblon'

One important aspect of the style of *Philobiblon* completely escaped Thomas, but has been ably pointed out by Dr. Denholm-Young.[2] This is the use of *clausulae* or deliberately rhythmical ends to sentences, or clauses in sentences. This is not the place to expound the system in full: for this inquirers are commended to Dr. Denholm-Young's article and other sources cited there. It is enough to say that there were three endings in common use, styled Planus, Tardus, and Velox. This manner of writing, often called the Cursus, was derived from the Papal Chancery: it was known to earlier and cosmopolitan writers like John of Salisbury, but only became at all common in this country in the fourteenth century.

'In an exact use of the Roman Cursus de Bury can rival Dante, Petrarch or Boccaccio, and in his use of compound *clausulae* he was probably never excelled', writes Dr. Denholm-Young. He goes on to point out that de Bury's book contains about 19,000 words, and that of these the Planus, Tardus, and Velox endings make a total of over 3,800 words,

[1] See Holcot's *Super sap.*, f. 103ª, where he writes of *De Vetula* 'An sit liber Ovidii, Deus novit'.

[2] Denholm-Young, *The Cursus in England* (Essays presented to H. E. Salter), but reprinted in Denholm-Young, *Collected Papers on Mediaeval Subjects*, pp. 26–55, and especially p. 45.

and occur in a ratio of approximately 3 : 4 : 5. It is tempting to suppose that this is additional reason for attributing the book to the much-travelled bishop, versed as he was in the language of diplomacy and the practice of the papacy. A cynic could reply that a well-trained clerk like Holcot was perfectly capable of writing in this manner, if instructed to do so. On margin, however, it appears to me slightly to strengthen the case for de Bury's authorship.

Bishop Richard de Bury

There can be no doubt that the circumstances of de Bury's career drew him away from scholarship. There is no need to rehearse them again, and he still lacks the biographer who shall give the various facets their relative importance. In public life it is clear that his talents must have been considerable and that it was the view of his master (and pupil) that they were better employed in diplomacy than in one of the routine great offices of state. De Bury's role as a politician has yet to be assessed, but it is difficult to resist the conclusion that he must have been one of the most important figures in the group which assisted the young king to break free from the tutelage of his mother and her paramour. Not long after this de Bury seems to have felt once again the lure of scholarship, for in August 1333 he obtained leave from the Pope to absent himself from the Deanery of Wells (then his highest preferment) in order to study for three years at a University;[1] this would presumably have entailed giving up his post as Keeper of the Privy Seal. In September the see of Durham

[1] *Cal. Pap. Lett.* ii, p. 392.

Foreword

became vacant: de Bury was promoted, and, after his brief periods as Lord Treasurer and Lord Chancellor, pursued his career of diplomacy.

It must not be forgotten that in the intervals of his appearance on the stage of national affairs he was carrying out at least two other important roles. In the north of England, like all bishops of Durham, he was the most important servant of the Crown, a bulwark against Scottish invasion and a royal agent in every form of activity. De Bury did not shirk those tasks: the public records attest the variety of his duties. But in addition he maintained around himself and in his *familia* a group of scholars whose learning and importance has been widely recognized.[1] These scholars the bishop made dispute before him daily after dinner, and he was also active in promoting their interests: on one visit to the Pope he is recorded as having obtained over 300 favours for his clerks.[2] And all these learned men must in their turn have profited from their bishop's great collection of books. They repaid him with their dedications, as that of Walter Burley's commentary on the *Politics* of Aristotle.

The last years of the life of Richard de Bury were, as we have seen, clouded by sickness according to Chambre. We do not know the nature of his malady, but it certainly led to some withdrawal from public life noticeable from about 1342. It is at least plausible that he used this leisure to compile the *Philobiblon*, which he only finished shortly before his death on 14 April 1345. No fresh evidence can be brought

[1] Pantin, op. cit., p. 139. See also the important series of articles (already cited) by J. de Ghellinck in *Revue d'Histoire Ecclésiastique*, vols. xviii and xix.

[2] *Scriptores Tres* (Surtees Soc. IX), pp. 127, 128.

Foreword

forward as to the fate of his beloved library: it must remain most likely that it was sold to pay his debts.[1]

The 'Philobiblon'

Every reader of the *Philobiblon* will have his own favourite passages. No one can deny that its writer was in love with books. Those who have suffered even mildly from this affection will understand the *Philobiblon* the more fully. For those who have not so suffered, we can do 'Nothing but sympathise'. It is clear from Chapter XVII that the outrages committed by borrowers were little different in the fourteenth century from the crimes which they commit today. Equally modern is the Bishop's love of Paris, 'the Paradise of the world', as a centre of learning and of libraries. What collector has not suffered the same anguish when an unclean hand approaches a beloved volume: and yet de Bury realizes full well that books are made to be seen and to be lent. His sense of humour, if perhaps a slightly malicious one, shows clearly in his description of the pustular clergy. Over and above all shines out the pleasure in owning and acquiring books. 'No man, therefore, can serve both books and Mammon.' It is small wonder that the Bishop died in debt. Perhaps he would in a sense have been happy that his great collection should have been dispersed: for if all libraries are held together, whence may the collector of tomorrow find his treasures?

The Present Edition

The present edition of the *Philobiblon* is to mark the seventieth birthday of a bibliophile of today, one who has not

[1] See Rashdall, *Universities of Europe in the Middle Ages*, ed. Powicke and Emden, vol. iii, pp. 186–7.

Foreword

only loved books in their own right and made them nobly at the Shakespeare Head Press, but has also done much to make them available to thousands of readers of all classes and races. Sir Basil Blackwell would have been welcome at Bishop Auckland in the early 1340's.

Time has not allowed the preparation of a new text, the collation of the manuscripts, or even a new translation. The reader is therefore entitled to know that what is before him is mainly based on the 1888 edition of Thomas, and also to know what has been done to that edition. First, the Introduction, the Latin text, and the English translation of Thomas have been reprinted almost unaltered. It is certain that one could improve on Thomas's text, but it was difficult to decide how far to go and again time stood in the path, as it did also in the way of attempting a new translation. Where the text and the English were concerned our first thought was for the reader. We have been anxious to produce a printed page which would encourage the curious to find out what Bishop de Bury actually said. In an ideal world all would do this in his original language, but the Latinity of many today is rusty or even non-existent and so the two tongues have been set *en regard* and without either textual variants or foot-notes on the page. Those who seek these may be referred to Thomas himself (if they can come by a copy of this now rare book) or to the more modern editions of Nelson or Altamura.

I have ventured to deal more harshly with Thomas's foot-notes. Those to the text itself tended to be verbose or tangential: of the briefer ones many simply identified passages of scripture or other writing to which de Bury alluded. Like all

Foreword

medieval writers, he knew the Bible from cover to cover: he was steeped in it: his verbiage is impregnated with it. Most readers will recognize many such allusions spontaneously and will half recognize others. They would not always have been helped by Thomas, who, somewhat perversely, employed the Vulgate terminology for the Old Testament chronicle books and the Vulgate numbering of the Psalms. A limited number of Thomas's notes, though I hope enough to show the flavour of his scholarship, together with a few suggestions of my own, follow the Latin and English texts. I am particularly conscious that my few textual emendations are of a haphazard character.

The two sections of Thomas's Introduction on Printed Editions and MSS. I have tried to bring more or less up to date. Again I have virtually eliminated his footnotes which added little to his argument and were in many cases references to authorities now obsolete. Furthermore, I have provided a new set of notes to the first part of his Introduction, dealing with the career of Richard de Bury. Many of these notes incorporate material from Thomas, but in the others I have sought to include references to views advanced or writings about Richard de Bury which have been produced in the seventy years since Thomas laid down his pen. I have not attempted a formal bibliography, but one may be found in Altamura. It is my hope that the ghost of a former scholar of Trinity will forgive a fellow of his college for these liberties.

Conclusion

Sir Basil Blackwell was born when Thomas's book was still fresh and white from its printer. It has long been one of

Foreword

his favourite books and we hope he will enjoy it in this form.

Where it is of value or beauty, the work is by other hands than mine, living or dead. They are the same to booklovers—'In libris mortuos quasi vivos invenio' says de Bury in his very first chapter—but I must express my gratitude to both. Where there are imperfections they are mine.

I would end with words which are written on the second page of the manuscript in St. John Baptist College:

Hic aurum tibi non ualet ubi nitet Philobiblon.

M. M.

Philobiblon
Ricardi de Bury

INCIPIUNT CAPITULA

A LIST OF CHAPTERS

Incipiunt Capitula

A List of Chapters

Incipit Prologus

VNIVERSIS Christi fidelibus, ad quos tenor praesentis scripturae pervenerit, Ricardus de Bury, miseratione divina Dunelmensis episcopus, salutem in Domino sempiternam, piamque ipsius praesentare memoriam iugiter coram Deo in vita pariter et post fata.

℣ Quid retribuam Domino pro omnibus quae retribuit mihi? devotissimus investigat psalmista, rex invictus et eximius prophetarum: in qua quaestione gratissima semetipsum redditorem voluntarium, debitorem multifarium et sanctiorem optantem consiliarium recognoscit, concordans cum Aristotele, philosophorum principe, qui omnem de agibilibus quaestionem consilium probat esse: 3° et 6° Ethicorum.

℣ Sane si propheta tam mirabilis, secretorum praescius divinorum, praeconsulere volebat tam sollicite quomodo grate posset gratis data refundere, quid nos rudes regratiatores et avidissimi receptores, onusti divinis beneficiis infinitis, poterimus digne velle? Proculdubio deliberatione sollerti et circumspectione multiplici, invitato primitus spiritu septiformi, quatenus in nostra meditatione ignis illuminans exardescat, viam non impedibilem providere debemus attentius, quo largitor omnium de collatis muneribus suis sponte veneretur reciproce, proximus relevetur ab onere et reatus contractus per peccantes cotidie eleemosynarum remediis redimatur.

Prologue

TO all the faithful of Christ to whom the tenor of these presents may come, Richard de Bury, by the divine mercy Bishop of Durham, wisheth everlasting salvation in the Lord and to present continually a pious memorial of himself before God, alike in his lifetime and after his death.

⸿ What shall I render unto the Lord for all His benefits toward me? asks the most devout psalmist, an invincible king and first among the prophets: in which most grateful question he approves himself a willing thank-offerer, a multifarious debtor, and one who wishes for a holier counsellor than himself: agreeing with Aristotle, the chief of philosophers, who shows (in the 3rd and 6th books of his Ethics) that all action depends upon counsel.

⸿ And indeed if so wonderful a prophet, having a foreknowledge of divine secrets, wished so anxiously to consider how he might gratefully repay the blessings graciously bestowed, what can we fitly do, who are but rude thanksgivers and most greedy receivers, laden with infinite divine benefits? Assuredly we ought with anxious deliberation and abundant consideration, having first invoked the Sevenfold Spirit, that it may burn in our musings as an illuminating fire, fervently to prepare a way without hindrance, that the bestower of all things may be cheerfully worshipped in return for the gifts that He has bestowed, that our neighbour may be relieved of his burden, and that the guilt contracted by sinners every day may be redeemed by the atonement of almsgiving.

The Philobiblon

℃ Huius igitur devotionis monitione praeventi ab eo qui solus bonam hominis et praevenit voluntatem et perficit, sine quo nec sufficientia suppetit cogitandi solummodo, cuius quicquid boni fecerimus non ambigimus esse munus, diligenter tam penes nos quam cum aliis inquirendo discussimus quid inter diversorum generum pietatis officia primo gradu placeret Altissimo, prodessetque potius Ecclesiae militanti. Et ecce mox nostrae considerationis aspectibus grex occurrit scholarium elegorum quin potius electorum, in quibus Deus artifex et ancilla natura morum optimorum et scientiarum celebrium plantaverunt radices, sed ita rei familiaris oppressit penuria, quod obstante fortuna contraria semina tam fecunda virtutum in culto iuventutis agro, roris debiti non rigata favore, arescere compelluntur. Quo fit ut lateat in obscuris condita virtus clara, ut verbis alludamus Boetii, et ardentes lucernae non ponantur sub modio, sed prae defectu olei penitus exstinguantur.

℃ Sic ager in vere floriger ante messem exaruit, sic frumenta in lollium et vites degenerant in labruscas, ac sic in oleastros olivae silvescunt. Marcescunt omnino tenellae trabeculae et qui in fortes columnas Ecclesiae poterant excrevisse, subtilis ingenii capacitate dotati, studiorum gymnasia derelinquunt. Sola inedia novercante, repelluntur a philosophiae nectareo poculo violenter, quam primo gustaverint, ipso gustu ferventius sitibundi: liberalibus artibus habiles et scripturis tantum dispositi contemplandis, orbati

Prologue

❡ Forewarned therefore through the admonition of the psalmist's devotion by Him who alone prevents and perfects the goodwill of man, without whom we have no power even so much as to think, and whose gift we doubt not it is, if we have done anything good, we have diligently inquired and considered in our own heart as well as with others, what among the good offices of various works of piety would most please the Almighty and would be more beneficial to the Church Militant. And lo! there soon occurred to our contemplation a host of unhappy, nay rather of elect scholars, in whom God the Creator and Nature His handmaid planted the roots of excellent morals and of famous sciences, but whom the poverty of their circumstances so oppressed that before the frown of adverse fortune the seeds of excellence, so fruitful in the cultivated field of youth, not being watered by the rain that they require, are forced to wither away. Thus it happens that 'bright virtue lurks buried in obscurity', to use the words of Boethius, and burning lights are not put under a bushel, but for want of oil are utterly extinguished.

❡ Thus the field, so full of flower in spring, has withered up before harvest-time; thus wheat degenerates to tares, and vines into the wild vine, and thus olives run into the wild olive; the tender stems rot away altogether, and those who might have grown up into strong pillars of the Church, being endowed with the capacity of a subtle intellect, abandon the schools of learning. With poverty only as their stepmother, they are repelled violently from the nectared cup of philosophy, as soon as they have tasted of it and have become more fiercely thirsty by the very taste. Though fit for the liberal arts and disposed to study the sacred writings alone, being

9

necessariorum subsidiis, quasi quadam apostasiae specie ad artes mechanicas, propter victus solius suffragia ad Ecclesiae dispendium et totius cleri vilipendium revertuntur.

℄ Sic mater Ecclesia pariendo filios abortiri compellitur, quinimmo ab utero foetus informis monstruose dirumpitur, et pro paucis minimisque quibus contentatur natura, alumnos amittit egregios, postea promovendos in pugiles fidei et athletas. Heu quam repente tela succiditur, dum texentis manus orditur! Heu quod sol eclipsatur in aurora clarissima et planeta progrediens regiratur retrograde ac naturam et speciem verae stellae praetendens subito decidit et fit assub! Quid poterit pius homo intueri miserius? Quid misericordiae viscera penetrabit acutius? Quid cor congelatum ut incus in calentes guttas resolvet facilius?

℄ Amplius arguentes a sensu contrario, quantum profuit toti reipublicae Christianae, non quidem Sardanapali deliciis, neque Croesi divitiis enervare studentes, sed melius mediocritate scholastica suffragari pauperibus, ex eventu praeterito recordemur. Quot oculis vidimus, quot ex scripturis collegimus, nulla suorum natalium claritate fulgentes, nullius haereditatis successione gaudentes, sed tantum proborum virorum pietate suffultos, apostolicas cathedras meruisse! subiectis fidelibus praefuisse probissime! superborum et sublimium colla jugo ecclesiastico subiecisse et procurasse propensius Ecclesiae libertatem!

Prologue

deprived of the aid of their friends, by a kind of apostasy they return to the mechanical arts solely to gain a livelihood, to the loss of the Church and the degradation of the whole clergy.

℩ Thus Mother Church conceiving sons is compelled to miscarry, nay some misshapen monster is born untimely from her womb, and for lack of that little with which nature is contented, she loses excellent pupils, who might afterwards become champions and athletes of the faith. Alas, how suddenly the woof is cut, while the hand of the weaver is beginning his work! Alas, how the sun is eclipsed in the brightness of the dawn, and the planet in its course is hurled backwards, and while it bears the nature and likeness of a star suddenly drops and becomes a meteor! What more piteous sight can the pious man behold? What can more sharply stir the bowels of his pity? What can more easily melt a heart hard as an anvil into hot tears?

℩ On the other hand, let us recall from past experience how much it has profited the whole Christian commonwealth, not indeed to enervate students with the delights of a Sardanapalus or the riches of a Croesus, but rather to support them in their poverty with the frugal means that become the scholar. How many have we seen with our eyes, how many have we read of in books, who distinguished by no pride of birth, and rejoicing in no rich inheritance, but supported only by the piety of the good, have made their way to apostolic chairs, have most worthily presided over faithful subjects, have bent the necks of the proud and lofty to the ecclesiastical yoke and have extended further the liberties of the Church!

The Philobiblon

(Quamobrem perlustratis humanis egestatibus usque-
quaque caritativae considerationis intuitu, huic tandem cala-
mitoso generi hominum, in quibus tamen tanta redolet spes
profectus Ecclesiae, praeelegit peculiariter nostrae compassionis affectio pium ferre praesidium et eisdem non solum
de necessariis victui, verum multo magis de libris utilissimis
studio providere. Ad hunc effectum acceptissimum coram
Deo nostra iam ab olim vigilavit intentio indefessa. Hic amor
ecstaticus tam potenter nos rapuit ut, terrenis aliis abdicatis
ab animo, acquirendorum librorum solummodo flagraremus
affectu.

(Vt igitur nostri finis intentio tam posteris pateat quam
modernis, et ora loquentium perversa quantum ad nos pertinet obstruamus perpetuo, tractatum parvulinum edidimus
stilo quidem levissimo modernorum—est enim ridiculosum
rhetoricis quando levis materia grandi describitur stilo; qui
tractatus amorem quem ad libros habuimus ab excessu pur-
gabit, devotionis intentae propositum propalabit et circum-
stantias facti nostri, per viginti divisus capitula, luce clarius
enarrabit. Quia vero de amore librorum principaliter disserit,
placuit nobis more veterum Latinorum ipsum Graeco vocabulo Philobiblon amabiliter nuncupare.

Explicit Prologus. Incipiunt Capitula.

Prologue

₵ Accordingly, having taken a survey of human necessities in every direction, with a view to bestow our charity upon them, our compassionate inclinations have chosen to bear pious aid to this calamitous class of men, in whom there is nevertheless such hope of advantage to the Church, and to provide for them not only in respect of things necessary to their support, but much more in respect of the books so useful to their studies. To this end, most acceptable in the sight of God, our attention has long been unweariedly devoted. This ecstatic love has carried us away so powerfully, that we have resigned all thoughts of other earthly things, and have given ourselves up to a passion for acquiring books.

₵ That our intent and purpose, therefore, may be known to posterity as well as to our contemporaries, and that we may for ever stop the perverse tongues of gossipers as far as we are concerned, we have published a little treatise written in the lightest style of the moderns; for it is ridiculous in authors to find a slight matter treated of in a pompous style. And this treatise (divided into twenty chapters) will clear the love we have had for books from the charge of excess, will expound the purpose of our intense devotion, and will narrate more clearly than light all the circumstances of our undertaking. And because it principally treats of the love of books, we have chosen after the fashion of the ancient Romans fondly to name it by a Greek word, *Philobiblon*.

Here ends the Prologue.

CAPITULUM I

Quod thesaurus sapientiae potissime sit in libris

THESAURUS desiderabilis sapientiae et scientiae, quem omnes homines per instinctum naturae deside-rant, cunctas mundi transcendit divitias infinite: cuius respectu lapides pretiosi vilescunt; cuius comparatione argentum lutescit et aurum obryzum exigua fit arena; cuius splendore tenebrescunt visui sol et luna; cuius dulcore mirabili amarescunt gustui mel et manna.

(O valor sapientiae non marcescens ex tempore, virtus virens assidue, omne virus evacuans ab habente! O munus caeleste liberalitatis divinae, descendens a Patre luminum, ut mentem rationalem provehas usque in caelum! Tu es intellectus caelestis alimonia, quam qui edunt adhuc esurient, quam qui bibunt adhuc sitient, et languentis animae harmonia laetificans, quam qui audit nullatenus confundetur. Tu es morum moderatrix et regula, secundum quam operans non peccabit. Per te reges regnant et legum conditores iusta decernunt. Per te deposita ruditate nativa, elimatis ingeniis atque linguis, vitiorum sentibus coeffossis radicitus, apices consequuntur honoris, fiuntque patres patriae et comites principum, qui sine te conflassent lanceas in ligones et

CHAPTER I

That the Treasure of Wisdom is chiefly contained in Books

THE desirable treasure of wisdom and science, which all men desire by an instinct of nature, infinitely surpasses all the riches of the world; in respect of which precious stones are worthless; in comparison with which silver is as clay and pure gold is as a little sand; at whose splendour the sun and moon are dark to look upon; compared with whose marvellous sweetness honey and manna are bitter to the taste.

(O value of wisdom that fadeth not away with time, virtue ever flourishing, that cleanseth its possessor from all venom! O heavenly gift of the divine bounty, descending from the Father of lights, that thou mayest exalt the rational soul to the very heavens! Thou art the celestial nourishment of the intellect, which those who eat shall still hunger and those who drink shall still thirst, and the gladdening harmony of the languishing soul, which he that hears shall never be confounded. Thou art the moderator and rule of morals, which he who follows shall not sin. By thee kings reign and princes decree justice. By thee, rid of their native rudeness, their minds and tongues being polished, the thorns of vice being torn up by the roots, those men attain high places of honour and become fathers of their country and companions of princes, who without thee would have melted their spears

vomeres, vel cum filio prodigo pascerent forte sues.

℄ Quo lates potissime, praeelecte thesaure, et ubi te reperient animae sitibundae?

℄ In libris proculdubio posuisti tabernaculum tuum, ubi te fundavit Altissimus, lumen luminum, liber vitae. Ibi te omnis qui petit accipit, et qui quaerit invenit, et pulsantibus improbe citius aperitur. In his cherubin alas suas extendunt ut intellectus studentis ascendat, et a polo usque ad polum prospiciat, a solis ortu et occasu, ab aquilone et mari. In his incomprehensibilis ipse Deus altissimus apprehensibiliter continetur et colitur; in his patet natura caelestium, terrestrium et infernorum; in his cernuntur iura quibus omnis regitur politia, hierarchiae caelestis distinguuntur officia et daemonum tyrannides describuntur, quos nec ideae Platonis exsuperant nec Cratonis cathedra continebat.

℄ In libris mortuos quasi vivos invenio; in libris futura praevideo; in libris res bellicae disponuntur; de libris prodeunt iura pacis. Omnia corrumpuntur et intabescunt in tempore; Saturnus quos generat devorare non cessat: omnem mundi gloriam operiret oblivio, nisi Deus mortalibus librorum remedia providisset.

℄ Alexander, orbis domitor, Iulius et urbis et orbis invasor, qui et Marte et arte primus in unitate personae assumpsit imperium, fidelis Fabricius et Cato rigidus hodie

into pruning-hooks and ploughshares, or would perhaps be feeding swine with the prodigal.

℆ Where dost thou chiefly lie hidden, O most elect treasure, and where shall thirsting souls discover thee?

℆ Certes, thou hast placed thy tabernacle in books, where the Most High, the Light of lights, the Book of Life, has established thee. There everyone who asks receiveth thee, and everyone who seeks finds thee, and to everyone that knocketh boldly it is speedily opened. Therein the cherubim spread out their wings, that the intellect of the student may ascend and look from pole to pole, from the east and west, from the north and from the south. Therein the mighty and incomprehensible God Himself is apprehensibly contained and worshipped; therein is revealed the nature of things celestial, terrestrial, and infernal; therein are discerned the laws by which every state is administered, the offices of the celestial hierarchy are distinguished and the tyrannies of demons described, such as neither the ideas of Plato transcend nor the chair of Crato contained.

℆ In books I find the dead as if they were alive; in books I foresee things to come; in books warlike affairs are set forth; from books come forth the laws of peace. All things are corrupted and decay in time; Saturn ceases not to devour the children that he generates: all the glory of the world would be buried in oblivion, unless God had provided mortals with the remedy of books.

℆ Alexander, the conqueror of the earth, Julius the invader of Rome and of the world, who, the first in war and arts, assumed universal empire under his single rule, faithful Fabricius and stern Cato, would now have been unknown

caruissent memoria, si librorum suffragia defuissent. Turres ad terram sunt dirutae; civitates eversae; putredine perierunt fornices triumphales; nec quicquam reperiet vel Papa vel Rex quo perennitatis privilegium conferatur commodius quam per libros. Reddit auctori vicissitudinem liber factus, ut quamdiu liber supererit auctor manens athanatos nequeat interire, teste Ptolemaeo in prologo Almagesti: non fuit, inquit, mortuus qui scientiam vivificavit.

℄ Quis igitur infinito thesauro librorum, de quo scriba doctus profert nova et vetera, per quodcunque alterius speciei pretium limitabit? Veritas vincens super omnia, quae regem, vinum et mulierem supergreditur, quam amicis praehonorare officium obtinet sanctitatis, quae est et via sine devio et vita sine termino, cui sacer Boetius attribuit triplex esse, in mente, voce et scripto, in libris videtur manere utilius et fructificare fecundius ad profectum. Nam virtus vocis perit cum sonitu; veritas mente latens est sapientia absconsa et thesaurus invisus; veritas vero quae lucet in libris omni se disciplinabili sensui manifestare desiderat. Visui dum legitur, auditui dum auditur, amplius et tactui se commendat quodammodo, dum transcribi se sustinet, colligari, corrigi et servari.

℄ Veritas mentis clausa, licet sit possessio nobilis animi, quia tamen caret socio, non constat esse iocunda, de qua nec visus iudicat nec auditus. Veritas vero vocis soli patet auditui, visum latens, qui plures nobis differentias rerum mon-

to fame, if the aid of books had been wanting. Towers have been razed to the ground; cities have been overthrown; triumphal arches have perished from decay; nor can either pope or king find any means of more easily conferring the privilege of perpetuity than by books. The book that he has made renders its author this service in return, that so long as the book survives its author remains immortal and cannot die, as Ptolemy declares in the Prologue to his Almagest: He is not dead, he says, who has given life to science.

❡ Who therefore will limit by anything of another kind the price of the infinite treasure of books, from which the scribe who is instructed bringeth forth things new and old? Truth that triumphs over all things, which overcomes the king, wine, and women, which it is reckoned holy to honour before friendship, which is the way without turning and the life without end, which holy Boethius considers to be three-fold in thought, speech, and writing, seems to remain more usefully and to fructify to greater profit in books. For the meaning of the voice perishes with the sound; truth latent in the mind is wisdom that is hid and treasure that is not seen; but truth which shines forth in books desires to manifest itself to every impressionable sense. It commends itself to the sight when it is read, to the hearing when it is heard, and moreover in a manner to the touch, when it suffers itself to be transcribed, bound, corrected, and preserved.

❡ The undisclosed truth of the mind, although it is the possession of the noble soul, yet because it lacks a companion, is not certainly known to be delightful, while neither sight nor hearing takes account of it. Further, the truth of the voice is patent only to the ear and eludes the sight, which

strat, affixaque subtilissimo motui incipit et desinit quasi simul. Sed veritas scripta libri, non successiva sed permanens, palam se praebet aspectui et per sphaerulas pervias oculorum, vestibula sensus communis et imaginationis atria transiens, thalamum intellectus ingreditur, in cubili memoriae se recondens, ubi aeternam mentis congenerat veritatem.

℃ Postremo pensandum, quanta doctrinae commoditas sit in libris, quam facilis, quam arcana. Quam tuto libris humanae ignorantiae paupertatem sine verecundia denudamus! Hi sunt magistri qui nos instruunt sine virgis et ferula, sine verbis et cholera, sine pannis et pecunia. Si accedis, non dormiunt; si inquirens interrogas, non abscondunt; non remurmurant, si oberres; cachinnos nesciunt, si ignores.

℃ O libri soli liberales et liberi, qui omni petenti tribuitis et omnes manumittitis vobis sedulo servientes, quot rerum millibus typice viris doctis recommendamini in scriptura nobis divinitus inspirata! Vos enim estis profundissimae sophiae fodinae, ad quas sapiens filium suum mittit ut inde thesauros effodiat: Proverbiorum 2°; vos putei aquarum viventium, quos pater Abraham primo fodit, Isaac eruderavit, quosque nituntur obstruere Palestini: Genesis 26°. Vos estis revera spicae gratissimae, plenae granis, solis apostolicis manibus confricandae, ut egrediatur cibus suavissimus famelicis animabus: Matt. 12°.

℃ Vos estis urnae aureae, in quibus manna reconditur, atque petrae mellifluae, immo potius favi mellis, ubera

Richard de Bury

reveals to us more of the qualities of things, and linked with the subtlest of motions begins and perishes as it were in a breath. But the written truth of books, not transient but permanent, plainly offers itself to be observed, and by means of the pervious spherules of the eyes, passing through the vestibule of perception and the courts of imagination, enters the chamber of intellect, taking its place in the couch of memory, where it engenders the eternal truth of the mind.

℘ Finally, we must consider what pleasantness of teaching there is in books, how easy, how secret! How safely we lay bare the poverty of human ignorance to books without feeling any shame! They are masters who instruct us without rod or ferule, without angry words, without clothes or money. If you come to them they are not asleep; if you ask and inquire of them, they do not withdraw themselves; they do not chide if you make mistakes; they do not laugh at you if you are ignorant.

℘ O books who alone are liberal and free, who give to all who ask of you and enfranchise all who serve you faithfully! By how many thousand types are ye commended to learned men in the scriptures given us by inspiration of God! For ye are the mines of profoundest wisdom, to which the wise man sends his son that he may dig out treasures: Prov. 2. Ye are the wells of living waters, which father Abraham first digged, Isaac digged again, and which the Philistines strive to fill up: Gen. 26. Ye are indeed the most delightful ears of corn, full of grain, to be rubbed only by apostolic hands, that the sweetest food may be produced for hungry souls: Matt. 12.

℘ Ye are the golden pots in which manna is stored, and rocks flowing with honey, nay combs of honey, most plente-

uberrima lactis vitae, promptuaria semper plena; vos lignum
et quadripartitus fluvius paradisi, quo mens humana pa-
scitur et aridus intellectus imbuitur et rigatur; vos arca Noae
et scala Iacob, canalesque quibus foetus intuentium coloran-
tur; vos lapides testimonii et lagenae servantes lampadas
Gedeonis, pera David, de qua limpidissimi lapides extrahun-
tur ut Goliath prosternatur. Vos estis aurea vasa templi,
arma militiae clericorum, quibus tela nequissimi hostis de-
struuntur, olivae fecundae, vineae Engadi, ficus sterilescere
nescientes, lucernae ardentes, semper in manibus praeten-
dendae,—et optima quaeque scripturae libris adaptare poterimus, si loqui libeat figurate.

ous udders of the milk of life, garners ever full; ye are the tree of life and the fourfold river of Paradise, by which the human mind is nourished and the thirsty intellect is watered and refreshed. Ye are the ark of Noah and the ladder of Jacob, and the troughs by which the young of those who look therein are coloured; ye are the stones of testimony and the pitchers holding the lamps of Gideon, the scrip of David, from which the smoothest stones are taken for the slaying of Goliath. Ye are the golden vessels of the temple, the arms of the soldiers of the Church, with which to quench all the fiery darts of the wicked, fruitful olives, vines of Engadi, figtrees that are never barren, burning lamps always to be held in readiness—and all the noblest comparisons of scripture may be applied to books, if we choose to speak in figures.

CAPITULUM II

Qualis amor libris rationabiliter debeatur

SI quidlibet iuxta gradum valoris gradum mereatur amoris, valorem vero librorum ineffabilem persuadet praecedens capitulum; palam liquet lectori quid sit inde probabiliter concludendum. Non enim demonstrationibus in morali materia nitimur, recordantes quoniam disciplinati hominis est certitudinem quaerere, sicut rei naturam perspexerit tolerare, archiphilosopho attestante: 1º Ethicorum. Quoniam nec Tullius requirit Euclidem, nec Euclidi Tullius facit fidem; hoc revera sive logice sive rhetorice suadere conamur, quod quaecunque divitiae vel deliciae cedere debent libris in anima spiritali, ubi spiritus, qui est caritas, ordinat caritatem.

℃ Primo quidem quia in libris sapientia continetur potissime, plus quam omnes mortales naturaliter comprehendunt; sapientia vero divitias parvipendit, sicut capitulum antecedens allegat. Praeterea Aristoteles, De problematibus, particula 3ª, problemate 10º, istam determinat quaestionem propter quid antiqui, qui pro gymnasticis et corporalibus agoniis praemia statuerunt potioribus, nullum unquam praemium sapientiae decreverunt. Hanc quaestionem responsione tertia ita solvit: in gymnasticis exercitiis praemium est melius et eligibilius illo, pro quo datur; sapientia autem nihil melius esse potest; quamobrem sapientiae nullum potuit praemium

CHAPTER II

The degree of Affection that is properly due to Books

SINCE the degree of affection a thing deserves depends upon the degree of its value, and the previous chapter shows that the value of books is unspeakable, it is quite clear to the reader what is the probable conclusion from this. I say probable, for in moral science we do not insist upon demonstration, remembering that the educated man seeks such degree of certainty as he perceives the subject-matter will bear, as Aristotle testifies in the first book of his Ethics. For Tully does not appeal to Euclid, nor does Euclid rely upon Tully. This at all events we endeavour to prove whether by logic or rhetoric, that all riches and all delights whatsoever yield place to books in the spiritual mind, wherein the Spirit which is charity ordereth charity.

⸿ Now in the first place, because wisdom is contained in books more than all mortals understand, and wisdom thinks lightly of riches, as the foregoing chapter declares. Furthermore, Aristotle in his Problems determines the question, why the ancients proposed prizes to the stronger in gymnastic and corporeal contests, but never awarded any prize for wisdom. This question he solves as follows: In gymnastic exercises the prize is better and more desirable than that for which it is bestowed; but it is certain that nothing is better than wisdom: wherefore no prize could be assigned for wisdom.

assignari. Ergo nec divitiae nec deliciae sapientiam antecellunt.

℆ Rursus amicitiam divitiis praeponendam solus negabit insipiens, cum sapientissimus hoc testetur; amicitiae vero veritatem hierophilosophus praehonorat et verus Zorobabel omnibus anteponit. Subsunt igitur divitiae veritati. Veritatem vero potissime et tuentur et continent sacri libri, immo sunt veritas ipsa scripta; quoniam pro nunc librorum asseres librorum non asserimus esse partes. Quamobrem divitiae subsunt libris, praesertim cum pretiosissimum genus divitiarum omnium sint amici, sicut secundo de Consolatione testatur Boetius, quibus tamen librorum veritas est per Aristotelem praeferenda.

℆ Amplius cum divitiae ad solius corporis subsidia primo et principaliter pertinere noscantur, virtus vero librorum sit perfectio rationis, quae bonum humanum proprie nominatur, apparet quod libri sunt homini ratione utenti divitiis cariores. Praeterea illud quo fides defenderetur commodius, dilataretur diffusius, praedicaretur lucidius, diligibilius debet esse fideli. Hoc autem est veritas libris inscripta, quod evidentius figuravit Salvator, quando contra Tentatorem praeliaturus viriliter scuto se circumdedit veritatis, non cuiuslibet immo scripturae, scriptum esse praemittens quod vivae vocis oraculo erat prolaturus: Matt. 4°.

℆ Rursus autem felicitatem nemo dubitat divitiis praeponendam. Consistit autem felicitas in operatione nobilissimae et divinioris potentiae quam habemus, dum videlicet intellectus vacat totaliter veritati sapientiae contemplandae, quae est delectabilissima omnium operationum secundum

Richard de Bury

And therefore neither riches nor delights are more excellent than wisdom.

❦ Again, only the fool will deny that friendship is to be preferred to riches, since the wisest of men testifies this; but the chief of philosophers honours truth before friendship, and the truthful Zorobabel prefers it to all things. Riches then are less than truth. Now truth is chiefly maintained and contained in holy books—nay they are written truth itself, since by books we do not now mean the materials of which they are made. Wherefore riches are less than books, especially as the most precious of all riches are friends, as Boethius testifies in the second book of his *Consolation*; to whom the truth of books according to Aristotle is to be preferred.

❦ Moreover, since we know that riches first and chiefly appertain to the support of the body only, while the virtue of books is the perfection of reason, which is properly speaking the happiness of man, it appears that books to the man who uses his reason are dearer than riches. Furthermore, that by which the faith is more easily defended, more widely spread, more clearly preached, ought to be more desirable to the faithful. But this is the truth written in books, which our Saviour plainly showed, when he was about to contend stoutly against the Tempter, girding himself with the shield of truth and indeed of written truth, declaring 'it is written' of what he was about to utter with his voice: Matt. 4.

❦ And, again, no one doubts that happiness is to be preferred to riches. But happiness consists in the operation of the noblest and diviner of the faculties that we possess— when the whole mind is occupied in contemplating the truth of wisdom, which is the most delectable of all our virtuous

virtutem, sicut princeps philosophorum determinat 10°
Ethicorum, propter quod et philosophia videtur habere
admirabiles delectationes puritate et firmitate, ut scribitur
consequenter. Contemplatio autem veritatis nunquam est
perfectior quam per libros, dum actualis imaginatio con-
tinuata per librum actum intellectus super visas veritates
non sustinet interrumpi. Quamobrem libri videntur esse
felicitatis speculativae immediatissima instrumenta, unde
Aristoteles, sol philosophicae veritatis, ubi de eligendis dis-
tribuit methodos, docet quod philosophari est simpliciter
eligibilius quam ditari, quamvis in casu ex circumstantia,
puta necessariis indigenti, ditari quam philosophari sit
potius eligendum: 3° Topicorum.

❡ Adhuc cum libri sint nobis commodissimi magistri, ut
praecedens assumit capitulum, eisdem non immerito tam
honorem quam amorem tribuere convenit magistralem. Tandem cum omnes homines natura scire desiderent ac per libros
scientiam veterum praeoptandam divitiis omnibus adipisci
possimus, quis homo secundum naturam vivens librorum
non habeat appetitum? Quamvis vero porcos margaritas sper-
nere sciamus, nihil in hoc prudentis laedetur opinio, quo-
minus oblatas comparet margaritas. Pretiosior est igitur cunctis opibus sapientiae libraria, et omnia quae desiderantur
huic non valent comparari: Proverbiorum 3°. Quisquis igitur
se fatetur veritatis, felicitatis, sapientiae vel scientiae, seu
etiam fidei zelatorem, librorum necesse est se faciat amatorem.

Richard de Bury

activities, as the prince of philosophers declares in the tenth book of the Ethics, on which account it is that philosophy is held to have wondrous pleasures in respect of purity and solidity, as he goes on to say. But the contemplation of truth is never more perfect than in books, where the act of imagination perpetuated by books does not suffer the operation of the intellect upon the truths that it has seen to suffer interruption. Wherefore books appear to be the most immediate instruments of speculative delight, and therefore Aristotle, the sun of philosophic truth, in considering the principles of choice, teaches that in itself to philosophize is more desirable than to be rich, although in certain cases, as where for instance one is in need of necessaries, it may be more desirable to be rich than to philosophize: Topica 3.

❡ Moreover, since books are the aptest teachers, as the previous chapter assumes, it is fitting to bestow on them the honour and the affection that we owe to our teachers. In fine, since all men naturally desire to know, and since by means of books we can attain the knowledge of the ancients, which is to be desired beyond all riches, what man living according to nature would not feel the desire of books? And although we know that swine trample pearls under foot, the wise man will not therefore be deterred from gathering the pearls that lie before him. A library of wisdom, then, is more precious than all wealth, and all things that are desirable cannot be compared to it. Whoever therefore claims to be zealous of truth, of happiness, of wisdom or knowledge, aye even of the faith, must needs become a lover of books.

Qualiter in libris emendis sit pretium aestimandum

COROLLARIUM nobis gratum de praedictis elicimus, paucis tamen (ut credimus) acceptandum: nullam videlicet debere caristiam hominem impedire ab emptione librorum, cum sibi suppetat quod petitur pro eisdem, nisi ut obsistatur malitiae venditoris, vel tempus emendi opportunius expectetur. Quoniam, si sola sapientia pretium facit libris, quae est infinitus thesaurus hominibus, et si valor librorum est ineffabilis, ut praemissa supponunt, qualiter probabitur carum esse commercium, ubi bonum emitur infinitum? Quapropter libros libenter emendos et invite vendendos sol hominum Salomon nos hortatur, Prov. 23°: veritatem, inquit, eme et noli vendere sapientiam.

❧ Sed quod rhetorice suademus vel logice, adstruamus historiis rei gestae. Archiphilosophus Aristoteles, quem Averroes datum putat quasi regulam in natura, paucos libros Speusippi post ipsius decessum pro septuaginta duobus millibus sestertiis statim emit. Plato, prior tempore sed doctrinis posterior, Philolai Pythagorici librum emit pro decem millibus denariorum, de quo dicitur Timaei dialogum excerpsisse, sicut refert A. Gellius, Noctium Atticarum libro tertio, capitulo 17°. Haec autem narrat A. Gellius, ut perpendat insipiens quam nihilipendant sapientes pecuniam comparatione libro-

30

CHAPTER III

What we are to think of the Price in the buying of Books

FROM what has been said we draw this corollary welcome to us, but (as we believe) acceptable to few: namely, that no dearness of price ought to hinder a man from the buying of books, if he has the money that is demanded for them, unless it be to withstand the malice of the seller or to await a more favourable opportunity of buying. For if it is wisdom only that makes the price of books, which is an infinite treasure to mankind, and if the value of books is unspeakable, as the premises show, how shall the bargain be shown to be dear where an infinite good is being bought? Wherefore, that books are to be gladly bought and unwillingly sold, Solomon, the sun of men, exhorts us in the *Proverbs: Buy the truth,* he says, *and sell not wisdom.*

❡ But what we are trying to show by rhetoric or logic, let us prove by examples from history. The arch-philosopher Aristotle, whom Averroes regards as the law of Nature, bought a few books of Speusippus straightway after his death for seventy-two thousand sesterces. Plato, before him in time, but after him in learning, bought the book of Philolaus the Pythagorean, from which he is said to have taken the *Timæus,* for ten thousand denaries, as Aulus Gellius relates in the *Noctes Atticæ*. Now Aulus Gellius relates this that the foolish may consider how wise men despise money in comparison

rum. Et e contrario, ut omni superbiae stultitiam cognoscamus annexam, libet hic Tarquinii Superbi stultitiam recensere in parvipensione librorum, quam refert idem A. Gellius, Noctium Atticarum libro primo, cap. 19°.

(Vetula quaedam omnino incognita ad Tarquinium Superbum, regem Romanum septimum, dicitur accessisse, venales offerens novem libros, in quibus (ut asseruit) divina continebantur oracula, sed immensam pro eisdem poposcit pecuniam, in tantum ut rex eam diceret delirare. Illa commota tres libros in ignem proiecit et pro residuis summam quam prius exegit. Rege negante, rursus tres alios in ignem proiecit et adhuc pro tribus residuis primam summam poposcit. Tandem stupefactus supra modum, Tarquinius summam pro tribus gaudet exsolvere, pro qua novem poterat redemisse. Vetula statim disparuit, quae nec prius, nec postea visa fuit. Hi sunt libri Sibyllini, quos quasi quoddam divinum oraculum per aliquem de quindecim viris consulebant Romani, et quindecimviratus creditur officium originem habuisse. Quid aliud haec Sibylla prophetissa tam vafro facto superbum regem edocuit, nisi quod vasa sapientiae, sacri libri, omnem humanam aestimationem excedunt, et sicut de regno caelorum dicit Gregorius: Tantum valent, quantum habes?

Richard de Bury

with books. And on the other hand, that we may know that folly and pride go together, let us here relate the folly of Tarquin the Proud in despising books, as also related by Aulus Gellius.

⸿ An old woman, utterly unknown, is said to have come to Tarquin the Proud, the seventh king of Rome, offering to sell nine books, in which (as she declared) sacred oracles were contained, but she asked an immense sum for them, insomuch that the king said she was mad. In anger she flung three books into the fire, and still asked the same sum for the rest. When the king refused it, again she flung three others into the fire and still asked the same price for the three that were left. At last, astonied beyond measure, Tarquin was glad to pay for three books the same price for which he might have bought nine. The old woman straightway disappeared, and was never seen before or after. These were the Sibylline books, which the Romans consulted as a divine oracle by some one of the Quindecimvirs, and this is believed to have been the origin of the Quindecimvirate. What did this Sibyl teach the proud king by this bold deed, except that the vessels of wisdom, holy books, exceed all human estimation; and as Gregory says of the kingdom of Heaven: They are worth all that thou hast?

CAPITULUM IV

Querimonia librorum contra clericos iam promotos

PROGENIES viperarum parentes proprios perimens atque semen nequam ingratissimi cuculi, qui, cum vires acceperit, virium largitricem nutriculam suam necat, sunt clerici degeneres erga libros. Reddite praevaricatores ad cor et quid per libros recipitis fideliter computetis et invenietis libros totius nobilis status vestri quodammodo creatores, sine quibus proculdubio defecissent caeteri promotores.

℘ Ad nos nempe rudes penitus et inertes reptastis, ut parvuli loquebamini, ut parvuli sapiebatis, ut parvuli eiulantes implorastis participes fieri lactis nostri. Nos vero protinus lacrimis vestris tacti mamillam grammaticae porreximus exsugendam, quam dentibus atque lingua contrectastis assidue, donec dempta nativa barbarie nostris linguis inciperetis magnalia Dei fari. Post haec philosophiae vestibus valde bonis, rhetorica et dialectica, quas apud nos habuimus et habemus, vos induimus, cum essetis nudi, quasi tabula depingenda. Omnes enim philosophiae domestici sunt vestiti duplicibus, ut tegatur tam nuditas quam ruditas intellectus. Post haec, ut alati more seraphico super cherubin scanderetis, quadrivialium pennas vobis quatuor adiungentes,

CHAPTER IV

The Complaint of Books against the Clergy already promoted

A GENERATION of vipers destroying their own parents and base offspring of the ungrateful cuckoo, who when he has grown strong slays his nurse, the giver of his strength, are degenerate clerks with regard to books. Bring it again to mind and consider faithfully what ye receive through books, and ye will find that books are as it were the creators of your distinction, without which other favourers would have been wanting.

❡ In sooth, while still untrained and helpless ye crept up to us, ye spake as children, ye thought as children, ye cried as children and begged to be made partakers of our milk. But we being straightway moved by your tears gave you the breast of grammar to suck, which ye plied continually with teeth and tongue, until ye lost your native barbarousness and learned to speak with our tongues the mighty things of God. And next we clad you with the goodly garments of philosophy, rhetoric and dialectic, of which we had and have a store, while ye were naked as a tablet to be painted on. For all the household of philosophy are clothed with twofold garments, that the nakedness and rawness of the intellect may be covered. After this, providing you with the fourfold wings of the quadrivials that ye might be winged like the seraphs and so mount above the cherubim, we sent you to a friend

transmisimus ad amicum, ad cuius ostium, dum tamen improbe pulsaretis, tres panes commodarentur intelligentiae Trinitatis, in qua consistit finalis felicitas cuiuslibet viatoris.

ℭ Quod si vos haec munera non habere dixeritis, confidenter asserimus, quod vel ea per incuriam perdidistis collata, vel in principio desides respuistis oblata. Si huiusmodi videantur ingratis pusilla, adicimus his maiora. Vos estis genus electum, regale sacerdotium, gens sancta, vos populus peculiaris in sortem Domini computati, vos sacerdotes et ministri Dei, immo vos antonomatice ipsa Ecclesia Dei dicimini, quasi laici non sint ecclesiastici nuncupandi. Vos, laicis postpositis, psalmos et hymnos concinitis in cancellis et altari deservientes, cum altario participantes, verum conficitis corpus Christi, in quo Deus ipse vos non solum laicis, immo paulo magis angelis honoravit. Cui enim aliquando angelorum dixit: Tu es sacerdos in aeternum secundum ordinem Melchisedech? Vos crucifixi patrimonium dispensatis pauperibus, ubi iam quaeritur inter dispensatores ut fidelis quis inveniatur. Vos estis pastores gregis dominici tam exemplo vitae quam verbo doctrinae, qui vobis tenentur rependere lac et lanam.

ℭ Qui sunt istorum omnium largitores, O clerici, nonne libri? Reminisci libeat, supplicamus, quot per nos clericis sint concessa egregia privilegia libertatum. Per nos siquidem vasa sapientiae et intellectus imbuti cathedras scanditis magistrales, vocati ab hominibus Rabbi. Per nos, in oculis laicorum mirabiles velut magna mundi luminaria, dignitates ecclesiae secundum sortes varias possidetis. Per nos, cum

at whose door, if only ye importunately knocked, ye might borrow the three loaves of the Knowledge of the Trinity, in which consists the final felicity of every sojourner below.

ℂ Nay, if ye deny that ye had these privileges, we boldly declare that ye either lost them by your carelessness, or that through your sloth ye spurned them when offered to you. If these things seem but a light matter to you, we will add yet greater things. Ye are a chosen people, a royal priesthood, a holy race, ye are a peculiar people chosen into the lot of God, ye are priests and ministers of God, nay, ye are called the very Church of God, as though the laity were not to be called churchmen. Ye, being preferred to the laity, sing psalms and hymns in the chancel, and serving the altar and living by the altar, make the true body of Christ, wherein God Himself has honoured you not only above the laity, but even a little higher than the angels. For to whom of His angels has He said at any time: Thou art a priest for ever after the order of Melchisedech? Ye dispense the patrimony of the crucified one to the poor, wherein it is required of stewards that a man be found faithful. Ye are shepherds of the Lord's flock, as well in example of life as in the word of doctrine, which is bound to repay you with milk and wool.

ℂ Who are the givers of all these things, O clerks? Is it not books? Do ye remember therefore, we pray, how many and how great liberties and privileges are bestowed upon the clergy through us. In truth, taught by us who are the vessels of wisdom and intellect, ye ascend the teacher's chair and are called of men Rabbi. By us ye become marvellous in the eyes of the laity, like great lights in the world, and possess the dignities of the Church according to your various stations.

adhuc careatis genarum lanugine, in aetate tenera constituti tonsuram portatis in vertice, prohibente statim ecclesiastica sententia formidanda: Nolite tangere christos meos et in prophetis meis nolite malignari; et qui eos tetigerit temere violenter anathematis vulnere ictu proprio protinus feriatur.

℣ Tandem aetate succumbente malitiae, figurae Pythagoricae bivium attingentes ramum laevum eligitis et retrorsum abeuntes sortem Domini praeassumptam dimittitis, socii facti furum; sicque semper proficientes in peius, latrociniis, homicidiis et multigenis impudicitiis maculati, tam fama quam conscientia tabefacta sceleribus, compellente iustitia, in manicis et compedibus coarctati, servamini morte turpissima puniendi. Tunc elongatur amicus et proximus, nec est qui doleat vicem vestram. Petrus iurat se hominem non novisse: vulgus clamat iusticiario: Crucifige, crucifige eum! quoniam si hunc dimittis, Caesaris amicus non eris. Iam periit omnis fuga, nam ante tribunal oportet assisti, nec locus suppetit appellandi sed solum suspendium exspectatur.

℣ Dum sic tristitia complevit cor miseri et solae Camenae lacerae fletibus ora rigant, fit balatus angustiis undique memor nostri et ut evitet mortis propinquae periculum antiquatae tonsurae, quam dedimus, parvum praefert signaculum, supplicans ut vocemur in medium et collati muneris testes simus. Tunc misericordia statim moti occurrimus filio prodigo et a portis mortis servum eripimus fugitivum. Legendus liber porrigitur non ignotus et ad modicam balbutientis prae

Richard de Bury

By us, while ye still lack the first down upon your cheeks, ye are established in your early years and bear the tonsure on your heads, while the dread sentence of the Church is heard: *Touch not mine anointed and do my prophets no harm*, and he who has rashly touched them let him forthwith by his own blow be smitten violently with the wound of an anathema.

⁋ At length yielding your lives to wickedness, reaching the two paths of Pythagoras, ye choose the left branch, and going backward ye let go the lot of God which ye had first assumed, becoming companions of thieves. And thus ever going from bad to worse, dyed with theft and murder and manifold impurities, your fame and conscience stained by sins, at the bidding of justice ye are confined in manacles and fetters, and are kept to be punished by a most shameful death. Then your friend is put far away, nor is there any to mourn your lot. Peter swears that he knows not the man: the people cry to the judge: *Crucify, crucify him! if thou let this man go, thou art not Cæsar's friend.* Now all refuge has perished, for ye must stand before the judgment-seat, and there is no appeal, but only hanging is in store for you.

⁋ While the wretched man's heart is thus filled with woe and only the sorrowing Muses bedew their cheeks with tears, in his strait is heard on every side the wailing appeal to us, and to avoid the danger of impending death he shows the slight sign of the ancient tonsure which we bestowed upon him, begging that we may be called to his aid and bear witness to the privilege bestowed upon him. Then straightway touched with pity we run to meet the prodigal son and snatch the fugitive slave from the gates of death. The book he has not forgotten is handed to him to be read, and while with

timore lecturam iudicis potestas dissolvitur, accusator subtrahitur, mors fugatur.

℃ O carminis empirici mira virtus! O dirae cladis antidotum salutare! O lectio pretiosa psalterii, quod meretur
hoc ipso liber vitae deinceps appellari! Sustineant laici saecu-
lare iudicium, ut vel insuti culleis enatent ad Neptunum, vel
in terra plantati Plutoni fructificent, aut Vulcano per incen-
dia holocaustum se offerant medullatum, vel certe suspensi
victima sint Iunoni; dum noster alumnus ad lectionem uni-
cam libri vitae pontificis commendatur custodiae et rigor in
favorem convertitur, ac dum forum transfertur a laico, a librorum alumno clerico mors differtur.

℃ Caeterum iam de clericis, qui sunt vasa virtutis, loqua-
mur. Quis de vobis pulpitum seu scabellum praedicaturus
ascendit nobis penitus inconsultis? Quis scholas lecturus vel
disputaturus ingreditur, qui nostris conatibus non fulcitur?
Primum oportet volumen cum Ezechiele comedere, quo venter memoriae dulcescat intrinsecus et sic more pantherae
refectae redoleat extrinsecus conceptorum aromatum odor
suavis, ad cuius anhelitum coanhelent accedere omnes bestiae
et iumenta. Sic nostra natura in nostris familiaribus operante
latenter, auditores accurrunt benevoli, sicut adamas trahit
ferrum nequaquam invite. O virtus infinita librorum! Iacent
Parisius vel Athenis simulque resonant in Britannia et in
Roma. Quiescentes quippe moventur, dum ipsis loca sua
tenentibus, auditorum intellectibus circumquaque feruntur.

Richard de Bury

lips stammering with fear he reads a few words the power of the judge is loosed, the accuser is withdrawn, and death is put to flight.

℄ O marvellous virtue of an empiric verse! O saving antidote of dreadful ruin! O precious reading of the psalter, which for this alone deserves to be called the book of life! Let the laity undergo the judgment of the secular arm, that either sewn up in sacks they may be carried out to Neptune, or planted in the earth may fructify for Pluto, or may be offered amid the flames as a fattened holocaust to Vulcan, or at least may be hung up as a victim to Juno; while our nursling at a single reading of the book of life is handed over to the custody of the bishop, and rigour is changed to favour, and the forum being transfer.ed from the laity, death is routed by the clerk who is the nursling of books.

℄ But now let us speak of the clerks who are vessels of virtue. Which of you about to preach ascends the pulpit or the rostrum without in some way consulting us? Which of you enters the schools to teach or to dispute without relying upon our support? First of all it behoves you to eat the book with Ezechiel, that the belly of your memory may be sweetened within, and thus as with the panther refreshed, to whose breath all beasts and cattle long to approach, the sweet savour of the spices it has eaten may shed a perfume without. Thus our nature secretly working in our own, listeners hasten up gladly, as the loadstone draws the iron nothing loth. What an infinite host of books lie at Paris or Athens, and at the same time resound in Britain and in Rome! In truth, while resting they yet move, and while retaining their own places they are carried about every way to the minds of listeners.

The Philobiblon of

℃ Nos denique sacerdotes, pontifices, cardinales et papam, ut cuncta in hierarchia ecclesiastica collocentur in ordine, litterarum scientia stabilimus. A libris namque sumit originem quicquid boni provenit statui clericali. Sed haec hactenus: piget enim reminisci quae dedimus populo clericorum degeneri, quia magis videntur perdita quam collata, quaecumque munera tribuuntur ingratis.

℃ Deinceps insistemus parumper recitandis iniuriis quas rependunt, vilipensionibus et iacturis, de quibus nec singula generum recitare sufficimus, immo vix proxima genera singulorum. Inprimis de domiciliis clericorum nobis iure haereditario debitis vi et armis expellimur, qui quondam in interiori cubiculo cellulas habebamus quietis, sed proh dolor! his nefandis temporibus penitus exsulantes improperium patimur extra portas.

℃ Occupant etenim loca nostra nunc canes, nunc aves, nunc bestia bipedalis, cuius cohabitatio cum clericis vetabatur antiquitus, a qua semper super aspidem et basiliscum alumnos nostros docuimus esse fugiendum; quamobrem ista nostris semper studiis aemula, nullo die placanda, finaliter nos conspectos in angulo iam defunctae araneae sola tela protectos, in rugam fronte collecta, virulentis sermonibus detrahit et subsannat, ac nos in tota domus suppellectili supervacaneos hospitari demonstrat et ad unumquodque oeconomiae servitium conqueritur otiosos, mox in capitegia pretiosa, sindonem et sericum et coccum bis tinctum, vestes et varias furraturas, linum et lanam, nos consulit commutandos: et quidem merito, si videret intrinseca cordis nostri, si nostris

Richard de Bury

❡ Finally, by the knowledge of literature, we establish priests, bishops, cardinals, and the Pope, that all things in the ecclesiastical hierarchy may be fitly disposed. For it is from books that everything of good that befalls the clerical condition takes its origin. But let this suffice: for it pains us to recall what we have bestowed upon the degenerate clergy, because whatever gifts are distributed to the ungrateful seem to be lost rather than bestowed.

❡ Let us next dwell a little on the recital of the wrongs with which they requite us, the contempts and cruelties of which we cannot recite an example in each kind, nay, scarcely the main classes of the several wrongs. In the first place, we are expelled by force and arms from the homes of the clergy, which are ours by hereditary right, who were used to have cells of quietness in the inner chamber, but alas! in these unhappy times we are altogether exiled, suffering poverty without the gates.

❡ For our places are seized now by dogs, now by hawks, now by that biped beast whose cohabitation with the clergy was forbidden of old, from which we have always taught our nurslings to flee more than from the asp and cockatrice; wherefore she, always jealous of the love of us, and never to be appeased, at length seeing us in some corner protected only by the web of some dead spider, with a frown abuses and reviles us with bitter words, declaring us alone of all the furniture in the house to be unnecessary, and complaining that we are useless for any household purpose, and advises that we should speedily be converted into rich caps, sendal and silk and twice-dyed purple, robes and furs, wool and linen: and, indeed, not without reason, if she could see our

privatis interfuisset consiliis, si Theophrasti vel Valerii perlegisset volumen, vel saltem 25 capitulum Ecclesiastici auri-
bus intellectus audisset.

⟪ Quapropter conquerimur de hospitiis nobis iniuste
ablatis, de vestibus, non quidem non datis sed de datis
antiquitus, violentis manibus laceratis. Adhaesit pavimento
anima nostra, conglutinatus est in terra venter noster, et
gloria nostra in pulverem est deducta. Morbis variis labora-
mus, dorsa dolentes et latera, et iacemus membratim para-
lysi dissoluti, nec est qui recogitet, nec est ullus qui malagma
procuret. Candor nativus et luce perspicuus iam in fuscum et
croceum est conversus, ut nemo medicus dubitet ictericia
nos infectos. Arthriticam patiuntur nonnulli de nobis, sicut
extremitates retortae insinuant evidenter. Fumus et pulvis,
quibus infestamur assidue, radiorum visualium aciem hebe-
tarunt et iam lippientibus oculis ophthalmiam superducunt.

⟪ Ventres nostri duris torsionibus viscerum, quae vermes
edaces non cessant corrodere, consumuntur et utriusque
Lazari sustinemus putredinem, nec invenitur quisquam, qui
cedri resina nos liniat vel qui quatriduano iam putrido
clamans dicat, Lazare veni foras! Nullo circumligantur medi-
camine vulnera nostra saeva, quae nobis innoxiis inferuntur
atrociter, nec est ullus qui super nostra ulcera cataplasmet;
sed pannosi et algidi in angulos tenebrosos abicimur, in
lacrimis cum sancto Iob in sterquilinio collocamur, vel, quod

44

Richard de Bury

inmost hearts, if she had listened to our secret counsels, if she had read the book of Theophrastus or Valerius, or only heard the twenty-fifth chapter of Ecclesiasticus with understanding ears.

ℭ And hence it is that we have to mourn for the homes of which we have been unjustly robbed; and as to our coverings, not that they have not been given to us, but that the coverings anciently given to us have been torn by violent hands, insomuch that our soul is bowed down to the dust, our belly cleaveth unto the earth. We suffer from various diseases, enduring pains in our backs and sides; we lie with our limbs unstrung by palsy, and there is no man who layeth it to heart, and no man who provides a mollifying plaster. Our native whiteness that was clear with light has turned to dun and yellow, so that no leech who should see us would doubt that we are diseased with jaundice. Some of us are suffering from gout, as our twisted extremities plainly show. The smoke and dust by which we are continuously plagued have dulled the keeness of our visual rays, and are now infecting our bleared eyes with ophthalmia.

ℭ Within we are devoured by the fierce gripings of our entrails, which hungry worms cease not to gnaw, and we undergo the corruption of the two Lazaruses, nor is there anyone to anoint us with balm of cedar, nor to cry to us who have been four days dead and already stink, Lazarus come forth! No healing drug is bound around our cruel wounds, which are so atrociously inflicted upon the innocent, and there is none to put a plaster upon our ulcers; but ragged and shivering we are flung away into dark corners, or in tears take our place with holy Job upon his dunghill, or—too horrible

nefas videtur effatu, in abyssis abscondimur cloacarum. Pulvinar subtrahitur evangelicis supponendum lateribus, quibus primo deberent de sortibus clericorum provenire subsidia et sic ad nos suo famulatui deputandos pro semper communis victus necessarius derivari.

℃ Rursus de alio genere calamitatis conquerimur, quae personis nostris crebrius irrogatur iniuste. Nam in servos vendimur et ancillas et obsides in tabernis absque redemptore iacemus. Macellariis crudelibus subdimur, ubi mactari tam pecora quam iumenta sine piis lacrimis non videmus et ubi millesies morimur ipso metu, qui cadere posset in constantem. Iudaeis committimur, Sarracenis, haereticis et paganis, quorum super omnia toxicum formidamus, per quos nonnullos de nostris parentibus per venenum pestiferum constat esse corruptos. Sane nos, qui architectonici reputari debemus in scientiis et subiectis nobis omnibus mechanicis imperamus, subalternatorum regimini vice versa committimur, tanquam si monarcha summe nobilis rusticanis calcaneis substernatur. Sartor et sutor et scissor quicunque ac cuiuslibet artifex operis inclusos nos custodit in carcere pro superfluis et lascivis deliciis clericorum.

℃ Iam volumus prosequi novum genus iniuriae, quo tam in nostris personis laedimur quam in fama, qua nihil carius possidemus. Generositati nostrae omni die detrahitur, dum per pravos compilatores, translatores et transformatores nova nobis auctorum nomina imponuntur et, antiqua nobilitate mutata, regeneratione multiplici renascentes degeneramus omnino. Sicque vilium vitricorum nobis nolentibus affigun-

to relate—are buried in the depths of the common sewers. The cushion is withdrawn that should support our evangelical sides, which ought to have the first claim upon the incomes of the clergy, and the common necessaries of life thus be for ever provided for us, who are entrusted to their charge.

℩ Again, we complain of another sort of injury which is too often unjustly inflicted upon our persons. We are sold for bondmen and bondwomen, and lie as hostages in taverns with no one to redeem us. We fall a prey to the cruel shambles, where we see sheep and cattle slaughtered not without pious tears, and where we die a thousand times from such terrors as might frighten even the brave. We are handed over to Jews, Saracens, heretics and infidels, whose poison we always dread above everything, and by whom it is well known that some of our parents have been infected with pestiferous venom. In sooth, we who should be treated as masters in the sciences, and bear rule over the mechanics who should be subject to us, are instead handed over to the government of subordinates, as though some supremely noble monarch should be trodden under foot by rustic heels. Any seamster or cobbler or tailor or artificer of any trade keeps us shut up in prison for the luxurious and wanton pleasures of the clergy.

℩ Now we would pursue a new kind of injury by which we suffer alike in person and in fame, the dearest thing we have. Our purity of race is diminished every day, while new authors' names are imposed upon us by worthless compilers, translators, and transformers, and losing our ancient nobility, while we are reborn in successive generations, we become wholly degenerate; and thus against our will the name of some

tur vocabula et verorum patrum nomina filiis subducuntur. Versus Vergilii, adhuc ipso vivente quidam pseudoversificus usurpavit, et Martialis Coci libellos Fidentinus quidam sibi mendaciter arrogavit, quem idem Martialis redarguit merito sub his verbis:

Quem recitas, meus est, O Fidentine, libellus;
Sed male quum recitas, incipit esse tuus.

Quid ergo mirum, si defunctis nostris auctoribus suas per nos fimbrias simiae clericorum magnificant, cum eisdem superstitibus nos recenter editos rapere moliantur. Ah, quoties nos antiquos fingitis nuper natos, et qui patres sumus filios nominare conamini, quique vos ad esse clericale creavimus studiorum vestrorum fabricas appellatis! Revera de Athenis exstitimus oriundi, qui fingimur nunc de Roma, semper namque Carmentis latruncula fuit Cadmi, et qui nuper nascebamur in Anglia cras Parisius renascemur, et inde delati Bononiam Italicam sortiemur originem, nulla consanguinitate suffultam.

ℂ Heu, quam falsis scriptoribus nos exarandos committitis; quam corrupte nos legitis et medicando necatis, quos pro zelo corrigere credebatis! Interpretes barbaros sustinemus multotiens et qui linguarum idiomata nesciunt nos de lingua ad linguam transferre praesumunt; sicque proprietate sermonis ablata fit sententia contra sensum auctoris turpiter mutilata. Bene gratiosa fuisset librorum conditio, si turris Babel nullatenus obfuisset praesumptio, si totius humani generis unica descendisset sermonis species propagata.

Richard de Bury

wretched stepfather is affixed to us, and the sons are robbed of the names of their true fathers. The verses of Vergil, while he was yet living, were claimed by an impostor; and a certain Fidentinus mendaciously usurped the works of Martial, whom Martial thus deservedly rebuked:

> The book you read is, Fidentinus, mine,
> Though, read so badly, 't well may pass for thine!

What marvel, then, if when our authors are dead clerical apes use us to make broad their phylacteries, since even while they are alive they try to seize us as soon as we are published? Ah! how often ye pretend that we who are ancient are but lately born, and try to pass us off as sons who are really fathers, calling us who have made you clerks the production of your studies. Indeed, we derived our origin from Athens, though we are now supposed to be from Rome; for Carmentis was always the pilferer of Cadmus, and we who were but lately born in England, will tomorrow be born again in Paris; and thence being carried to Bologna, will obtain an Italian origin, based upon no affinity of blood.

ℂ Alas! how ye commit us to treacherous copyists to be written, how corruptly ye read us and kill us by medication, while ye supposed ye were correcting us with pious zeal. Oftentimes we have to endure barbarous interpreters, and those who are ignorant of foreign idioms presume to translate us from one language into another; and thus all propriety of speech is lost and our sense is shamefully mutilated contrary to the meaning of the author! Truly noble would have been the condition of books, if it had not been for the presumption of the tower of Babel, if but one kind of speech had been transmitted by the whole human race.

49

The Philobiblon of

❡ Ultimam nostrae prolixae querelae, sed pro materia quam habemus brevissimae, clausulam subiungemus. In nobis etenim commutatur naturalis usus in eum usum qui est contra naturam, dum passim pictoribus subdimur litterarum ignaris et aurifabris, proh dolor! commendamur nos, qui sumus lumen fidelium animarum, ut fiamus, ac si non essemus sapientiae sacra vasa, repositoria bractearum. Devolvimur indebite in laicorum dominium, quod est nobis amarius omni morte, quoniam hi vendiderunt populum nostrum sine pretio et inimici nostri iudices nostri sunt.

❡ Liquet omnibus ex praedictis quam infinita possemus in clericos invectiva conicere, si non honestati propriae parceremus. Nam miles emeritus clipeum veneratur et arma gratusque Corydon aratro tabescenti, bigae, trahae, tribulae ac ligoni, etiam omnis artifex manualis hyperduliam propriam suis exhibet instrumentis. Solus ingratus clericus parvipendit et negligit ea, per quae sui honoris auspicia semper sumit.

Richard de Bury

❲ We will add the last clause of our long lament, though far too short for the materials that we have. For in us the natural use is changed to that which is against nature, while we who are the light of faithful souls everywhere fall a prey to painters knowing nought of letters, and are entrusted to goldsmiths to become, as though we were not sacred vessels of wisdom, repositories of gold-leaf. We fall undeservedly into the power of laymen, which is more bitter to us than any death, since they have sold our people for nought, and our enemies themselves are our judges.

❲ It is clear from what we have said what infinite invectives we could hurl against the clergy, if we did not think of our own reputation. For the soldier whose campaigns are over venerates his shield and arms, and grateful Corydon shows regard for his decaying team, harrow, flail and mattock, and every manual artificer for the instruments of his craft; it is only the ungrateful cleric who despises and neglects those things which have ever been the foundation of his honours.

CAPITULUM V

Querimonia librorum contra religiosos possessionatos

RELIGIONUM veneranda devotio in librorum cultu solet esse sollicita et in eorum eloquiis sicut in omnibus divitiis delectari. Scribebant namque nonnulli manibus propriis inter horas canonicas, intervallis captatis, et tempora pro quiete corporis commodata fabricandis codicibus concesserunt. De quorum laboribus hodie in plerisque splendent monasteriis illa sacra gazophylacia, cherubicis libris plena, ad dandam scientiam salutis studentibus atque lumen delectabile semitis laicorum. O labor manualis, felicior omni cura georgica! O devota sollicitudo, ubi nec meretur Martha corripi nec Maria! O domus iocunda, in qua Racheli formosae Lya fecunda non invidet, sed contemplatio cum activa gaudia sua miscet. Felix providentia pro futuro infinitis posteris valitura, cui nulla virgultorum plantatio, nulla seminum satio comparatur, nulla bucolica curiositas quorumlibet armentorum, nulla castrorum constructio munitorum!

℃ Quamobrem immortalis debet esse patrum illorum memoria, quos solius sapientiae delectabat thesaurus, qui contra futuras caligines luminosas lucernas artificiosissime providerunt et contra famem audiendi verbum Dei panes non subcinericeos neque hordeaceos nec muscidos, sed panes

CHAPTER V

The Complaint of Books against the Possessioners

THE venerable devotion of the religious orders is wont to be solicitous in the care of books and to delight in their society, as if they were the only riches. For some used to write them with their own hands between the hours of prayer, and gave to the making of books such intervals as they could secure and the times appointed for the recreation of the body. By whose labours there are resplendent today in most monasteries these sacred treasuries full of cherubic letters, for giving the knowledge of salvation to the student and a delectable light to the paths of the laity. O manual toil, happier than any agricultural task! O devout solicitude, where neither Martha nor Mary deserves to be rebuked! O joyful house, in which the fruitful Leah does not envy the beauteous Rachel, but action and contemplation share each other's joys! O happy charge, destined to benefit endless generations of posterity, with which no planting of trees, no sowing of seeds, no pastoral delight in herds, no building of fortified camps can be compared!

℆ Wherefore the memory of those fathers should be immortal, who delighted only in the treasures of wisdom, who most laboriously provided shining lamps against future darkness, and against hunger of hearing the word of God most carefully prepared not bread baked in the ashes, nor of barley,

azymos de purissima simila sacrae sophiae confectos accuratissime paraverunt, quibus esurientes animae feliciter cibarentur. Hi fuerunt probissimi pugiles Christianae militiae, qui nostram infirmitatem armis fortissimis munierunt. Hi fuerunt suis temporibus vulpium venatores cautissimi, qui iam nobis sua retia reliquerunt, ut parvulas caperemus vulpeculas, quae non cessant florentes vineas demoliri. Vere, patres egregii, benedictione perpetua recolendi, felices merito fuissetis, si vobis similem sobolem genuisse, si prolem non degenerem nec aequivocam reliquisse ad sequentis temporis subsidium licuisset.

℄ Sed, quod dolentes referimus, iam Thersites ignavus arma contrectat Achillis et dextrariorum phalerae praeelectae pigritantibus asinis substernuntur, aquilarum nidis caecutientes noctuae dominantur et in accipitris pertica residet vecors miluus.

> *Liber Bacchus respicitur*
> *et in ventrem traicitur*
> *nocte dieque;*
> *liber codex despicitur*
> *et a manu reicitur*
> *longe lateque.*

Tanquam si cuiusdam aequivocationis multiplicitate fallatur simplex monachica plebs moderna, dum Liber pater praeponitur libro patrum, calicibus epotandis non codicibus emendandis indulget hodie studium monachorum; quibus lasciviam musicam Timothei pudicis moribus aemulam non verentur adiungere, sicque cantus ludentis non planctus lugentis officium efficitur monachale.

Richard de Bury

nor musty, but unleavened loaves made of the finest wheat of divine wisdom, with which hungry souls might be joyfully fed. These men were the stoutest champions of the Christian army, who defended our weakness by their most valiant arms; they were in their time the most cunning takers of foxes, who have left us their nets, that we might catch the young foxes, who cease not to devour the growing vines. Of a truth, noble fathers, worthy of perpetual benediction, ye would have been deservedly happy, if ye had been allowed to beget offspring like yourselves, and to leave no degenerate or doubtful progeny for the benefit of future times.

℄ But, painful to relate, now slothful Thersites handles the arms of Achilles and the choice trappings of war-horses are spread upon lazy asses, winking owls lord it in the eagle's nest, and the cowardly kite sits upon the perch of the hawk.

> *Liber Bacchus is ever loved,*
> *And is into their bellies shoved,*
> *By day and by night;*
> *Liber Codex is neglected,*
> *And with scornful hand rejected,*
> *Far out of their sight.*

And as if the simple monastic folk of modern times were deceived by a confusion of names, while *Liber Pater* is preferred to *Liber Patrum*, the study of the monks nowadays is in the emptying of cups and not the emending of books; to which they do not hesitate to add the wanton music of Timotheus, jealous of chastity, and thus the song of the merry-maker and not the chant of the mourner is become the office of the monks.

The Philobiblon of

❡ Greges et vellera, fruges et horrea, porri et olera, potus et patera, lectiones sunt hodie et studia monachorum, exceptis quibusdam paucis electis, in quibus patrum praecedentium non imago sed vestigium remanet aliquale. Rursus nulla nobis materia ministratur omnino, qua de nostro cultu vel studio commendentur hodie canonici regulares, qui licet a geminata regula nomen portent eximium, Augustini tamen regulae notabilem neglexere versiculum, quo sub his verbis suis clericis commendamur: Codices certa hora singulis diebus petantur; extra horam qui petierit, non accipiat.

❡ Hunc devotum studii canonem vix observat aliquis post ecclesiastica cantica repetita, sed sapere quae sunt saeculi et relictum aratrum intueri summa prudentia reputatur. Tollunt pharetram et arcum, apprehendunt arma et scutum, eleemosynarum tributum canibus tribuunt non egenis, inserviunt aleis et taxillis et his quae nos saecularibus inhibere solemus, ut non miremur, si nos non dignentur respicere, quos sic suis cernerent moribus contraire.

❡ Patres igitur reverendi, patrum vestrorum dignemini reminisci et librorum propensius indulgete studio, sine quibus quaelibet vacillabit religio, sine quibus ut testa virtus devotionis arescet, sine quibus nullum lumen poteritis mundo praebere.

Richard de Bury

⁋ Flocks and fleeces, crops and granaries, leeks and pot-herbs, drink and goblets, are nowadays the reading and study of the monks, except a few elect ones, in whom lingers not the image but some slight vestige of the fathers that preceded them. And again, no materials at all are furnished us to commend the canons regular for their care or study of us, who though they bear their name of honour from their twofold rule, yet have neglected the notable clause of Augustine's rule, in which we are commended to his clergy in these words: *Let books be asked for each day at a given hour; he who asks for them after the hour is not to receive them.*

⁋ Scarcely anyone observes this devout rule of study after saying the prayers of the Church, but to care for the things of this world and to look at the plough that has been left is reckoned the highest wisdom. They take up bow and quiver, embrace arms and shield, devote the tribute of alms to dogs and not to the poor, become the slaves of dice and draughts, and of all such things as we are wont to forbid even to the secular clergy, so that we need not marvel if they disdain to look upon us, whom they see so much opposed to their mode of life.

⁋ Come then, reverend fathers, deign to recall your fathers and devote yourselves more faithfully to the study of holy books, without which all religion will stagger, without which the virtue of devotion will dry up like a sherd, and without which ye can afford no light to the world.

CAPITULUM VI

Querimonia librorum contra religiosos mendicantes

PAUPERES spiritu sed in fide ditissimi, mundi peri-psema et sal terrae, saeculi contemptores et hominum piscatores, quam beati estis, si penuriam patientes pro Christo animas vestras scitis in patientia possidere! Non enim vos ultrix iniquitatis inopia, nec parentum adversa fortuna, nec ulla violenta necessitas sic oppressit inedia, sed devota voluntas et electio Christiformis, qua vitam illam optimam aestimastis, quam Deus omnipotens factus homo tam verbo quam exemplo optimam praedicavit. Sane vos estis semper parientis ecclesiae novus fetus, pro patribus et prophetis noviter substituti divinitus, ut in omnem terram exeat sonus vester, et nostris instituti salutaribus doctrinis coram gentibus et regibus promulgetis inexpugnabilem fidem Christi.

℩ Porro fidem patrum potissime libris esse inclusam secundum capitulum supra satis asseruit, quo constat luce clarius quod librorum deberetis esse zelotypi prae caeteris Christianis. Seminare iubemini super omnes aquas, quoniam non est personarum acceptor Altissimus nec vult mortem peccatorum Piissimus, qui occidi voluit pro eisdem, sed contritos corde mederi desiderat atque lapsos erigi et perversos corrigi

CHAPTER VI

The Complaint of Books against the Mendicants

POOR in spirit but most rich in faith, offscourings of the world and salt of the earth, despisers of the world and fishers of men, how happy are ye, if suffering penury for Christ ye know how to possess your souls in patience! For it is not want the avenger of iniquity, nor the adverse fortune of your parents, nor violent necessity that has thus oppressed you with beggary, but a devout will and Christ-like election, by which ye have chosen that life as the best, which God Almighty made man as well by word as by example declared to be the best. In truth, ye are the latest offspring of the ever-fruitful Church, of late divinely substituted for the Fathers and the Prophets, that your sound may go forth into all the earth, and that instructed by our healthful doctrines ye may preach before all kings and nations the invincible faith of Christ.

❡ Moreover, that the faith of the Fathers is chiefly enshrined in books the second chapter has sufficiently shown, from which it is clearer than light that ye ought to be zealous lovers of books above all other Christians. Ye are commanded to sow upon all waters, because the Most High is no respecter of persons, nor does the Most Holy desire the death of sinners, who offered Himself to die for them, but desires to heal the contrite in heart, to raise the fallen, and

spiritu lenitatis. Ad quem effectum saluberrimum alma mater Ecclesia vos plantavit gratuito, plantatosque rigavit favoribus, et rigatos privilegiis suffulcivit, ut cum pastoribus et curatis coadiutores essetis ad procurandum salutem fidelium animarum. Unde et Praedicatorum ordinem propter sacrae scripturae studium et proximorum salutem principaliter institutum constitutiones pronunciant eorundem, ut non solum ex regula reverendi praesulis Augustini, quae codices singulis diebus iubet esse petendos, verum mox cum earundem constitutionum prologum legerint ex ipsius libri capite ad amorem librorum se noverint obligatos.

℀ Sed proh dolor! tam hos quam alios istorum sectantes effigiem a paterna cultura librorum et studio subtrahit triplex cura superflua, ventris videlicet, vestium et domorum. Sunt enim, neglecta Salvatoris providentia, quem psalmista circa pauperem et mendicum promittit esse sollicitum, circa labentis corporis indigentias occupati, ut sint epulae splendidae, vestesque contra regulam delicatae, necnon aedificiorum fabricae et castrorum propugnacula tali proceritate, quae paupertati non convenit, exaltatae. Propter haec tria nos libri, qui semper eos proveximus ad profectum, et inter potentes et nobiles sedes honoris concessimus, elongati a cordis affectibus quasi inter supervacanea reputamur, excepto quod quibusdam quaternis parvi valoris insistunt, de quibus Hiberas naenias et apocrypha deliramenta producunt, non ad refocillativum animarum edulium, sed ad pruritum potius aurium auditorum.

to correct the perverse in the spirit of lenity. For which most salutary purpose our kindly Mother Church has planted you freely, and having planted has watered you with favours, and having watered you has established you with privileges, that ye may be co-workers with pastors and curates in procuring the salvation of faithful souls. Wherefore, that the order of Preachers was principally instituted for the study of the holy scriptures and the salvation of their neighbours, is declared by their constitutions, so that not only from the rule of Bishop Augustine, which directs books to be asked for every day, but as soon as they have read the prologue of the said constitutions they may know from the very title of the same that they are pledged to the love of books.

¶ But alas! a threefold care of superfluities, viz., of the stomach, of dress, and of houses, has seduced these men and others following their example from the paternal care of books, and from their study. For forgetting the providence of the Saviour (who is declared by the Psalmist to think upon the poor and needy), they are occupied with the wants of the perishing body, that their feasts may be splendid and their garments luxurious, against the rule, and the fabrics of their buildings, like the battlements of castles, carried to a height incompatible with poverty. Because of these three things, we books, who have ever procured their advancement and have granted them to sit among the powerful and noble, are put far from their heart's affection and are reckoned as superfluities; except that they rely upon some treatises of small value, from which they derive strange heresies and apocryphal imbecilities, not for the refreshment of souls, but rather for tickling the ears of the listeners.

The Philobiblon of

❦ Sacra scriptura non exponitur, sed omnino seponitur; quasi trita per vicos et omnibus divulgata supponitur, cuius tamen fimbrias vix paucissimi tetigerunt; cuius etiam tanta est litterarum profunditas, ut ab humano intellectu, quantumcunque invigilet, summo otio et maximo studio nequeat comprehendi, sicut sanctus asserit Augustinus. De hac mille moralis disciplinae sententias enucleare poterit qui indulget assidue, si tamen ostium aperire dignetur Ille, qui condidit spiritum pietatis, quae et recentissima novitate pollebunt et sapidissima suavitate auditorum intelligentias refovebunt.

❦ Quamobrem paupertatis evangelicae professores primarii, post utcunque salutatas scientias saeculares, toto mentis ingenio recollecto, huius se scripturae laboribus devoverunt, nocte dieque in lege Domini meditantes. Quicquid vero poterant a famescente ventre furari, vel corpori semitecto surripere, illud lucrum praecipuum arbitrantes, vel emendis vel edendis codicibus adscripserunt. Quorum contemporanei saeculares, tam officium intuentes quam studium, libros eis, quos in diversis mundi partibus sumptuose collegerant, ad totius aedificationem ecclesiae contulerunt.

❦ Sane diebus istis, cum sitis tota diligentia circa quaestus intenti, praesumptione probabili credi potest, si per anthropospatos sermo fiat, Deum circa vos minorem sollicitudinem gerere, quos de sua promissione perpendit diffidere, in humanis providentiis spem habentes. Corvum non consideratis nec lilia, quos pascit et vestit Altissimus; Danielem et Habacuc cocti pulmenti discophorum non pensatis, nec Eliam recolitis nunc in torrente per corvos, nunc in deserto

Richard de Bury

❧ The holy scripture is not expounded, but is neglected and treated as though it were commonplace and known to all, though very few have touched its hem, and though its depth is such, as Holy Augustine declares, that it cannot be understood by the human intellect, however long it may toil with the utmost intensity of study. From this he who devotes himself to it assiduously, if only He will vouchsafe to open the door who has established the spirit of piety, may unfold a thousand lessons of moral teaching, which will flourish with the freshest novelty and will cherish the intelligence of the listeners with the most delightful savours.

❧ Wherefore the first professors of evangelical poverty, after some slight homage paid to secular science, collecting all their force of intellect, devoted themselves to labours upon the sacred scripture, meditating day and night on the law of the Lord. And whatever they could steal from their famishing belly, or intercept from their half-covered body, they thought it the highest gain to spend in buying or correcting books. Whose worldly contemporaries observing their devotion and study, bestowed upon them for the edification of the whole Church the books which they had collected at great expense in the various parts of the world.

❧ In truth, in these days as ye are engaged with all diligence in pursuit of gain, it may be reasonably believed, if we speak according to human notions, that God thinks less upon those whom He perceives to distrust His promises, putting their hope in human providence, not considering the raven, nor the lilies, whom the Most High feeds and arrays. Ye do not think upon Daniel and the bearer of the mess of boiled pottage, nor recollect Elijah who was delivered from hunger

63

per angelum, nunc in Sarepta per viduam, largitate divina, quae dat escam omni carni tempore opportuno, a famis inedia liberatum. Climate miserabili, ut timetur, descenditis, dum divinae pietatis diffidentia prudentiae propriae producit innisum, innisus vero prudentiae propriae sollicitudinem generat terrenorum, nimiaque terrenorum sollicitudo librorum adimit tam amorem quam studium, et sic cedit paupertas hodie per abusum in verbi Dei dispendium, quam propter ipsius solum adminiculum elegistis.

℘ Vncinis pomorum, ut populus fabulatur, puerulos ad religionem attrahitis, quos professos doctrinis non instruitis vi et metu, sicut exigit aetas illa, sed mendicativis discursibus sustinetis intendere atque tempus quo possent addiscere, in captandis favoribus amicorum consumere sinitis, in offensam parentum, puerorum periculum et ordinis detrimentum. Sicque nimirum contingit quod qui parvuli discere minime cogebantur inviti, grandiores effecti docere praesumunt, indigni penitus et indocti, et parvus error in principio maximus fit in fine. Succrescit namque in grege vestro promiscuo laicorum quaedam multitudo plurimum onerosa, qui tamen se ad praedicationis officium tanto improbius ingerunt, quanto minus ea quae loquuntur intelligunt, in contemptum sermonis divini et in perniciem animarum.

℘ Sane contra legem in bove aratis et asino, cum indoctis et doctis culturam agri dominici committitis pari passu. Scriptum est: Boves arabant et asinae pascebantur iuxta eos;

once in the desert by angels, again in the torrent by ravens, and again in Sarepta by the widow, through the divine bounty, which gives to all flesh their meat in due season. Ye descend (as we fear) by a wretched anticlimax, distrust of the divine goodness producing reliance upon your own prudence, and reliance upon your own prudence begetting anxiety about worldly things, and excessive anxiety about worldly things taking away the love as well as the study of books; and thus poverty in these days is abused to the injury of the word of God, which ye have chosen only for profit's sake.

❦ With summer fruit, as the people gossip, ye attract boys to religion, whom when they have taken the vows ye do not instruct by fear and force, as their age requires, but allow them to devote themselves to begging expeditions, and suffer them to spend the time, in which they might be learning, in procuring the favour of friends, to the annoyance of their parents, the danger of the boys, and the detriment of the order. And thus no doubt it happens that those who were not compelled to learn as unwilling boys, when they grow up presume to teach though utterly unworthy and unlearned, and a small error in the beginning becomes a very great one in the end. For there grows up among your promiscuous flock of laity a pestilent multitude of creatures, who nevertheless the more shamelessly force themselves into the office of preaching, the less they understand what they are saying, to the contempt of the divine word and the injury of souls.

❦ In truth against the law ye plough with an ox and an ass together, in committing the cultivation of the Lord's field to learned and unlearned. *Side by side*, it is written, *the oxen*

quoniam discretorum interest praedicare, simplicium vero
per auditum sacri eloquii sub silentio se cibare. Quot lapides mittitis in acervum Mercurii his diebus! quot eunuchis
sapientiae nuptias procuratis! quot caecos speculatores super
Ecclesiae muros circumire praecipitis!

℆ O piscatores inertes! solis retibus alienis utentes, qui
rupta vix imperite reficitis, nova vero nullatenus connodatis,
aliorum labores intratis, aliorum studia recitatis, aliorum
sapientiam superficialiter repetitam theatrali strepitu labiatis.
Quemadmodum psittacus idiota auditas voces effigiat, sic
tales recitatores fiunt omnium sed nullius auctores, asinam
Balaam imitantes, quae licet esset intrinsecus insensata, lingua tamen diserta facta est, tam domini quam prophetae
magistra. Resipiscite pauperes Christi et nos libros inspicite
studiose, sine quibus in praeparatione evangelii pacis nunquam poteritis debite calceari.

℆ Paulus apostolus, praedicator veritatis et doctor eximius
gentium, ista sibi per Timotheum pro omni supellectile tria
iussit afferri, paenulam, libros et membranas, 2ª ad Tim.
ul°, viris evangelicis formam praebens, ut habitum deferant
ordinatum, libros habeant ad studendi subsidium et membranas, quas apostolus maxime ponderat, ad scribendum:
maxime, inquit, membranas.

℆ Revera mancus est clericus et ad multorum iacturam
turpiter mutilatus, qui artis scribendi totaliter est ignarus.
Aërem vocibus verberat et praesentes tantum aedificat, ab-
sentibus et posteris nihil parat. Atramentarium scriptoris

were ploughing and the asses feeding beside them: since it is the duty of the discreet to preach, but of the simple to feed themselves in silence by the hearing of sacred eloquence. How many stones ye fling upon the heap of Mercury nowadays! How many marriages ye procure for the eunuchs of wisdom! How many blind watchmen ye bid go round about the walls of the Church!

℟ O idle fishermen, using only the nets of others, which when torn it is all ye can do to clumsily repair, but can net no new ones of your own! ye enter on the labours of others, ye repeat the lessons of others, ye mouth with theatric effort the superficially repeated wisdom of others. As the silly parrot imitates the words that he has heard, so such men are mere reciters of all, but authors of nothing, imitating Balaam's ass, which, though senseless of itself, yet became eloquent of speech and the teacher of its master though a prophet. Recover yourselves, O poor in Christ, and studiously regard us books, without which ye can never be properly shod in the preparation of the gospel of peace.

℟ Paul the apostle, preacher of the truth and excellent teacher of the nations, for all his gear bade three things to be brought to him by Timothy, his cloak, books and parchments, affording an example to ecclesiastics that they should wear dress in moderation, and should have books for aid in study, and parchments, which the apostle especially esteems, for writing: *and especially*, he says, the parchments.

℟ And truly that clerk is crippled and maimed to his disablement in many ways, who is entirely ignorant of the art of writing. He beats the air with words and edifies only those who are present, but does nothing for the absent and for

gestabat in renibus vir qui frontes gementium Tau signabat,
Ezechiel. 9°; insinuans figurate quod, si quis scribendi peritia
careat, praedicandi paenitentiam officium non praesumat.

ℂ Tandem in praesentis calce capituli supplicant vobis
libri: Iuvenes vestros aptos ingenio studiis applicate, neces-
saria ministrantes, quos non solummodo bonitatem verum
etiam disciplinam et scientiam doceatis, verberibus terreatis,
attrahatis blanditiis, molliatis munusculis et poenosis rigori-
bus urgeatis, ut et Socratici moribus et doctrinis Peripatetici
simul fiant. Heri quasi hora xiª vos discretus paterfamilias
introduxit in vineam; ante sero penitus pigeat otiari. Utinam
cum prudenti villico mendicandi tam improbe verecundiam
haberetis! Tunc enim proculdubio libris et studio propensius
vacaretis.

Richard de Bury

posterity. The man bore a writer's ink-horn upon his loins, who set a mark *Tau* upon the foreheads of the men that sigh and cry, *Ezechiel* 9; teaching in a figure that if any lack skill in writing, he shall not undertake the task of preaching repentance.

❡ Finally, in conclusion of the present chapter, books implore of you: make your young men who though ignorant are apt of intellect apply themselves to study, furnishing them with necessaries, that ye may teach them not only goodness but discipline and science, may terrify them by blows, charm them by blandishments, mollify them by gifts, and urge them on by painful rigour, so that they may become at once Socratics in morals and Peripatetics in learning. Yesterday, as it were at the eleventh hour, the prudent householder introduced you into his vineyard. Repent of idleness before it is too late: would that with the cunning steward ye might be ashamed of begging so shamelessly; for then no doubt ye would devote yourselves more assiduously to us books and to study.

Querimonia librorum contra bella

PACIS auctor et amator Altissime! dissipa gentes bella volentes, quae super omnes pestilentias libris nocent. Bella namque carentia rationis iudicio furiosos efficiunt impetus in adversa et dum rationis moderamine non utuntur, sine differentia discretionis progressa, vasa destruunt rationis.

℃ Tunc prudens Apollo Pythoni subicitur et tunc Phronesis pia mater in phrenesis redigitur potestatem. Tunc pennatus Pegasus stabulo Corydonis includitur et facundus Mercurius suffocatur. Tunc Pallas prudens erroris mucrone conciditur et iocundae Pierides truculenta furoris tyrannide supprimuntur.

℃ O crudele spectaculum! ubi Phoebum philosophorum, archisophum Aristotelem, cui in orbis dominum Deus ipse commisit dominium, scelerosis manibus vinculatum, ferramentis infamibus compeditum lanistarum humeris a sacratis aedibus asportari, et qui in mundi magistratum magisterium atque super imperatorem imperium meruit obtinere, iniustissimo belli iure videres subici vili scurrae.

℃ O potestas iniquissima tenebrarum, quae Platonis non veretur pessumdare deitatem probatam, qui solus conspectui Creatoris prius quam bellantis chaos placaret litigium, et

CHAPTER VII

The Complaint of Books against Wars

ALMIGHTY Author and Lover of peace, scatter the nations that delight in war, which is above all plagues injurious to books. For wars being without the control of reason make a wild assault on everything they come across, and lacking the check of reason they push on without discretion or distinction to destroy the vessels of reason.

⸿ Then the wise Apollo becomes the Python's prey, and Phronesis, the pious mother, becomes subject to the power of Phrenzy. Then winged Pegasus is shut up in the stall of Corydon, and eloquent Mercury is strangled. Then wise Pallas is struck down by the dagger of error, and the charming Pierides are smitten by the truculent tyranny of madness.

⸿ O cruel spectacle! where you may see the Phoebus of philosophers, the all-wise Aristotle, whom God Himself made master of the master of the world, enchained by wicked hands and borne in shameful irons on the shoulders of gladiators from his sacred home. There you may see him who was worthy to be lawgiver to the lawgiver of the world and to hold empire over its emperor made the slave of vile buffoons by the most unrighteous laws of war.

⸿ O most wicked power of darkness, which does not fear to undo the approved divinity of Plato, who alone was worthy to submit to the view of the Creator, before he assuaged the strife of warring chaos, and before form had put

71

ante quam hylen endelechia induisset, species ideales obicere dignus fuit, ut mundum archetypum demonstraret auctori, quo de superno exemplo mundus sensibilis duceretur. O lacrimosus intuitus! quo moralis Socrates, cuius actus virtus et sermo doctrina, qui de naturae principiis politiae produxit iustitiam, vitiosi vispilionis addictus cernitur servituti. Pythagoram plangimus, harmoniae parentem, bellorum incentricibus furiis flagellatum atrociter vice cantus gemitus edere columbinos. Miseremur Zenonis, principis Stoicorum, qui ne consilium proderet linguam morsu secuit et exspuit in tyrannum intrepide. Heu, iam rursus a Diomedonte tritus in mortario pistillatur!

⁋ Certe non sufficimus singulos libros luctu lamentari condigno, qui in diversis mundi partibus bellorum discrimine perierunt. Horribilem tamen stragem, quae per auxiliares milites secundo bello Alexandrino contigit in Aegypto, stilo flebili memoramus, ubi septinginta millia voluminum ignibus conflagrarunt, quae sub regibus Ptolemaeis per multa curricula temporum sunt collecta, sicut recitat Aulus Gellius, Noctium Atticarum lib. 6°, cap. 16°.

⁋ Quanta proles Atlantica tunc occubuisse putabitur, orbium motus omnes, coniunctiones planetarum, galaxiae naturam et generationes prognosticas cometarum ac quaecunque in caelo fiunt vel aethere, comprehendens! Quis tam infaustum holocaustum, ubi loco cruoris incaustum offertur, non exhorreat? ubi prunae candentes pergameni crepitantis sanguine vernabantur, ubi tot innocentium millia, in quorum

Richard de Bury

on its garb of matter, the ideal types, in order to demonstrate the archetypal universe to its author, so that the world of sense might be modelled after the supernal pattern. O tearful sight! where the moral Socrates, whose acts were virtue and whose discourse was science, who deduced political justice from the principles of nature, is seen enslaved to some rascal robber. We bemoan Pythagoras, the parent of harmony, as, brutally scourged by the harrying furies of war, he utters not a song but the wailings of a dove. We mourn, too, for Zeno, who lest he should betray his secret bit off his tongue and fearlessly spat it out at the tyrant, and now, alas! is brayed and crushed to death in a mortar by Diomedon.

❡ In sooth we cannot mourn with the grief that they deserve all the various books that have perished by the fate of war in various parts of the world. Yet we must tearfully recount the dreadful ruin which was caused in Egypt by the auxiliaries in the Alexandrian war, when seven hundred thousand volumes were consumed by fire. These volumes had been collected by the royal Ptolemies through long periods of time, as Aulus Gellius relates.

❡ What an Atlantean progeny must be supposed to have then perished: including the motions of the spheres, all the conjunctions of the planets, the nature of the galaxy, and the prognostic generations of comets, and all that exists in the heavens or in the ether! Who would not shudder at such a hapless holocaust, where ink is offered up instead of blood, where the glowing ashes of crackling parchment were encarnadined with blood, where the devouring flames consumed so many thousands of innocents in whose mouth was

73

ore non est inventum mendacium, flamma vorax consumpsit, ubi tot scrinia veritatis aeternae ignis parcere nesciens in faetentem cinerem commutavit.

℀ Minoris facinoris aestimatur tam Jeptae quam Agamemnonis victima, ubi pia filia virgo patris gladio iugulatur. Quot labores celebris Herculis tunc periisse putabimus, qui ob astronomiae peritiam collo irreflexo caelum describitur sustulisse, cum iam secundo flammis Hercules sit iniectus.

℀ Arcana caelorum, quae Ionithus non ab homine neque per hominem didicit sed divinitus inspiratus accepit; quaeque Zoroastes germanus eiusdem, immundorum servitor spirituum, Bactrianis disseruit; quae etiam sanctus Enoch Paradisi praefectus prius quam transferretur de saeculo prophetavit; immo quae primus Adam filios docuit, sicut raptus in ecstasi in libro aeternitatis praeviderat, flammis illis nefandis probabiliter aestimantur destructa.

℀ Aegyptiorum religio, quam liber Logostilios sic commendat egregie, politia veterum Athenarum, quae novem millibus annorum Athenas Graeciae praecesserunt; carmina Chaldaeorum; considerationes Arabum et Indorum; caerimoniae Iudaeorum; architectura Babyloniorum; Noe georgica; Moysis praestigia; Iosuae planimetria; Samsonis aenigmata; Salomonis problemata, a cedro Libani usque ad hyssopum planissime disputata; Aesculapii antidota; Cadmi grammatica; Parnasi poemata; Apollinis oracula; Argonautica Iasonis; strategematon Palamedis; et alia infinita scientiarum secreta huius incendii tempestate creduntur sublata.

no guile, where the unsparing fire turned into stinking ashes so many shrines of eternal truth?

❡ A lesser crime than this is the sacrifice of Jephthah or Agamemnon, where a pious daughter is slain by a father's sword. How many labours of the famous Hercules shall we suppose then perished, who because of his knowledge of astronomy is said to have sustained the heaven on his unyielding neck, when Hercules was now for the second time cast into the flames.

❡ The secrets of the heavens, which Jonithus learnt not from man or through man but received by divine inspiration; what his brother Zoroaster, the servant of unclean spirits, taught the Bactrians; what holy Enoch, the prefect of Paradise, prophesied before he was taken from the world, and finally, what the first Adam taught his children of the things to come, which he had seen when caught up in an ecstasy in the book of eternity, are believed to have perished in those horrid flames.

❡ The religion of the Egyptians, which the book of the Perfect Word so commends; the excellent polity of the older Athens, which preceded by nine thousand years the Athens of Greece; the charms of the Chaldaeans; the observations of the Arabs and Indians; the ceremonies of the Jews; the architecture of the Babylonians; the agriculture of Noah; the magic arts of Moses; the geometry of Joshua; the enigmas of Samson; the problems of Solomon from the cedar of Lebanon to the hyssop; the antidotes of Aesculapius; the grammar of Cadmus; the poems of Parnassus; the oracles of Apollo; the argonautics of Jason; the stratagems of Palamedes, and infinite other secrets of science are believed to have perished at the time of this conflagration.

The Philobiblon of

℩ Numquid Aristotelem de circuli quadratura syllogismus apodicticon latuisset, si libros veterum methodos naturae totius habentium permisissent nefanda praelia superesse? Nec enim de mundi aeternitate problema neutrum fecisset, nec de intellectuum humanorum pluralitate eorundemque perpetuitate, ut verisimiliter creditur, dubitasset ullatenus, si perfectae scientiae veterum invisorum bellorum pressuris obnoxiae non fuissent. Per bella namque ad patrias peregrinas distrahimur, obtruncamur, vulneramur et enormiter mutilamur, sub terra suffodimur, in mari submergimur, flammis exurimur et omni necis genere trucidamur.

℩ Quantum sanguinis nostri fudit Scipio bellicosus, cum eversioni Carthaginis, Romani imperii impugnatricis et aemulae, anxius incumbebat! Quot millia millium praelium decennale Troianum ab hac luce transmisit! Quot per Antonium, Tullio iam occiso, externarum provinciarum latebras adierunt! Quot de nobis per Theodoricum, exulante Boetio, in diversa mundi climata, sicut oves pastore percusso, sunt dispersi! Quot Seneca succumbente Neronis malitiae, cum et volens et nolens portas mortis adiret, ab eo divisi retrocessimus lacrimantes et in quibus partibus hospitari possemus penitus ignorantes!

℩ Felix fuit illa librorum translatio, quam in Persas de Athenis Xerxes fecisse describitur, quos rursus de Persis in Athenas Seleucus reduxit. O postliminium gratiosum! O mira laetitia! quam tunc cerneres in Athenis, cum proli suae

76

Richard de Bury

❡ Nay, Aristotle would not have missed the quadrature of
the circle, if only baleful conflicts had spared the books of
the ancients, who knew all the methods of nature. He would
not have left the problem of the eternity of the world an open
question, nor, as is credibly conceived, would he have had
any doubts of the plurality of human intellects and of their
eternity, if the perfect sciences of the ancients had not been
exposed to the calamities of hateful wars. For by wars we are
scattered into foreign lands, are mutilated, wounded, and
shamefully disfigured, are buried under the earth and over-
whelmed in the sea, are devoured by the flames and destroyed
by every kind of death.

❡ How much of our blood was shed by warlike Scipio,
when he was eagerly compassing the overthrow of Carthage,
the opponent and rival of the Roman empire! How many
thousands of thousands of us did the ten years' war of Troy
dismiss from the light of day! How many were driven by
Antony, after the murder of Tully, to seek hiding places in
foreign provinces! How many of us were scattered by Theo-
doric, while Boethius was in exile, into the different quarters
of the world, like sheep whose shepherd has been struck
down! How many, when Seneca fell a victim to the cruelty
of Nero, and willing yet unwilling passed the gates of death,
took leave of him and retired in tears, not even knowing in
what quarter to seek for shelter!

❡ Happy was that translation of books which Xerxes is
said to have made to Persia from Athens, and which Seleucus
brought back again from Persia to Athens. O glad and joyful
return! O wondrous joy, which you might then see in Athens,
when the mother went in triumph to meet her progeny, and

genitrix obviaret tripudians matricemque thalamum sene-
scenti iam soboli denuo demonstraret. Reassignatis hospitiis
veteribus inquilinis, mox tabulata cedrina cum lignis et trabi-
bus levigatis aptissime complanantur; auro et ebore epigrammata designantur camerulis singulis, quibus ipsa volumina re-
verenter illata suavissime collocantur sic, ut nullum alterius
ingressum impediat vel propinquitate nimia fratrem laedat.

℅ Caeterum infinita sunt dispendia quae per seditiones
bellorum librorum generi sunt illata. Et quoniam infinita
nullatenus pertransire contingit, hic statuemus finaliter que-
rimoniae nostrae Gades, et ad preces a quibus incepimus
regiramus habenas, rogantes suppliciter ut rector Olympi ac
mundi totius dispensator altissimus firmet pacem et bella
removeat ac tempora faciat sua protectione tranquilla.

again showed the chambers in which they had been nursed to her now ageing children! Their old homes were restored to their former inmates, and forthwith boards of cedar with shelves and beams of gopher wood are most skilfully planed; inscriptions of gold and ivory are designed for the several compartments, to which the volumes themselves are reverently brought and pleasantly arranged, so that no one hinders the entrance of another or injures its brother by excessive crowding.

❦ But in truth infinite are the losses which have been inflicted upon the race of books by wars and tumults. And as it is by no means possible to enumerate and survey infinity, we will here finally set up the Gades of our complaint, and turn again to the prayers with which we began, humbly imploring that the Ruler of Olympus and the Most High Governor of all the world will establish peace and dispel wars and make our days tranquil under His protection.

CAPITULUM VIII

De multiplici opportunitate quam habuimus librorum copiam conquirendi

CUM omni negotio tempus sit et opportunitas, ut testatur sapiens Ecclesiastes, 8°, iam progredimur enarrare multiplices opportunitates, quibus in adquisitione librorum, nostris propositis divinitate propitia, iuvabamur.

⁋ Quamvis enim ab adolescentia nostra semper socialem communionem cum viris litteratis et librorum dilectoribus delectaremur habere, succedentibus tamen prosperis, regiae maiestatis consecuti notitiam et in ipsius acceptati familia, facultatem accepimus ampliorem ubilibet visitandi pro libito et venandi quasi saltus quosdam delicatissimos, tum privatas, tum communes, tum regularium, tum saecularium librarias.

⁋ Sane dum invictissimi principis ac semper magnifice triumphantis regis Angliae Eduardi Tertii post conquestum, cuius tempora serenare dignetur Altissimus diutine et tranquille, primo quidem suam concernentibus curiam, deinde vero rempublicam regni sui, cancellarii videlicet ac thesaurarii, fungeremur officiis, patescebat nobis aditus facilis, regalis favoris intuitu, ad librorum latebras libere perscrutandas.

⁋ Amoris quippe nostri fama volatilis iam ubique percre-

CHAPTER VIII

Of the numerous Opportunities we have had of collecting a store of Books

SINCE to everything there is a season and an opportunity, as the wise Ecclesiastes witnesseth, let us now proceed to relate the manifold opportunities through which we have been assisted by the divine goodness in the acquisition of books.

❡ Although from our youth upwards we had always delighted in holding social commune with learned men and lovers of books, yet when we prospered in the world and made acquaintance with the King's majesty and were received into his household, we obtained ampler facilities for visiting everywhere as we would, and of hunting as it were certain most choice preserves, libraries private as well as public and of the regular as well as of the secular clergy.

❡ And indeed while we filled various offices to the victorious Prince and splendidly triumphant King of England, Edward the Third from the Conquest—whose reign may the Almighty long and peacefully continue—first those about his court, but then those concerning the public affairs of his kingdom, namely the offices of Chancellor and Treasurer, there was afforded to us, in consideration of the royal favour, easy access for the purpose of freely searching the retreats of books.

❡ In fact, the fame of our love of them had been soon

buit, tantumque librorum et maxime veterum ferebamur
cupiditate languescere, posse vero quemlibet nostrum per
quaternos facilius quam per pecuniam adipisci favorem.
Quamobrem cum supra dicti principis recolendae memoriae
bonitate suffulti possemus obesse et prodesse, officere et pro-
ficere vehementer tam maioribus quam pusillis, affluxerunt
loco xeniorum et munerum locoque donorum et iocalium
caenulenti quaterni ac decrepiti codices, nostris tam aspectibus quam affectibus pretiosi.

℀ Tunc nobilissimorum monasteriorum aperiebantur armaria, reserabantur scrinia et cistulae solvebantur, et per
longa saecula in sepulcris soporata volumina expergiscunt
attonita, quaeque in locis tenebrosis latuerant novae lucis
radiis perfunduntur. Delicatissimi quondam libri, corrupti
et abominabiles iam effecti, murium quidem foetibus co-
operti et vermium morsibus terebrati, iacebant exanimes; et
qui olim purpura vestiebantur et bysso, nunc in cinere et
cilicio recubantes oblivioni traditi videbantur domicilia
tinearum.

℀ Inter haec nihilominus, captatis temporibus, magis vo-
luptuose consedimus quam fecisset medicus delicatus inter
aromatum apothecas, ubi amoris nostri obiectum reperimus
et fomentum. Sic sacra vasa scientiae ad nostrae dispensatio-
nis provenerunt arbitrium, quaedam data, quaedam vendita
ac nonnulla pro tempore commodata.

℀ Nimirum cum nos plerique de huiusmodi donariis cernerent contentatos, ea sponte nostris usibus studuerunt tri-

Richard de Bury

winged abroad everywhere, and we were reported to burn with such desire for books, and especially old ones, that it was more easy for any man to gain our favour by means of books than of money. Wherefore, since supported by the goodness of the aforesaid Prince of worthy memory we were able to requite a man well or ill, to benefit or injure mightily great as well as small, there flowed in, instead of presents and guerdons, and instead of gifts and jewels, soiled tracts and battered codices, gladsome alike to our eye and heart.

¶ Then the aumbries of the most famous monasteries were thrown open, cases were unlocked and caskets were undone, and volumes that had slumbered through long ages in their tombs wake up and are astonished, and those that had lain hidden in dark places are bathed in the ray of unwonted light. These long lifeless books, once most dainty, but now become corrupt and loathsome, covered with litters of mice and pierced with the gnawings of the worms, and who were once clothed in purple and fine linen, now lying in sackcloth and ashes, given up to oblivion, seemed to have become habitations of the moth.

¶ Natheless among these, seizing the opportunity, we would sit down with more delight than a fastidious physician among his stores of gums and spices, and there we found the object and the stimulus of our affections. Thus the sacred vessels of learning came into our control and stewardship; some by gift, others by purchase, and some lent to us for a season.

¶ No wonder that when people saw that we were contented with gifts of this kind, they were anxious of their own accord to minister to our needs with those things that they

buere, quibus ipsi libentius caruerunt, quam ea quae nostris assistentes servitiis abstulerunt. Quorum tamen negotia sic expedire curavimus gratiose, ut et eisdem emolumentum accresceret, nullum tamen detrimentum iustitia sentiret. Porro, si scyphos aureos et argenteos, si equos egregios, si nummorum summas non modicas amassemus, tunc temporis dives nobis aerarium instaurasse possemus. Sed revera libros non libras maluimus, codicesque plus dileximus quam florenos, ac panfletos exiguos incrassatis praetulimus palefridis.

℀ Ad haec eiusdem principis illustrissimi sempiternae memoriae legationibus crebris functi, et ob multiplicia regni negotia nunc ad sedem Romanam, nunc ad curiam Franciae, nunc ad mundi diversa dominia, taediosis ambassiatibus ac periculosis temporibus mittebamur, circumferentes tamen ubique illam, quam aquae plurimae nequiverunt exstinguere, caritatem librorum. Haec omnium peregrinationum absinthia quasi quaedam pigmentaria potio dulcoravit. Haec post perplexas intricationes et scrupulosos causarum anfractus ac vix egressibiles rei publicae labyrinthos ad respirandum parumper temperiem aurae lenis aperuit.

℀ O beate Deus Deorum in Sion, quantus fluminis impetus voluptatis laetificavit cor nostrum, quotiens paradisum mundi Parisius visitare vacavimus moraturi, ubi nobis semper dies pauci prae amoris magnitudine videbantur! Ibi bibliothecae iocundae super cellas aromatum redolentes, ibi virens viridarium universorum voluminum, ibi prata academica terrae motu trementia, Athenarum diverticula, Peripateticorum itinera, Parnasi promontoria et porticus Stoicorum.

Richard de Bury

were more willing to dispense with than the things they secured by ministering to our service. And in good will we strove so to forward their affairs that gain accrued to them, while justice suffered no disparagement. Indeed, if we had loved gold and silver goblets, highbred horses, or no small sums of money, we might in those days have furnished forth a rich treasury. But in truth we wanted manuscripts not moneyscripts; we loved codices more than florins, and preferred slender pamphlets to pampered palfreys.

⁋ Besides all this, we were frequently made ambassador of this most illustrious Prince of everlasting memory, and were sent on the most various affairs of state, now to the Holy See, now to the Court of France, and again to various powers of the world, on tedious embassies and in times of danger, always carrying with us, however, that love of books which many waters could not quench. For this like a delicious draught sweetened the bitterness of our journeyings and after the perplexing intricacies and troublesome difficulties of causes and the all but inextricable labyrinths of public affairs afforded us a little breathing space to enjoy a balmier atmosphere.

⁋ O Holy God of Gods in Sion, what a mighty stream of pleasure made glad our hearts whenever we had leisure to visit Paris, the Paradise of the world, and to linger there; where the days seemed ever few for the greatness of our love! There are delightful libraries, more aromatic than stores of spicery; there are luxuriant parks of all manner of volumes; there are Academic meads shaken by the tramp of scholars; there are lounges of Athens; walks of the Peripatetics; peaks of Parnassus; and porches of the Stoics.

The Philobiblon of

℩ Ibi cernitur tam artis quam scientiae mensurator Aristoteles, cuius est totum quod est optimum in doctrinis, in regione dumtaxat transmutabili sublunari; ibi Ptolemaeus epicyclos et eccentricos auges atque geuzahar planetarum figuris et numeris emetitur; ibi Paulus arcana revelat; ibi Dionysius convicinus hierarchias coordinat et distinguit; ibi quicquid Cadmus grammate recolligit Phoeniceo, totum virgo Carmenta charactere repraesentat Latino; ibi revera, apertis thesauris et sacculorum corrigiis resolutis, pecuniam laeto corde dispersimus, atque libros impretiabiles luto redemimus et arena. Nequaquam malum est, malum est, insonuit omnis emptor; sed ecce quam bonum et quam iocundum arma clericalis militiae congregare in unum, ut suppetat nobis, unde haereticorum bella conterere, si insurgant!

℩ Amplius opportunitatem maximam nos captasse cognoscimus per hoc, quod ab aetate tenera magistrorum et scholarium ac diversarum artium professorum quos ingenii perspicacitas ac doctrinae celebritas clariores effecerant, relegato quolibet partiali favore, exquisitissima sollicitudine nostrae semper coniunximus comitivae, quorum consolativis colloquiis confortati, nunc argumentorum ostensivis investigationibus, nunc physicorum processuum ac catholicorum doctorum tractatuum recitationibus, nunc moralitatum excitativis collationibus, velut alternatis et multiplicatis ingenii ferculis, dulcius fovebamur.

℩ Tales in nostro tirocinio commilitones elegimus, tales in thalamo collaterales habuimus, tales in itinere comites, tales in hospitio commensales, et tales penitus in omni fortuna

Richard de Bury

¶ There is seen the surveyor of all arts and sciences Aristotle, to whom belongs all that is most excellent in doctrine, so far as relates to this passing sublunary world; there Ptolemy measures epicycles and eccentric apogees and the nodes of the planets by figures and numbers; there Paul reveals the mysteries; there his neighbour Dionysius arranges and distinguishes the hierarchies; there the virgin Carmenta reproduces in Latin characters all that Cadmus collected in Phoenician letters; there indeed opening our treasuries and unfastening our purse-strings we scattered money with joyous heart and purchased inestimable books with mud and sand. It is naught, it is naught, saith every buyer. But in vain; for behold how good and how pleasant it is to gather together the arms of the clerical warfare, that we may have the means to crush the attacks of heretics, if they arise!

¶ Further, we are aware that we obtained most excellent opportunities of collecting in the following way. From our early years we attached to our society with the most exquisite solicitude and discarding all partiality all such masters and scholars and professors in the several faculties as had become most distinguished by their subtlety of mind and the fame of their learning. Deriving consolation from their sympathetic conversation, we were delightfully entertained, now by demonstrative chains of reasoning, now by the recital of physical processes and the treatises of the doctors of the Church, now by stimulating discourses on the allegorical meanings of things, as by a rich and well-varied intellectual feast.

¶ Such men we chose as comrades in our years of learning, as companions in our chamber, as associates on our journeys, as guests at our table, and, in short, as helpmates in all the

sodales. Verum quia nulla felicitas diu durare permittitur, privabamur nonnunquam luminum aliquorum praesentia corporali, cum eisdem promotiones ecclesiasticae ac dignitates debitae, prospiciente de caelo iustitia, provenerunt. Quo fiebat, ut incumbentes sicut oportuit curae propriae se a nostris cogerentur obsequiis absentare.

℄ Rursus compendiosissimam semitam subiungemus, per quam ad manus nostras pervenit librorum tam veterum quam novorum plurima multitudo. Religiosorum siquidem mendicantium paupertatem susceptam pro Christo nunquam indignantes horruimus, verum ipsos ubique terrarum in nostrae compassionis ulnas admisimus mansuetas, affabilitate familiarissima in personae nostrae devotionem alleximus, allectosque beneficiorum liberalitate munifica fovimus propter Deum; quorum sic eramus omnium benefactores communes, ut nihilominus videremur quadam paternitatis proprietate singulos adoptasse.

℄ Istis in statu quolibet facti sumus refugium, istis nunquam clausimus gratiae nostrae sinum; quamobrem istos votorum nostrorum peculiarissimos zelatores meruimus habere, et tam opere quam opera promotores. Qui circuentes mare et aridam ac orbis ambitum perlustrantes, universitates quoque diversarumque provinciarum generalia studia perscrutantes, nostris desideriis militare studebant certissima spe mercedis.

℄ Quis inter tot argutissimos venatores lepusculus delitesceret? Quis pisciculus istorum nunc hamos, nunc retia, nunc

vicissitudes of life. But as no happiness is permitted to endure for long, we were sometimes deprived of the bodily companionship of some of these shining lights when, justice looking down from heaven, the ecclesiastical preferments and dignities that they deserved fell to their portion. And thus it happened, as was only right, that in attending to their own cures they were obliged to absent themselves from attendance upon us.

❡ We will add yet another very convenient way by which a great multitude of books old as well as new came into our hands. For we never regarded with disdain or disgust the poverty of the mendicant orders, adopted for the sake of Christ; but in all parts of the world took them into the kindly arms of our compassion, allured them by the most friendly familiarity into devotion to ourselves, and having so allured them cherished them with munificent liberality of beneficence for the sake of God, becoming benefactors of all of them in general in such wise that we seemed none the less to have adopted certain individuals with a special fatherly affection.

❡ To these men we were as a refuge in every case of need, and never refused to them the shelter of our favour, wherefore we deserved to find them most special furtherers of our wishes and promoters thereof in act and deed, who compassing land and sea, traversing the circuit of the world, and ransacking the universities and high schools of various provinces, were zealous in combating for our desires, in the sure and certain hope of reward.

❡ What leveret could escape amidst so many keen-sighted hunters? What little fish could evade in turn their hooks and

sagenas evaderet? A corpore sacrae legis divinae usque ad quaternum sophismatum hesternorum, nihil istos praeterire potuit scrutatores. Si in fonte fidei Christianae, curia sacrosancta Romana, sermo devotus insonuit, vel si pro novis causis quaestio ventilabatur extranea, si Parisiensis soliditas, quae plus antiquitati discendae quam veritati subtiliter producendae iam studet, si Anglicana perspicacitas, quae antiquis perfusa luminaribus novos semper radios emittit veritatis, quicquam ad augmentum scientiae vel declarationem fidei promulgabat, hoc statim nostris recens infundebatur auditibus nullo denigratum seminiverbio nulloque nugace corruptum, sed de praelo purissimi torcularis in nostrae memoriae dolia defaecandum transibat.

℃ Cum vero nos ad civitates et loca contingeret declinare, ubi praefati pauperes conventus habebant, eorum armaria ac quaecunque librorum repositoria visitare non piguit; immo ibi in altissima paupertate altissimas divitias sapientiae thesaurizatas invenimus, et non solum in eorum sarcinulis et sportellis micas de mensa dominorum cadentes repperimus pro catellis, verum panes propositionis absque fermento panemque angelorum omne delectamentum in se habentem, immo horrea Ioseph plena frumentis totamque Aegypti supellectilem atque dona ditissima, quae regina Saba detulit Salomoni.

℃ Hi sicut formicae continue congregantes in messem et apes argumentosae fabricantes iugiter cellas mellis. Hi successores Bezeleel ad excogitandum quicquid fabrefieri poterit in argento et auro ac gemmis, quibus templum Ecclesiae

nets and snares? From the body of the Sacred Law down to the booklet containing the fallacies of yesterday, nothing could escape these searchers. Was some devout discourse uttered at the fountain-head of Christian faith, the holy Roman Curia, or was some strange question ventilated with novel arguments; did the solidity of Paris, which is now more zealous in the study of antiquity than in the subtle investigation of truth, did English subtlety, which illumined by the lights of former times is always sending forth fresh rays of truth, produce anything to the advancement of science or the declaration of the faith, this was instantly poured still fresh into our ears, ungarbled by any babbler, unmutilated by any trifler, but passing straight from the purest of wine-presses into the vats of our memory to be clarified.

℃ But whenever it happened that we turned aside to the cities and places where the mendicants we have mentioned had their convents, we did not disdain to visit their libraries and any other repositories of books; nay, there we found heaped up amid the utmost poverty the utmost riches of wisdom. We discovered in their fardels and baskets not only crumbs falling from the masters' table for the dogs, but the shewbread without leaven and the bread of angels having in it all that is delicious; and indeed the garners of Joseph full of corn, and all the spoil of the Egyptians and the very precious gifts which Queen Sheba brought to Solomon.

℃ These men are as ants ever preparing their meat in the summer, and ingenious bees continually fabricating cells of honey. They are successors of Bezeleel in devising all manner of workmanship in silver and gold and precious stones for decorating the temple of the Church. They are cunning em-

decoretur. Hi prudentes polymitarii, qui superhumerale et rationale pontificis sed et vestes varias efficiunt sacerdotum. Hi cortinas, saga pellesque arietum rubricatas resarciunt, quibus Ecclesiae militantis tabernaculum contegatur. Hi agricolae seminantes, boves triturantes, tubae buccinantes, pleiades emicantes et stellae manentes in ordine suo, quae Sisaram expugnare non cessant. Et ut veritas honoretur, salvo praeiudicio cuiuscunque, licet hi nuper hora undecima vineam sint ingressi dominicam, sicut amantissimi nobis libri cap° 6° supra anxius allegabant, plus tamen in hac hora brevissima sacratorum librorum adiecerunt propagini quam omnes residui vinitores; Pauli sectantes vestigia, qui vocatione novissimus praedicatione primus, multo latius aliis evangelium Christi sparsit.

⁋ De istis ad statum pontificalem assumpti nonnullos habuimus de duobus ordinibus, Praedicatorum videlicet et Minorum, nostris assistentes lateribus nostraeque familiae commensales, viros utique tam moribus insignitos quam litteris, qui diversorum voluminum correctionibus, expositionibus, tabulationibus ac compilationibus indefessis studiis incumbebant.

⁋ Sane quamvis omnium religiosorum communicatione multiplici plurimorum operum copiam tam novorum quam veterum assecuti fuerimus, Praedicatores tamen extollimus merito speciali praeconio in hac parte, quod eos prae cunctis religiosis suorum sine invidia gratissime communicativos invenimus, ac divina quadam liberalitate perfusos sapientiae luminosae probavimus non avaros sed idoneos possessores.

⁋ Praeter has omnes opportunitates praetactas, stationario-

broiderers, who fashion the breastplate and ephod of the high priest and all the various vestments of the priests. They fashion the curtains of linen and hair and coverings of rams' skins dyed red with which to adorn the tabernacle of the Church militant. They are husbandmen that sow, oxen treading out corn, sounding trumpets, shining Pleiades and stars remaining in their courses, which cease not to fight against Sisera. And to pay due regard to truth, without prejudice to the judgment of any, although they lately at the eleventh hour have entered the lord's vineyard, as the books that are so fond of us eagerly declared in our sixth chapter, they have added more in this brief hour to the stock of the sacred books than all the other vine-dressers; following in the footsteps of Paul, the last to be called but the first in preaching, who spread the gospel of Christ more widely than all others.

⁋ Of these men, when we were raised to the episcopate we had several of both orders, viz. the Preachers and Minors, as personal attendants and companions at our board, men distinguished no less in letters than in morals, who devoted themselves with unwearied zeal to the correction, exposition, tabulation and compilation of various volumes.

⁋ But although we have acquired a very numerous store of ancient as well as modern works by the manifold intermediation of the religious, yet we must laud the Preachers with special praise, in that we have found them above all the religious most freely communicative of their stores without jealousy, and proved them to be imbued with an almost divine liberality, not greedy but fitting possessors of luminous wisdom.

⁋ Besides all the opportunities mentioned above, we se-

rum ac librariorum notitiam, non solum infra natalis soli provinciam, sed per regnum Franciae, Teutoniae et Italiae dispersorum comparavimus, faciliter pecunia praevolante, nec eos ullatenus impedivit distantia, neque furor maris absterruit, nec aes eis pro expensa defecit, quin ad nos optatos libros transmitterent vel afferrent. Sciebant profecto quod spes eorum in sinu nostro reposita defraudari non poterat, sed restabat apud nos copiosa redemptio cum usuris.

⁋ Denique nec rectores scholarum ruralium puerorumque rudium paedagogos nostra neglexit communio, singulorum captatrix amoris; sed potius cum vacaret, eorum hortulos et agellos ingressi, flores superficietenus redolentes collegimus ac radices effodimus obsoletas, studiosis tamen accommodas et quae possent, digesta barbarie rancida, pectorales arterias eloquentiae munere medicari. Inter huiusmodi pleraque comperimus renovari dignissima quae, solerter elimata robigine turpi, larva vetustatis deposita, merebantur venustis vultibus denuo reformari. Quae nos, adhibita necessariorum sufficientia, in futurae resurrectionis exemplum resuscitata quodammodo redivivae reddidimus sospitati.

⁋ Caeterum apud nos in nostris maneriis multitudo non modica semper erat antiquariorum, scriptorum, correctorum, colligatorum, illuminatorum et generaliter omnium, qui poterant librorum servitiis utiliter insudare. Postremo omnis utriusque sexus omnisque status vel dignitatis conditio, cuius erat cum libris aliquale commercium, cordis nostri ianuas

cured the acquaintance of stationers and booksellers, not only within our own country, but of those spread over the realms of France, Germany, and Italy, money flying forth in abundance to anticipate their demands; nor were they hindered by any distance or by the fury of the seas, or by the lack of means for their expenses, from sending or bringing to us the books that we required. For they well knew that their expectations of our bounty would not be defrauded, but that ample repayment with usury was to be found with us.

❡ Nor, finally, did our good-fellowship, which aimed to captivate the affection of all, overlook the rectors of schools and the instructors of rude boys. But rather, when we had an opportunity, we entered their little plots and gardens and gathered sweet-smelling flowers from the surface and dug up their roots, obsolete indeed, but still useful to the student, which might when their rank barbarism was digested heal the pectoral arteries with the gift of eloquence. Amongst the mass of these things we found some greatly meriting to be restored, which when skilfully cleansed and freed from the disfiguring rust of age, deserved to be renovated into comeliness of aspect. And applying in full measure the necessary means, as a type of the resurrection to come, we resuscitated them and restored them again to new life and health.

❡ Moreover, we had always in our different manors no small multitude of copyists and scribes, of correctors, binders, illuminators, and generally of all who could usefully labour in the service of books. Finally, all of both sexes and of every rank or position who had any kind of association with books, could most easily open by their knocking the

pulsu poterat aperire facillime et in nostrae gratiae gremio commodosum reperire cubile.

℃ Sic omnes admisimus codices afferentes, ut nunquam praecedentium multitudo fastidium posterorum efficeret, vel hesternum beneficium praecollatum praeiudicium pareret hodierno. Quapropter cum omnibus memoratis personis quasi quibusdam adamantibus attractivis librorum iugiter uteremur, fiebat ad nos desideratus accessus vasorum scientiae et volatus multifarius voluminum optimorum. Et hoc est quod praesenti capitulo sumpsimus enarrare.

Richard de Bury

door of our heart, and find a fit resting-place in our affection and favour.

❡ In so much did we receive those who brought books, that the multitude of those who had preceded them did not lessen the welcome of the after-comers, nor were the favours we had awarded yesterday prejudicial to those of today. Wherefore, ever using all the persons we have named as a kind of magnets to attract books, we had the desired accession of the vessels of science and a multitudinous flight of the finest volumes. And this is what we undertook to narrate in the present chapter.

CAPITULUM IX

Quod licet opera veterum amplius amaremus non tamen damnavimus studia modernorum

LICET nostris desideriis novitas modernorum nunquam fuerit odiosa, qui vacantes studiis ac priorum patrum sententiis quicquam vel subtiliter vel utiliter adicientes grata semper affectione coluimus, antiquorum tamen examinatos labores securiori aviditate cupivimus perscrutari. Sive enim naturaliter viguerunt perspicaciori mentis ingenio, sive instantiori studio forsitan indulserunt, sive utriusque suffulti subsidio profecerunt, hoc unum comperimus evidenter, quod vix sufficiunt successores priorum comperta discutere, atque ea per doctrinae captare compendium, quae antiqui anfractuosis adinventionibus effoderunt.

⟨ Sicut enim in corporis probitate praestantiores legimus praecessisse, quam moderna tempora exhibere noscantur, ita luculentioribus sensibus praefulsisse plerosque veterum opinari nullatenus est absurdum, cum utrosque opera, quae gesserunt, inattingibiles posteris aeque probent. Unde Phocas in prologo Grammaticae suae scribit:

> *Omnia cum veterum sint explorata libellis,*
> *Multa loqui breviter sit novitatis opus.*

CHAPTER IX

How although we preferred the Works of the Ancients we have not condemned the Studies of the Moderns

ALTHOUGH the novelties of the moderns were never disagreeable to our desires, who have always cherished with grateful affection those who devote themselves to study and who add anything either ingenious or useful to the opinions of our forefathers, yet we have always desired with more undoubting avidity to investigate the well-tested labours of the ancients. For whether they had by nature a greater vigour of mental sagacity, or whether they perhaps indulged in closer application to study, or whether they were assisted in their progress by both these things, one thing we are perfectly clear about, that their successors are barely capable of discussing the discoveries of their forerunners, and of acquiring those things as pupils which the ancients dug out by difficult efforts of discovery.

❡ For as we read that the men of old were of a more excellent degree of bodily development than modern times are found to produce, it is by no means absurd to suppose that most of the ancients were distinguished by brighter faculties, seeing that in the labours they accomplished of both kinds they are inimitable by posterity. And so Phocas writes in the prologue to his Grammar:

> *Since all things have been said by men of sense,*
> *The only novelty is—to condense.*

❧ Nempe si de fervore discendi ac diligentia studii fiat sermo, illi philosophiae vitam totam integre devoverunt; nostri vero saeculi contemporanei paucos annos fervidae iuventutis, aestuantis vicissim incendiis vitiorum, segniter applicant, et cum, sedatis passionibus, discernendae ambiguae veritatis acumen attigerint, mox externis implicati negotiis retrocedunt et philosophiae gymnasiis valedicunt.

❧ Mustum fumosum iuvenilis ingenii philosophicae difficultati delibant, vinumque maturius defaecatum oeconomicae sollicitudini largiuntur. Amplius sicut Ovidius, primo De Vetula, merito lamentatur:

> Omnes declinant ad ea, quae lucra ministrant,
> Utque sciant discunt pauci, plures ut abundent;
> Sic te prostituunt, O virgo Scientia! sic te
> Venalem faciunt castis amplexibus aptam,
> Non te propter te quaerentes, sed lucra per te,
> Ditarique volunt potius, quam philosophari;

et infra:

> sic Philosophia
> Exilium patitur, et Philopecunia regnat,

quam constat esse violentissimum toxicum disciplinae.

❧ Qualiter vero non alium terminum studio posuerunt antiqui quam vitae, declarat Valerius ad Tiberium, lib. 8, cap. 7, per exempla multorum. Carneades, inquit, laboriosus ac diutinus sapientiae miles fuit; siquidem expletis nonaginta annis idem illi vivendi ac philosophandi finis fuit. Isocrates nonagesimum quartum annum agens nobilissimum librum scripsit; Sophocles prope centesimum annum agens; Simo-

Richard de Bury

❦ But in truth, if we speak of fervour of learning and diligence in study, they gave up all their lives to philosophy; while nowadays our contemporaries carelessly spend a few years of hot youth, alternating with the excesses of vice, and when the passions have been calmed, and they have attained the capacity of discerning truth so difficult to discover, they soon become involved in worldly affairs and retire, bidding farewell to the schools of philosophy.

❦ They offer the fuming must of their youthful intellect to the difficulties of philosophy, and bestow the clearer wine upon the money-making business of life. Further, as Ovid in the first book of the *De Vetula* justly complains:

> *The hearts of all men after gold aspire;*
> *Few study to be wise, more to acquire:*
> *Thus, Science! all thy virgin charms are sold,*
> *Whose chaste embraces should disdain their gold,*
> *Who seek not thee thyself, but pelf through thee,*
> *Longing for riches, not philosophy.*

And further on:

> *Thus Philosophy is seen*
> *Exiled, and Philopecuny is queen,*

which is known to be the most violent poison of learning.

❦ How the ancients indeed regarded life as the only limit of study, is shown by Valerius, in his book addressed to Tiberius, by many examples. Carneades, he says, was a laborious and lifelong soldier of wisdom: after he had lived ninety years, the same day put an end to his life and his philosophizing. Isocrates in his ninety-fourth year wrote a most noble work. Sophocles did the same when nearly a hundred years old. Simonides wrote poems in his eightieth year. Aulus

nides octogesimo anno carmina scripsit. A. Gellius non affectavit diutius vivere, quam esset idoneus ad scribendum, teste seipso in prologo Noctium Atticarum.

℟ Fervorem vero studii, quem habebat Euclides Socraticus, recitare solebat Taurus philosophus, ut iuvenes ad studium animaret, sicut refert A. Gellius lib. 6, cap. 10 voluminis memorati. Athenienses namque cum Megarenses odirent, decreverunt quod si quis de Megarensibus Athenas intraret, capite plecteretur. Tunc Euclides, qui Megarensis erat et ante illud decretum Socratem audierat, muliebri ornamento contectus de nocte, ut Socratem audiret, ibat de Megaris ad Athenas viginti millia passuum et redibat. Imprudens et nimius fuit fervor Archimedis, qui geometricae facultatis amator nomen edisserere noluit nec a figura protracta caput erigere, quo vitae mortalis fatum poterat prolongasse, sed indulgens studio plus quam vitae studiosam figuram vitali sanguine cruentavit.

℟ Quam plurima huius nostri propositi sunt exempla, nec ea quidem transcurrere brevitas affectata permittit. Sed, quod dolentes referimus, iter prorsus diversum incedunt clerici celebres his diebus. Ambitione siquidem in aetate tenera laborantes, ac praesumptionis pennas Icarias inexpertis lacertis fragiliter coaptantes, pileum magistralem immaturi praeripiunt, fiuntque pueruli facultatum plurium professores immeriti, quas nequaquam pedetentim pertranseunt, sed ad instar caprearum saltuatim ascendunt; cumque parum de grandi torrente gustaverint, arbitrantur se totum funditus sorbuisse, vix faucibus humectatis; et quia in primis rudimentis tempore congruo non fundantur, super debile funda-

Richard de Bury

Gellius did not desire to live longer than he should be able to write, as he says himself in the prologue to the *Noctes Atticæ*.

℄ The fervour of study which possessed Euclid the Socratic, Taurus the philosopher used to relate to incite young men to study, as Gellius tells in the book we have mentioned. For the Athenians, hating the people of Megara, decreed that if any of the Megarensians entered Athens, he should be put to death. Then Euclid, who was a Megarensian, and had attended the lectures of Socrates before this decree, disguising himself in a woman's dress, used to go from Megara to Athens by night to hear Socrates, a distance of twenty miles and back. Imprudent and excessive was the fervour of Archimedes, a lover of geometry, who would not declare his name, nor lift his head from the diagram he had drawn, by which he might have prolonged his life, but, thinking more of study than of life, dyed with his life-blood the figure he was studying.

℄ There are very many such examples of our proposition, but the brevity we aim at does not allow us to recall them. But, painful to relate, the clerks who are famous in these days pursue a very different course. Afflicted with ambition in their tender years, and slightly fastening to their untried arms the Icarian wings of presumption, they prematurely snatch the master's cap; and mere boys become unworthy professors of the several faculties, through which they do not make their way step by step, but like goats ascend by leaps and bounds; and having slightly tasted of the mighty stream, they think that they have drunk it dry, though their throats are hardly moistened. And because they are not grounded in the first rudiments at the fitting time, they build a tottering

mentum opus aedificant ruinosum. Iamque provectos pudet addiscere, quae tenellos decuerat didicisse, et sic profecto coguntur perpetuo luere quod ad fasces indebitos praepropere salierunt.

⁋ Propter haec et his similia, tirones scholastici soliditatem doctrinae, quam veteres habuerunt, tam paucis lucubratiunculis non attingunt, quantumcunque fungantur honoribus, censeantur nominibus, auctorizentur habitibus, locenturque solemniter in cathedris seniorum. Prisciani regulas et Donati statim de cunis erepti et celeriter ablactati perlingunt; Categorias, Perihermenias, in cuius scriptura summus Aristoteles calamum in corde tinxisse confingitur, infantili balbutie resonant impuberes et imberbes. Quarum facultatum itinera dispendioso compendio damnosoque diplomate transmeantes, in sacrum Moysen manus iniciunt violentas, ac se tenebrosis aquis in nubibus aëris facialiter aspergentes, ad pontificatus infulam caput parant, nulla decoratum canitie senectutis.

⁋ Promovent plurimum istam pestem iuvantque ad istum phantasticum clericatum tam pernicibus passibus attingendum papalis provisio seductivis precibus impetrata necnon et preces, quae repelli non possunt, cardinalium et potentum, amicorum cupiditas et parentum, qui aedificantes Sion in sanguinibus, prius suis nepotibus et alumnis ecclesiasticas dignitates anticipant, quam naturae successu vel doctrinae temperie maturescant.

⁋ Isto, pro dolor! paroxysmo, quem plangimus, Parisiense palladium nostris maestis temporibus cernimus iam sub-

Richard de Bury

edifice on an unstable foundation, and now that they have grown up, they are ashamed to learn what they ought to have learned while young, and thus they are compelled to suffer for ever for too hastily jumping at dignities they have not deserved.

℘ For these and the like reasons the tyros in the schools do not attain to the solid learning of the ancients in a few short hours of study, although they may enjoy distinctions, may be accorded titles, be authorized by official robes, and solemnly installed in the chairs of the elders. Just snatched from the cradle and hastily weaned, they mouth the rules of Priscian and Donatus; while still beardless boys they gabble with childish stammering the Categories and *Peri Hermeneias*, in the writing of which the great Aristotle is said to have dipped his pen in his heart's blood. Passing through these faculties with baneful haste and a harmful diploma, they lay violent hands upon Moses, and sprinkling about their faces dark waters and thick clouds of the skies, they offer their heads, unhonoured by the snows of age, for the mitre of the pontificate.

℘ This pest is greatly encouraged, and they are helped to attain this fantastic clericate with such nimble steps, by Papal provisions obtained by insidious prayers, and also by the prayers, which may not be rejected, of cardinals and great men, by the cupidity of friends and relatives who, building up Sion in blood, secure ecclesiastical dignities for their nephews and pupils, before they are seasoned by the course of nature or ripeness of learning.

℘ Alas! by the same disease which we are deploring, we see that the Palladium of Paris has been carried off in these sad

latum, ubi tepuit, immo fere friguit zelus scholae tam nobilis, cuius olim radii lucem dabant universis angulis orbis terrae. Quiescit ibidem iam calamus omnis scribae, nec librorum generatio propagatur ulterius, nec est qui incipiat novus auctor haberi. Involvunt sententias sermonibus imperitis, et omnis logicae proprietate privantur; nisi quod Anglicanas subtilitates, quibus palam detrahunt, vigiliis furtivis addiscunt.

ℂ Minerva mirabilis nationes hominum circuire videtur, et a fine usque ad finem attingit fortiter, ut se ipsam communicet universis. Indos, Babylonios, Aegyptios atque Graecos, Arabes et Latinos eam pertransisse iam cernimus. Iam Athenas deseruit, iam a Roma recessit, iam Parisius praeterivit, iam ad Britanniam, insularum insignissimam quin potius microcosmum, accessit feliciter, ut se Graecis et barbaris debitricem ostendat. Quo miraculo perfecto, conicitur a plerisque quod, sicut Galliae iam sophia tepescit, sic eiusdem militia penitus evirata languescit.

times of ours, wherein the zeal of that noble university, whose rays once shed light into every corner of the world, has grown lukewarm, nay, is all but frozen. There the pen of every scribe is now at rest, generations of books no longer succeed each other, and there is none who begins to take place as a new author. They wrap up their doctrines in unskilled discourse, and are losing all propriety of logic, except that our English subtleties, which they denounce in public, are the subject of their furtive vigils.

(Admirable Minerva seems to bend her course to all the nations of the earth, and reacheth from end to end mightily, that she may reveal herself to all mankind. We see that she has already visited the Indians, the Babylonians, the Egyptians and Greeks, the Arabs and the Romans. Now she has passed by Paris, and now has happily come to Britain, the most noble of islands, nay, rather a microcosm in itself, that she may show herself a debtor both to the Greeks and to the Barbarians. At which wondrous sight it is conceived by most men, that as philosophy is now lukewarm in France, so her soldiery are unmanned and languishing.

CAPITULUM X

De successiva perfectione librorum

SAPIENTIAM veterum exquirentes assidue, iuxta sapientis consilium, Ecclesiastici 39°: Sapientiam, inquit, omnium antiquorum exquiret sapiens, non in illam opinionem dignum duximus declinandum, ut primos artium fundatores omnem ruditatem elimasse dicamus, scientes adinventionem cuiusque fideli canonio ponderatam pusillam efficere scientiae portionem. Sed per plurimorum investigationes sollicitas, quasi datis symbolis singillatim, scientiarum ingentia corpora ad immensas, quas cernimus, quantitates successivis augmentationibus succreverunt. Semper namque discipuli, magistrorum sententias iterata fornace liquantes, praeneglectam scoriam excoxerunt, donec fieret aurum electum probatum terrae purgatum septuplum et perfecte, nullius erronei vel dubii admixtione fucatum.

℄ Neque enim Aristoteles, quamvis ingenio giganteo floreret, in quo naturae complacuit experiri quantum mortalitati rationis posset annectere, quemque paulo minus minoravit ab angelis Altissimus, illa mira volumina, quae totus vix capit orbis, ex digitis suis suxit. Quinimmo Hebraeorum, Babyloniorum, Aegyptiorum, Chaldaeorum, Persarum etiam

CHAPTER X

Of the gradual Perfecting of Books

WHILE assiduously seeking out the wisdom of the men of old, according to the counsel of the Wise Man (Eccli. 39: *The wise man, he says, will seek out the wisdom of all the ancients*), we have not thought fit to be misled into the opinion that the first founders of the arts have purged away all crudeness, knowing that the discoveries of each individual man, when weighed in a faithful balance, make a tiny portion of science, but that by the anxious investigations of a multitude of scholars, each as it were contributing his share, the mighty bodies of the sciences have grown by successive augmentations to the immense bulk that we now behold. For the disciples continually melting down the doctrines of their masters, and passing them again through the furnace, drove off the dross that had been previously overlooked, until there came out refined gold tried in a furnace of earth, purified seven times to perfection, and stained by no admixture of error or doubt.

℄ For not even Aristotle, although a man of gigantic intellect, in whom it pleased Nature to try how much of reason she could bestow upon mortality, and whom the Most High made only a little lower than the angels, sucked from his own fingers those wonderful volumes which the whole world can hardly contain. But, on the contrary, with lynx-eyed penetration he had seen through the sacred books of the Hebrews, the Babylonians, the Egyptians, the Chaldæans, the Persians

et Medorum, quos omnes diserta Graecia in thesauros suos transtulerat, sacros libros oculis lynceis penetrando perviderat. Quorum recte dicta recipiens, aspera complanavit, superflua resecavit, diminuta supplevit et errata delevit; ac non solum sincere docentibus sed etiam oberrantibus regratiandum censuit, quasi viam praebentibus veritatem facilius inquirendi, sicut ipsemet 2° Metaphysicae clare docet. Sic multi iurisperiti condidere Pandectam, sic medici multi Tegni, sic Avicenna Canonem, sic Plinius molem illam Historiae Naturalis, sic Ptolemaeus edidit Almagesti.

⟨Quemadmodum namque in scriptoribus annalium considerare non est difficile quod semper posterior praesupponit priorem, sine quo praelapsa tempora nullatenus enarrare valeret, sic est in scientiarum auctoribus aestimandum. Nemo namque solus quamcunque scientiam generavit, cum inter vetustissimos et novellos intermedios reperimus, antiquos quidem si nostris aetatibus comparentur, novos vero si ad studiorum fundamenta referantur, et istos doctissimos arbitramur.

⟨ Quid fecisset Vergilius, Latinorum poeta praecipuus, si Theocritum, Lucretium et Homerum minime spoliasset et in eorum vitula non arasset? quid nisi Parthenium Pindarumque, cuius eloquentiam nullo modo potuit imitari, aliquatenus lectitasset? Quid Sallustius, Tullius, Boetius, Macrobius, Lactantius, Martianus, immo tota cohors generaliter Latinorum, si Athenarum studia vel Graecorum volumina non vidissent?

Richard de Bury

and the Medes, all of which learned Greece had transferred into her treasuries. Whose true sayings he received, but smoothed away their crudities, pruned their superfluities, supplied their deficiencies, and removed their errors. And he held that we should give thanks not only to those who teach rightly, but even to those who err, as affording the way of more easily investigating truth, as he plainly declares in the second book of his Metaphysics. Thus many learned lawyers contributed to the Pandects, many physicians to the Tegni, and it was by this means that Avicenna edited his Canon, and Pliny his great work on Natural History, and Ptolemy the Almagest.

℄ For as in the writers of annals it is not difficult to see that the later writer always presupposes the earlier, without whom he could by no means relate the former times, so too we are to think of the authors of the sciences. For no man by himself has brought forth any science, since between the earliest students and those of the latter time we find intermediaries, ancient if they be compared with our own age, but modern if we think of the foundations of learning, and these men we consider the most learned.

℄ What would Vergil, the chief poet among the Latins, have achieved, if he had not despoiled Theocritus, Lucretius, and Homer, and had not ploughed with their heifer? What, unless again and again he had read somewhat of Parthenius and Pindar, whose eloquence he could by no means imitate? What could Sallust, Tully, Boethius, Macrobius, Lactantius, Martianus, and in short the whole troop of Latin writers, have done, if they had not seen the productions of Athens or the volumes of the Greeks?

The Philobiblon of

⁋ Parum certe in scripturae gazophylacium Hieronymus, trium linguarum peritus, Ambrosius, Augustinus, qui tamen Graecas litteras se fatetur odisse, immo Gregorius, qui prorsus eas se nescisse describit, ad doctrinam ecclesiae contulissent, si nihil eisdem doctior Graecia commodasset. Cuius rivulis Roma rigata, sicut prius generavit philosophos ad Graecorum effigiem, pari forma postea protulit orthodoxae fidei tractatores. Sudores sunt Graecorum symbola quae cantamus, eorundem declarata consiliis et multorum martyrio confirmata.

⁋ Cedit tamen ad gloriam Latinorum per accidens hebetudo nativa, quoniam sicut fuerunt in studiis minus docti, sic in erroribus minus mali. Ariana nempe malitia fere totam eclipsarat ecclesiam, Nestoriana nequitia, quae blasphema rabie debacchari praesumpsit in virginem, tam nomen quam definitionem Theotokos abstulisset reginae non pugnando sed disputando, nisi miles invictus Cyrillus, ad monomachiae congressum paratus, eam favente consilio Ephesino in spiritu vehementi penitus exsufflasset.

⁋ Innumerabiles nobis sunt Graecorum haeresium tam species quam auctores; nam sicut fuerunt sacrosanctae fidei primitivi cultores, ita et primi zizaniorum satores produntur historiis fide dignis. Sicque posterius profecerunt in peius quod, dum Domini inconsutilem tunicam scindere molirentur, claritatem doctrinae praehabitam perdiderunt totaliter ac novis tenebris excaecati decidunt in abyssum, nisi ille sua occulta dispenset potentia, cuius sapientiam numerus non metitur.

Richard de Bury

❡ Certes, little would Jerome, master of three languages, Ambrosius, Augustine, though he confesses that he hated Greek, or even Gregory, who is said to have been wholly ignorant of it, have contributed to the doctrine of the Church, if more learned Greece had not furnished them from its stores. As Rome, watered by the streams of Greece, had earlier brought forth philosophers in the image of the Greeks, in like fashion afterwards it produced doctors of the orthodox faith. The creeds we chant are the sweat of Grecian brows, promulgated by their Councils, and established by the martyrdom of many.

❡ Yet their natural slowness, as it happens, turns to the glory of the Latins, since as they were less learned in their studies, so they were less perverse in their errors. In truth, the Arian heresy had all but eclipsed the whole Church; the Nestorian wickedness presumed to rave with blasphemous rage against the Virgin, for it would have robbed the Queen of Heaven, not in open fight but in disputation, of her name and character as *Mother of God*, unless the invincible champion Cyril, ready to do single battle, with the help of the Council of Ephesus, had in vehemence of spirit utterly extinguished it.

❡ Innumerable are the forms as well as the authors of Greek heresies; for as they were the original cultivators of our holy faith, so too they were the first sowers of tares, as is shown by veracious history. And thus they went on from bad to worse, because in endeavouring to part the seamless vesture of the Lord, they totally destroyed primitive simplicity of doctrine, and blinded by the darkness of novelty would fall into the bottomless pit, unless He provide for them in His inscrutable prerogative, whose wisdom is past reckoning.

The Philobiblon of

❡ Haec hactenus; nam hic nobis subducitur iudicandi facultas. Unum tamen elicimus ex praedictis, quod damnosa nimis est hodie studio Latinorum Graeci sermonis inscitia, sine quo scriptorum veterum dogmata sive Christianorum sive gentilium nequeunt comprehendi. Idemque de Arabico in plerisque tractatibus astronomicis, ac de Hebraico pro textu sacrae bibliae, verisimiliter est censendum, quibus defectibus proinde Clemens quintus occurrit, si tamen praelati quae faciliter statuunt, fideliter observarent. Quamobrem grammaticam, tam Hebraeam quam Graecam, nostris scholaribus providere curavimus cum quibusdam adiunctis, quorum adminiculo studiosi lectores in dictarum linguarum scriptura, lectura necnon etiam intellectu, plurimum poterunt informari, licet proprietatem idiomatis solus auditus aurium animae repraesentet.

Richard de Bury

₡ Let this suffice; for here we reach the limit of our power of judgment. One thing, however, we conclude from the premises, that the ignorance of the Greek tongue is now a great hindrance to the study of the Latin writers, since without it the doctrines of the ancient authors, whether Christian or Gentile, cannot be understood. And we must come to a like judgment as to Arabic in numerous astronomical treatises, and as to Hebrew as regards the text of the Holy Bible, which deficiencies indeed Clement V provides for if only the bishops would faithfully observe what they so lightly decree. Wherefore we have taken care to provide a Greek as well as a Hebrew grammar for our scholars, with certain other aids, by the help of which studious readers may greatly inform themselves in the writing, reading, and understanding of the said tongues, although only the hearing of them can teach correctness of idiom.

CAPITULUM XI

Quare libros liberalium litterarum praetulimus libris iuris

IURIS positivi lucrativa peritia dispensandis terrenis accommoda, quanto huius saeculi filiis famulatur utilius, tanto minus ad capescenda sacrae scripturae mysteria et arcana fidei sacramenta filiis lucis confert, utpote quae disponit peculiariter ad amicitiam huius mundi, per quam homo, Iacobo attestante, Dei constituitur inimicus. Haec nimirum lites humanas, quas infinita producit cupiditas, intricatis legibus, quae ad utrumlibet duci possunt, extendit crebrius quam exstinguit; ad quas tamen sedandas a iurisconsultis et piis principibus noscitur emanasse.

¶ Sane cum contrariorum sit eadem disciplina potentiaque rationalis ad opposita valeat, simulque sensus humanus proclivior sit ad malum, huius facultatis exercitatoribus accidit, ut plerumque litibus intendendis indulgeant plus quam paci, et iura non ad legislatoris intentum referant sed ad suae machinationis effectum verba retorqueant violenter.

¶ Quamobrem, licet mentem nostram librorum amor hereos possideret a puero, quorum zelo languere vice voluptatis accepimus, minus tamen librorum civilium appetitus

CHAPTER XI

Why we have preferred Books of Liberal Learning to Books of Law

THAT lucrative practice of positive law, designed for the dispensation of earthly things, the more useful it is found by the children of this world, so much the less does it aid the children of light in comprehending the mysteries of holy writ and the secret sacraments of the faith, seeing that it disposes us peculiarly to the friendship of the world, by which man, as S. James testifies, is made the enemy of God. Law indeed encourages rather than extinguishes the contentions of mankind, which are the result of unbounded greed, by complicated laws, which can be turned either way; though we know that it was created by jurisconsults and pious princes for the purpose of assuaging these contentions.

❡ But in truth, as the same science deals with contraries, and the power of reason can be used to opposite ends, and at the same time the human mind is more inclined to evil, it happens with the practisers of this science that they usually devote themselves to promoting contention rather than peace, and instead of quoting laws according to the intent of the legislator, violently strain the language thereof to effect their own purposes.

❡ Wherefore, although the over-mastering love of books has possessed our mind from boyhood, and to rejoice in their delights has been our only pleasure, yet the appetite for the

nostris adhaesit affectibus minusque huiusmodi voluminibus adquirendis concessimus tam operae quam impensae. Sunt enim utilia, sicut scorpio in theriaca, quemadmodum libro de Pomo Aristoteles, sol doctrinae, de logica definivit.

⹂ Cernebamus etiam inter leges et scientias quamdam naturae differentiam manifestam, dum omnis scientia iocundatur et appetit quod suorum principiorum praecordia, introspectis visceribus, pateant et radices suae pullulationis emineant suaeque scaturiginis emanatio luceat evidenter; sic enim ex cognato et consono lumine veritatis conclusionis ad principia ipsum corpus scientiae lucidum fiet totum, non habens aliquam partem tenebrarum. At vero leges, cum sint pacta et humana statuta ad civiliter convivendum vel iuga principum superiecta cervicibus subditorum, recusant reduci ad ipsam synderesim, aequitatis originem, eo quod plus habere se timeant de voluntatis imperio quam de rationis arbitrio. Quapropter causas legum discutiendas non esse suadet in pluribus sententia sapientum.

⹂ Nempe consuetudine sola leges multae vigorem adquirunt non necessitate syllogistica, sicut artes, prout 2° Politicorum adstruit Aristoteles, Phoebus scholae, ubi politiam redarguit Hippodami, quae novarum legum inventoribus praemia pollicetur, quia leges veteres abrogare et novellas statuere est ipsarum, quae fiunt, valitudinem infirmare. Quae enim sola consuetudine stabilitatem accipiunt, haec necesse est desuetudine dirimantur.

⹂ Ex quibus liquido satis constat quod, sicut leges nec artes sunt nec scientiae, sic nec libri legum libri scientiarum

books of the civil law took less hold of our affections, and we have spent but little labour and expense in acquiring volumes of this kind. For they are useful only as the scorpion in treacle, as Aristotle, the sun of science, has said of logic in his book *De Pomo*.

℄ We have noticed a certain manifest difference of nature between law and science, in that every science is delighted and desires to open its inward parts and display the very heart of its principles, and to show forth the roots from which it buds and flourishes, and that the emanation of its springs may be seen of all men; for thus from the cognate and harmonious light of the truth of conclusion to principles, the whole body of science will be full of light, having no part dark. But laws, on the contrary, since they are only human enactments for the regulation of social life, or the yokes of princes thrown over the necks of their subjects, refuse to be brought to the standard of synteresis, the origin of equity, because they feel that they possess more of arbitrary will than rational judgment. Wherefore the judgment of the wise for the most part is that the causes of laws are not a fit subject of discussion.

℄ In truth, many laws acquire force by mere custom, not by syllogistic necessity, like the arts: as Aristotle, the Phoebus of the Schools, urges in the second book of the Politics, where he confutes the polity of Hippodamus, which holds out rewards to the inventors of new laws, because to abrogate old laws and establish new ones is to weaken the force of those which exist. For whatever receives its stability from use alone must necessarily be brought to nought by disuse.

℄ From which it is seen clearly enough, that as laws are neither arts nor sciences, so books of law cannot properly be

vel artium proprie dici possunt. Nec est haec facultas inter scientias recensenda, quam licet geologiam appropriato vocabulo nominare. Libri vero liberalium litterarum tam utiles sunt scripturae divinae, quod sine ipsorum subsidio frustra ad ipsius notitiam intellectus aspiret.

Richard de Bury

called books of art or science. Nor is this faculty which we may call by a special term *geologia,* or the *earthly* science, to be properly numbered among the sciences. Now the books of the liberal arts are so useful to the divine writings, that without their aid the intellect would vainly aspire to understand them.

CAPITULUM XII

Quare libros grammaticales curavimus tanta diligentia renovare

CUM librorum lectionibus foveremur assidue, quos moris erat cotidie legere vel audire, perpendimus evidenter quantum impediat intellectus officium vel unius vocabuli semiplena notitia, dum nullius enuntiationis sententia capitur, cuius pars quantalibet ignoratur. Quapropter exoticorum verborum interpretationes mira sedulitate iussimus annotari antiquorumque grammaticorum orthographiam, prosodiam, etymologiam ac diasyntheticam inconcussa curiositate consideravimus terminosque vetustate nimia caligantes descriptionibus congruis lucidare curavimus, quatenus iter planum nostris studentibus pararemus.

❡ Haec est sane summa totalis quare tot grammaticorum antiquata volumina emendatis codicibus renovare studuimus, ut stratas regias sterneremus, quibus ad artes quascunque nostri futuri scholares incederent inoffense.

CHAPTER XII

Why we have caused Books of Grammar to be so diligently prepared

WHILE we were constantly delighting ourselves with the reading of books, which it was our custom to read or have read to us every day, we noticed plainly how much the defective knowledge even of a single word hinders the understanding, as the meaning of no sentence can be apprehended, if any part of it be not understood. Wherefore we ordered the meanings of foreign words to be noted with particular care, and studied the orthography, prosody, etymology, and syntax in ancient grammarians with unrelaxing carefulness, and took pains to elucidate terms that had grown too obscure by age with suitable explanations, in order to make a smooth path for our students.

❧ This is the whole reason why we took care to replace the antiquated volumes of the grammarians by improved codices, that we might make royal roads, by which our scholars in time to come might attain without stumbling to any science.

CAPITULUM XIII

Quare non omnino negleximus fabulas poetarum

OMNIA genera machinarum quibus contra poetas solius nudae veritatis amatores obiciunt duplici refelluntur umbone, quia vel in obscena materia gratus cultus sermonis addiscitur vel, ubi ficta sed honesta tractatur sententia, naturalis vel historialis veritas indagatur sub eloquio typicae fictionis.

℘ Quamvis nimirum omnes homines natura scire desiderent, non tamen omnes aequaliter delectantur addiscere, quinimmo studii labore gustato et sensuum fatigatione percepta plerique nucem abiciunt inconsulte prius quam testa soluta nucleus attingatur. Innatus est enim homini duplex amor, videlicet propriae libertatis in regimine et aliquantae voluptatis in opere; unde nullus sine causa alieno se subdit imperio vel opus quodcunque exercet cum taedio sua sponte. Delectatio namque perficit operationem, sicut pulcritudo iuventutem: sicut Aristoteles verissime dogmatizat 10° Ethicorum.

℘ Idcirco prudentia veterum adinvenit remedium, quo lascivum humanum caperetur ingenium quodammodo pio dolo, dum sub voluptatis iconio delicata Minerva delitesceret in occulto. Muneribus parvulos assolemus allicere ut

124

CHAPTER XIII

Why we have not wholly neglected the Fables of the Poets

ALL the varieties of attack directed against the poets by the lovers of naked truth may be repelled by a two-fold defence: either that even in an unseemly subject-matter we may learn a charming fashion of speech, or that where a fictitious but becoming subject is handled, natural or historical truth is pursued under the guise of allegorical fiction.

℃ Although it is true that all men naturally desire know-ledge, yet they do not all take the same pleasure in learning. On the contrary, when they have experienced the labour of study and find their senses wearied, most men inconsider-ately fling away the nut, before they have broken the shell and reached the kernel. For man is naturally fond of two things, namely, freedom from control and some pleasure in his activity; for which reason no one without reason submits himself to the control of others, or willingly engages in any tedious task. For pleasure crowns activity, as beauty is a crown to youth, as Aristotle truly asserts in the tenth book of the Ethics.

℃ Accordingly the wisdom of the ancients devised a remedy by which to entice the wanton minds of men by a kind of pious fraud, the delicate Minerva secretly lurking beneath the mask of pleasure. We are wont to allure children

illa gratis velint addiscere, quibus eos vel invitos intendimus applicare. Non enim natura corrupta eo impetu, quo prona se pellit ad vitia, transmigrat ad virtutes. Hoc in brevi versiculo nobis declarat Horatius, ubi artem tradit poeticam, ita dicens:

Aut prodesse volunt aut delectare poetae.

Hoc idem in alio versu eiusdem libri patenter insinuat, ita scribens:

Omne tulit punctum qui miscuit utile dulci.

℧ Quot Euclidis discipulos retroiecit Elefuga, quasi scopulus eminens et abruptus, qui nullo scalarum suffragio scandi posset! Durus, inquiunt, est hic sermo; quis potest eum audire? Filius inconstantiae, qui tandem in asinum transformari volebat, philosophiae studium nullatenus forsitan dimisisset, si eidem contecta voluptatis velamine familiariter occurrisset. Sed mox Cratonis cathedra stupefactus et quaestionibus infinitis, quasi quodam fulmine subito repercussus, nullum prorsus videbat refugium nisi fugam.

℧ Haec in excusationem adduximus poetarum; iam studentes intentione debita in eisdem ostendimus inculpandos. Ignorantia quidem solius unius vocabuli praegrandis sententiae impedit intellectum, sicut proximo capitulo est assumptum. Cum igitur dicta sanctorum poetarum figmentis frequenter alludant, eveniet, necesse est ut nescito poemate introducto tota ipsius auctoris intentio penitus obstruatur. Et certe, sicut dicit Cassiodorus libro suo, De institutione

by rewards, that they may cheerfully learn what we force them to study even though they are unwilling. For our fallen nature does not tend to virtue with the same enthusiasm with which it rushes into vice. Horace has expressed this for us in a brief verse of the *Ars Poetica*, where he says:

All poets sing to profit or delight.

And he has plainly intimated the same thing in another verse of the same book, where he says:

He hits the mark, who mingles joy with use.

℩ How many students of Euclid have been repelled by the *Pons Asinorum*, as by a lofty and precipitous rock, which no help of ladders could enable them to scale! *This is a hard saying*, they exclaim, *and who can receive it?* The child of inconstancy, who ended by wishing to be transformed into an ass, would perhaps never have given up the study of philosophy, if she had met him in friendly guise veiled under the cloak of pleasure; but anon, astonished by Crato's chair and struck dumb by his endless questions, as by a sudden thunderbolt, he saw no refuge but in flight.

℩ So much we have alleged in defence of the poets; and now we proceed to show that those who study them with proper intent are not to be condemned in regard to them. For our ignorance of one single word prevents the understanding of a whole long sentence, as was assumed in the previous chapter. But as the sayings of the saints frequently allude to the inventions of the poets, it must needs happen that through our not knowing the poem referred to, the whole meaning of the author is completely obscured, and assuredly, as Cassiodorus says in his book *Of the Institutes of Sacred Litera-*

divinarum litterarum, non sunt parva censenda sine quibus magna constare non possunt. Restat igitur ut ignoratis poesibus ignoretur Hieronymus, Augustinus, Boetius, Lactantius, Sidonius et plerique alii, quorum litaniam prolixum capitulum non teneret.

℃ Venerabilis vero Beda huius dubitationis articulum distinctione declaravit dilucida, sicut recitat compilator egregius Gratianus, plurium repetitor auctorum, qui sicut fuit avarus in compilationis materia, sic confusus reperitur in forma. Scribit tamen sic distinctione 37, *Turbat acumen*: saeculares litteras quidam legunt ad voluptatem, poetarum figmentis et verborum ornatu delectati; quidam vero ad eruditionem eas addiscunt, ut errores gentium legendo detestentur et utilia, quae in eis invenerint, ad usum sacrae eruditionis devoti convertant: tales laudabiliter saeculares litteras addiscunt. Haec Beda.

℃ Hac institutione salutifera moniti sileant detrahentes studentibus in poetis ad tempus, nec ignorantes huiusmodi connescientes desiderent, quia hoc est simile solatio miserorum. Statuat igitur sibi quisque piae intentionis affectum et de quacunque materia, observatis virtutis circumstantiis, faciet studium Deo gratum; et si in poeta profecerit, quemadmodum magnus Maro se fatetur in Ennio, non amisit.

ture: Those things are not to be considered trifles without which great things cannot come to pass. It follows therefore that through ignorance of poetry we do not understand Jerome, Augustine, Boethius, Lactantius, Sidonius, and very many others, a catalogue of whom would more than fill a long chapter.

℄ The Venerable Bede has very clearly discussed and determined this doubtful point, as is related by that great compiler Gratian, the repeater of numerous authors, who is as confused in form as he was eager in collecting matter for his compilation. Now he writes in his 37th section: Some read secular literature for pleasure, taking delight in the inventions and elegant language of the poets; but others study this literature for the sake of scholarship, that by their reading they may learn to detest the errors of the Gentiles and may devoutly apply what they find useful in them to the use of sacred learning. Such men study secular literature in a laudable manner. So far Bede.

℄ Taking this salutary instruction to heart, let the detractors of those who study the poets henceforth hold their peace, and let not those who are ignorant of these things require that others should be as ignorant as themselves, for this is the consolation of the wretched. And therefore let every man see that his own intentions are upright, and he may thus make of any subject, observing the limitations of virtue, a study acceptable to God. And if he have found profit in poetry, as the great Vergil relates that he had done in Ennius, he will not have done amiss.

CAPITULUM XIV

Qui debent esse librorum potissimi dilectores

RECOLLIGENTI praedicta palam est et perspicuum qui deberent esse librorum praecipui dilectores. Qui namque sapientia magis egent ad sui status officium utiliter exsequendum, hi potissimum sacris vasis sapientiae propensiorem proculdubio exhibere tenentur sollicitum grati cordis affectum. Est autem sapientis officium bene ordinare et alios et seipsum: secundum Phoebum philosophorum, Aristotelem, primo Metaphysicae, qui nec fallit nec fallitur in humanis. Quapropter principes et praelati, iudices et doctores et quicunque rei publicae directores, sicut prae aliis sapientia opus habent, ita prae aliis vasis sapientiae zelum debent.

⸿ Philosophiam nimirum conspexit Boetius in sinistra quidem sceptrum et in dextra libros gestantem, per quod universis evidenter ostenditur nullum posse rempublicam debite regere sine libris. Tu, inquit Boetius loquens Philosophiae, hanc sententiam Platonis ore sanxisti beatas fore res publicas si eas vel studiosi sapientiae regerent vel earum rectores studere sapientiae contigisset. Rursus hoc nobis insinuat ipse gestus imaginis, quod quanto dextra sinistram

CHAPTER XIV

Who ought to be special Lovers of Books

TO him who recollects what has been said before, it is plain and evident who ought to be the chief lovers of books. For those who have most need of wisdom in order to perform usefully the duties of their position, they are without doubt most especially bound to show more abundantly to the sacred vessels of wisdom the anxious affection of a grateful heart. Now it is the office of the wise man to order rightly both himself and others, according to the Phoebus of philosophers, Aristotle, who deceives not nor is deceived in human things. Wherefore princes and prelates, judges and doctors, and all other leaders of the commonwealth, as more than others they have need of wisdom, so more than others ought they to show zeal for the vessels of wisdom.

℄ Boethius indeed beheld Philosophy bearing a sceptre in her left hand and books in her right, by which it is evidently shown to all men that no one can rightly rule a commonwealth without books. Thou, says Boethius, speaking to Philosophy, hast sanctioned this saying by the mouth of Plato, that states would be happy, if they were ruled by students of philosophy, or if their rulers would study philosophy. And again, we are taught by the very gesture of the figure that in so far as the right hand is better than the left,

praecellit, tanto contemplativa dignior est activa, simulque sapientis interesse monstratur nunc studio veritatis, nunc dispensationi temporalium indulgere vicissim.

❡ Philippum legimus diis regratiatum devote, quod Alexandrum concesserant temporibus Aristotelis esse natum, cuius instructionibus educatus regni paterni moderamine dignus esset. Dum Phaethon ignarus regiminis fit currus auriga paterni, nunc vicinitate nimia nunc remota distantia infeliciter administrat mortalibus aestum Phoebi ac, ne omnes periclitarentur subiecti propinquo regimine, iuste meruit fulminari.

❡ Referunt tam Graecorum quam Latinorum historiae, quod nobiles inter eos principes non fuerunt, qui litterarum peritia caruerunt. Sacra lex Mosaica, praescribens regi regulam, per quam regat, librum legis divinae sibi praecipit habere descriptum, Deut. 17°, secundum exemplar a sacerdotibus exhibendum, in quo sibi legendum esset omnibus diebus vitae suae. Sane labilitatem humanae memoriae et instabilitatem virtuosae voluntatis in homine satis noverat Deus ipse, qui condidit et qui fingit cotidie corda hominum singillatim. Quamobrem quasi omnium malorum antidotum voluit esse librum, cuius lectionem et usum tanquam saluberrimum spiritus alimentum cotidianum iugiter esse iussit, quo refocillatus intellectus nec enervis nec dubius trepidaret ullatenus in agendis. Istud eleganter Ioannes Saresberiensis pertractat in suo Policraticon, libro 4°.

Richard de Bury

so far the contemplative life is more worthy than the active life; and at the same time we are shown that the business of the wise man is to devote himself by turns, now to the study of truth, and now to the dispensation of temporal things.

❡ We read that Philip thanked the gods devoutly for having granted that Alexander should be born in the time of Aristotle, so that educated under his instruction he might be worthy to rule his father's empire. While Phaethon unskilled in driving becomes the charioteer of his father's car, he unhappily distributes to mankind the heat of Phoebus, now by excessive nearness, and now by withdrawing it too far, and so, lest all beneath him should be imperilled by the closeness of his driving, justly deserved to be struck by the thunderbolt.

❡ The history of the Greeks as well as Romans shows that there were no famous princes among them who were devoid of literature. The sacred law of Moses in prescribing to the king a rule of government, enjoins him to have a copy made of the book of Divine law (Deut. xvii) according to the copy shown by the priests, in which he was to read all the days of his life. Certes, God Himself, who hath made and who fashioneth every day the hearts of everyone of us, knows the feebleness of human memory and the instability of virtuous intentions in mankind. Wherefore He has willed that books should be as it were an antidote to all evil, the reading and use of which He has commanded to be the healthful daily nourishment of the soul, so that by them the intellect being refreshed and neither weak nor doubtful should never hesitate in action. This subject is elegantly handled by John of Salisbury in his *Policraticon*.

The Philobiblon of

℃ Caeterum omne genus hominum, qui tonsura vel signo clericali praefulgent, contra quos libri 4° 5° et 6° capitulis querebantur, libris tenentur veneratione perpetua famulari.

Richard de Bury

¶ In conclusion, all classes of men who are conspicuous by the tonsure or the sign of clerkship, against whom books lifted up their voices in the fourth, fifth, and sixth chapters, are bound to serve books with perpetual veneration.

CAPITULUM XV

Quot commoda confert amor librorum

HUMANUM transcendit ingenium, quantumcunque de fonte fuerit Pegaseo potatum, in-
stantis capituli titulum explicare perfecte. Si
linguis angelorum et hominum quis loquatur, si in Mer-
curium transformetur aut Tullium, si dulcescat Titi Livii
eloquentia lactea, si Demosthenis suavitate peroret, aut
Moysi balbutiem allegabit, vel cum Ieremia se puerum
nescientem fatebitur adhuc loqui, vel imitabitur resonantem
in montibus altis echo. Amorem namque librorum amorem
sapientiae constat esse, sicut 2° cap° est probatum.

℩ Hic autem amor philosophia Graeco vocabulo nun-
cupatur, cuius virtutem nulla creata intelligentia compre-
hendit, quoniam vere creditur bonorum omnium esse mater:
Sap. 7°. Aestus quippe carnalium vitiorum quasi caelicus ros
exstinguit, dum motus intensus virtutum animalium vires
naturalium virtutum remittit, otio penitus effugato, quo
sublato periere Cupidinis arcus omnes.

℩ Hinc Plato in Phaedone: In hoc, inquit, manifestus est
philosophus, si absolvit animam a corporis communione dif-
ferentius aliis hominibus. Ama, inquit Hieronymus, scientiam scripturarum et carnis vitia non amabis. Demonstravit
hoc Xenocrates, deiformis in constantia rationis, quem

CHAPTER XV

Of the Advantages of the Love of Books

IT transcends the power of human intellect, however deeply it may have drunk of the Pegasean fount, to develop fully the title of the present chapter. Though one should speak with the tongues of men and angels, though he should become a Mercury or Tully, though he should grow sweet with the milky eloquence of Livy, yet he will plead the stammering of Moses, or with Jeremiah will confess that he is but a boy and cannot speak, or will imitate Echo rebounding from the mountains. For we know that the love of books is the same thing as the love of wisdom, as was proved in the second chapter.

 ⁋ Now this love is called by the Greek word *philosophy*, the whole virtue of which no created intelligence can comprehend; for she is believed to be the mother of all good things: Wisdom, 7. She as a heavenly dew extinguishes the heats of fleshly vices, the intense activity of the mental forces relaxing the vigour of the animal forces, and slothfulness being wholly put to flight, which being gone all the bows of Cupid are unstrung.

 ⁋ Hence Plato says in the *Phaedo*: The philosopher is manifest in this, that he dissevers the soul from communion with the body. Love, says Jerome, the knowledge of the scriptures and thou wilt not love the vices of the flesh. The godlike Xenocrates showed this by the firmness of his reason, who

nobile scortum, Phryne nomine, statuam definivit non hominem cum nullis eum valeret illecebris evirare, quemadmodum
Valerius li° 4°, c° 3° plene refert. Hoc ipsum noster Ori-
genes ostendit, qui ne eum ab omnipotenti femina effeminari
contingeret, utriusque sexus medium per abnegationem ex-
tremorum elegit: animosum quippe remedium, nec naturae
tamen consentaneum nec virtuti, cuius est hominem non in-
sensibilem facere passionum sed subortas a fomite rationis
enecare mucrone.

❡ Rursus mundanas pecunias parvipendunt ex animo,
quotquot amor affecit librorum, dicente Hieronymo contra
Vigilantium, epistola 54ª: non est eiusdem hominis aureos
nummos et scripturas probare. Unde a quodam metrice sic
dictum est:

> *Nulla libris erit apta manus ferrugine tincta,*
> *Nec nummata queunt corda vacare libris.*
> *Non est eiusdem nummos librosque probare;*
> *Persequitur libros grex, Epicure, tuus.*
> *Nummipetae cum libricolis nequeunt simul esse;*
> *Ambos, crede mihi, non tenet una domus.*

Nullus igitur potest libris et Mammonae deservire.

❡ Vitiorum deformitas in libris maxime reprobatur, ut
inducatur omnimode vitia detestari, qui libros dilexerit perscrutari. Daemon, qui a scientia nomen habet, per librorum
scientiam potissime triumphatur, cuius fraudes multipliciter
flexuosae milleque perniciosi maeandri per libros panduntur
legentibus, ne se transfigurans in angelum lucis dolis circum-
veniat innocentes. Divina nobis per libros reverentia reve-
latur, virtutes quibus colitur propalantur expressius, atque

Richard de Bury

was declared by the famous hetaera Phryne to be a statue and not a man, when all her blandishments could not shake his resolve, as Valerius Maximus relates at length. Our own Origen showed this also, who chose rather to be unsexed by the mutilation of himself, than to be made effeminate by the omnipotence of woman—though it was a hasty remedy, repugnant alike to nature and to virtue, whose place it is not to make men insensible to passion, but to slay with the dagger of reason the passions that spring from instinct.

ℭ Again, all who are smitten with the love of books think cheaply of the world and wealth; as Jerome says to Vigilantius: The same man cannot love both gold and books. And thus it has been said in verse:

> No iron-stained hand is fit to handle books,
> Nor he whose heart on gold so gladly looks;
> The same men love not books and money both,
> And books thy herd, O Epicurus, loathe;
> Misers and bookmen make poor company,
> Nor dwell in peace beneath the same roof-tree.

No man, therefore, can serve both books and Mammon.

ℭ The hideousness of vice is greatly reprobated in books, so that he who loves to commune with books is led to detest all manner of vice. The demon, who derives his name from knowledge, is most effectually defeated by the knowledge of books, and through books his multitudinous deceits and the endless labyrinths of his guile are laid bare to those who read, lest he be transformed into an angel of light and circumvent the innocent by his wiles. The reverence of God is revealed to us by books, the virtues by which He is worshipped are more expressly manifested, and the rewards are described that

merces describitur, quam quae nec fallit nec fallitur veritas pollicetur.

⸿ Imago simillima futurae beatitudinis est sacrarum contemplatio litterarum, in quibus nunc Creator nunc creatura conspicitur, ac de torrente perpetuae iocunditatis hauritur. Fides fundatur potentia litterarum. Spes librorum solatio confirmatur, ut per patientiam et consolationem scripturarum spem habeamus. Caritas non inflatur sed aedificatur per veram notitiam litterarum; immo super libros sacros constat luce clarius Ecclesiam stabilitam.

⸿ Delectant libri, prosperitate feliciter arridente, consolantur individue, nubila fortuna terrente: pactis humanis robur attribuunt, nec feruntur sententiae graves sine libris. Artes et scientiae in libris consistunt, quarum emolumenta nulla mens sufficeret enarrare. Quanti pendenda est mira librorum potentia, dum per eos fines tam orbis quam temporis cernimus, et ea quae non sunt, sicut ea quae sunt, quasi in quodam aeternitatis speculo contemplamur.

⸿ Montes scandimus, abyssorum voragines perscrutamur, species piscium, quos communis aer nequaquam salubriter continet, intuemur codicibus; fluviorum et fontium diversarum terrarum proprietates distinguimus; metallorum atque gemmarum genera et minerae cuiusque materias de libris effodimus, herbarumque vires, arborum et plantarum addiscimus, prolemque totam pro libito cernimus Neptuni, Cereris et Plutonis.

⸿ Quod si nos caelicolas visitare delectat, suppeditantes

Richard de Bury

are promised by the truth, which deceives not, neither is deceived.

℃ The truest likeness of the beatitude to come is the contemplation of the sacred writings, in which we behold in turn the Creator and the creature, and draw from streams of perpetual gladness. Faith is established by the power of books; hope is strengthened by their solace, insomuch that by patience and the consolation of scripture we are in good hope. Charity is not puffed up, but is edified by the knowledge of true learning, and indeed it is clearer than light that the Church is established upon the sacred writings.

℃ Books delight us, when prosperity smiles upon us; they comfort us inseparably when stormy fortune frowns on us. They lend validity to human compacts, and no serious judgments are propounded without their help. Arts and sciences, all the advantages of which no mind can enumerate, consist in books. How highly must we estimate the wondrous power of books, since through them we survey the utmost bounds of the world and time, and contemplate the things that are as well as those that are not, as it were in the mirror of eternity.

℃ In books we climb mountains and scan the deepest gulfs of the abyss; in books we behold the finny tribes that may not exist outside their native waters, distinguish the properties of streams and springs and of various lands; from books we dig out gems and metals and the materials of every kind of mineral, and learn the virtues of herbs and trees and plants, and survey at will the whole progeny of Neptune, Ceres, and Pluto.

℃ But if we please to visit the heavenly inhabitants,

Taurum, Caucasum et Olympum, Iunonis regna transcendimus, ac septena territoria planetarum funiculis et circulis emetimur. Ipsum tandem firmamentum supremum, signis, gradibus et imaginibus varietate maxima decoratum, lustramus. Ibi polum antarcticum, quem nec oculus vidit nec auris audivit, inspicimus; luminosum iter galaxiae et animalibus caelestibus picturatum zodiacum delectabili iocunditate miramur.

(Hinc per libros ad separatas transimus substantias, ut cognatas intelligentias intellectus salutet primamque causam omnium ac motorem immobilem infinitae virtutis oculo mentis cernat et amore inhaereat sine fine. Ecce per libros adiuti beatitudinis nostrae mercedem attingimus, dum adhuc existimus viatores.

(Quid plura? proculdubio, sicut Seneca docente didicimus, otium sine litteris mors est et vivi hominis sepultura, ita revera a sensu contrario litterarum seu librorum negotium concludimus hominis esse vitam.

(Rursus per libros tam amicis quam hostibus intimamus, quae nequaquam secure nuntiis commendamus: quoniam libro plerumque ad principum thalamos ingressus conceditur, quo repelleretur penitus vox auctoris, sicut Tertullianus in principio Apologetici sui dicit. Carceribus et vinculis custoditi, ademptaque penitus corporis libertate, librorum legationibus utimur ad amicos, eisque causas nostras expediendas committimus, atque illuc transmittimus, quo nobis fieret causa mortis accessus. Per libros praeteritorum remi-

Richard de Bury

Taurus, Caucasus, and Olympus are at hand, from which we pass beyond the realms of Juno and mark out the territories of the seven planets by lines and circles. And finally we traverse the loftiest firmament of all, adorned with signs, degrees, and figures in the utmost variety. There we inspect the antarctic pole, which eye hath not seen, nor ear heard; we admire the luminous Milky way and the Zodiac, marvellously and delightfully pictured with celestial animals.

❡ Thence by books we pass on to separate substances, that the intellect may greet kindred intelligences, and with the mind's eye may discern the First Cause of all things and the Unmoved Mover of infinite virtue, and may immerse itself in love without end. See how with the aid of books we attain the reward of our beatitude, while we are yet sojourners below.

❡ Why need we say more? Certes, just as we have learnt on the authority of Seneca, leisure without letters is death and the sepulture of the living, so contrariwise we conclude that occupation with letters or books is the life of man.

❡ Again, by means of books we communicate to friends as well as foes what we cannot safely entrust to messengers; since the book is generally allowed access to the chambers of princes, from which the voice of its author would be rigidly excluded, as Tertullian observes at the beginning of his *Apologeticus*. When shut up in prison and in bonds, and utterly deprived of bodily liberty, we use books as ambassadors to our friends, and entrust them with the conduct of our cause, and send them where to go ourselves would incur the penalty of death. By the aid of books we remember things that are past, and even prophesy as to the future; and things present,

niscimur, de futuris quodammodo prophetamus, praesentia quae labuntur et fluunt scripturae memoria stabilimus.

℃ Felix studiositas et studiosa felicitas praepotentis eunuchi, de quo Actuum 8° narratur, quem amor propheticae lectionis succenderat tam ardenter, quod nec ratione itineris a legendo cessaret, reginae Candacis regiam populosam oblivioni tradiderat, gazas quibus praeerat a cura cordis semoverat, et tam iter quam currum quo ferebatur neglexerat. Solus amor libri totum sibi vindicaverat domicilium castitatis, quo disponente mox fidei ianuam meruit introire. O gratiosus amor librorum, qui Gehennae filium et alumnum Tartari per gratiam baptismalem filium fecit regni!

℃ Cesset iam stilus impotens infiniti negotii consummare tenorem, ne videatur aggredi temere, quod in principio fatebatur impossibile cuiquam esse.

which shift and flow, we perpetuate by committing them to writing.

❡ The felicitous studiousness and the studious felicity of the all-powerful eunuch, of whom we are told in the Acts, who had been so mightily kindled by the love of the prophetic writings, that he ceased not from his reading by reason of his journey, had banished all thought of the populous palace of Queen Candace, and had forgotten even the treasures of which he was the keeper, and had neglected alike his journey and the chariot in which he rode. Love of his book alone had wholly engrossed this domicile of chastity, under whose guidance he soon deserved to enter the gate of faith. O gracious love of books, which by the grace of baptism transformed the child of Gehenna and nursling of Tartarus into a son of the Kingdom!

❡ Let the feeble pen now cease from the tenor of an infinite task, lest it seem foolishly to undertake what in the beginning it confessed to be impossible to any.

CAPITULUM XVI

Quam sit meritorium libros novos scribere et veteres renovare

SICUT necessarium est reipublicae pugnaturis militibus arma providere Vulcania et congestas victualium copias praeparare, sic Ecclesiae militanti contra paganorum et haereticorum insultus operae pretium constat esse sanorum librorum multitudine communiri.

℄ Verum quia omne quod servit mortalibus, per prolapsum temporis mortalitatis dispendium patitur, necesse est vetustate tabefacta volumina innovatis successoribus instaurari, ut perpetuitas, quae naturae repugnat individui, concedatur privilegio speciei. Hinc est, quod signanter dicitur (Ecclesiastes, 12): faciendi plures libros nullus est finis. Sicut enim librorum corpora, ex contrariorum commixtione compacta, suae compositionis continuum sentiunt detrimentum, sic per prudentiam clericorum reperiri debet remedium, per quod liber sacer, solvens naturae debitum, haereditarium obtineat substitutum et simile semen fratri mortuo suscitetur verificeturque statim illud Ecclesiastici 30: Mortuus est pater illius et quasi non est mortuus, similem enim sibi reliquit post se.

℄ Sunt igitur transcriptiones veterum quasi quaedam propagationes recentium filiorum, ad quos paternum devolvatur officium, ne librorum municipium minuatur. Sane huius-

CHAPTER XVI

That it is meritorious to write new Books and to renew the old

JUST as it is necessary for the state to prepare arms and to provide abundant stores of victuals for the soldiers who are to fight for it, so it is fitting for the Church Militant to fortify itself against the assaults of pagans and heretics with a multitude of sound writings.

℄ But because all the appliances of mortal men with the lapse of time suffer the decay of mortality, it is needful to replace the volumes that are worn out with age by fresh successors, that the perpetuity of which the individual is by its nature incapable may be secured to the species; and hence it is that the Preacher says: *Of making many books there is no end.* For as the bodies of books, seeing that they are formed of a combination of contrary elements, undergo a continual dissolution of their structure, so by the forethought of the clergy a remedy should be found, by means of which the sacred book paying the debt of nature may obtain a natural heir and may raise up like seed to its dead brother, and thus may be verified that saying of Ecclesiasticus: *His father is dead, and he is as if he were not dead; for he hath left one behind him that is like himself.*

℄ Thus the transcription of ancient books is as it were the begetting of fresh sons, on whom the office of the father may devolve, lest the commonwealth of books suffer detriment.

modi transcriptores antiquarii nominantur, quorum studia inter ea quae complentur labore corporeo plus sibi placere Cassiodorus confitetur, De institutione divinarum litterarum, capitulo 30, ita subdens: Felix, inquit, intentio, laudanda sedulitas, manu hominibus praedicare, linguas digitis aperire, salutem mortalibus tacitum dare, et contra diaboli surreptiones illicitas calamo et atramento pugnare. Haec ille. Porro scriptoris officium Salvator exercuit, dum inclinans se deorsum digito scribebat in terra, Ioh. 8°, ut nullus quantumcunque nobilis dedignetur hoc facere, quod sapientiam Dei patris intuetur fecisse.

℣ O scripturae serenitas singularis, ad cuius fabricam inclinatur artifex orbis terrae, in cuius tremendo nomine flectitur omne genu! O venerandum artificium singulariter prae cunctis praxibus, quae hominis manu fiunt, cui pectus Dominicum incurvatur humiliter, cui digitus Dei applicatur vice calami functus! Sevisse Dei filium vel arasse, texuisse vel fodisse non legimus; nec quicquam aliud de mechanicis divinam decebat sapientiam humanatam, nisi scribendo litteras exarare, ut discat quilibet generosus aut sciolus, quod hominibus digiti tribuuntur divinitus ad scribendi negotium potius quam ad bellum. Unde librorum sententiam plurimum approbamus, qua clericum inertem scripturae censuerunt quodammodo fore mancum, cap° 6° supra.

℣ Scribit iustos in libro viventium Deus ipse; lapideas quidem tabulas digito Dei scriptas Moyses accepit. Scribat librum ipse qui iudicat, Iob proclamat; digitos scribentis in pariete *Mane Thecel Phares* Nabuchodonosor tremens vidit, Danielis 5°. Ego, inquit Ieremias, scribebam in volu-

Richard de Bury

Now such transcribers are called *antiquarii*, whose occupations Cassiodorus confesses please him above all the tasks of bodily labour, adding: 'Happy effort,' he says, 'laudable industry, to preach to men with the hand, to let loose tongues with the fingers, silently to give salvation to mortals, and to fight with pen and ink against the illicit wiles of the Evil One.' So far Cassiodorus. Moreover, our Saviour exercised the office of the scribe when He stooped down and with His finger wrote on the ground (John viii.), that no one, however exalted, may think it unworthy of him to do what he sees the wisdom of God the Father did.

ℂ O singular serenity of writing, to practise which the Artificer of the world stoops down, at whose dread name every knee doth bow! O venerable handicraft pre-eminent above all other crafts that are practised by the hand of man, to which our Lord humbly inclines His breast, to which the finger of God is applied, performing the office of a pen! We do not read of the Son of God that He sowed or ploughed, wove or digged; nor did any other of the mechanic arts befit the divine wisdom incarnate except to trace letters in writing, that every gentleman and sciolist may know that fingers are given by God to men for the task of writing rather than for war. Wherefore we entirely approve the judgment of books, wherein they declared in our sixth chapter the clerk who cannot write to be as it were disabled.

℃ God Himself inscribes the just in the book of the living; Moses received the tables of stone written with the finger of God. Job desires that he himself that judgeth would write a book. Belshazzar trembled when he saw the fingers of a man's hand writing upon the wall, *Mene tekel phares.* I wrote, says

mine atramento, Ieremiae 36°. Quod vides, scribe in libro, Christus Ioanni praecipit caro suo: Apoc. primo. Sic Isaiae, sic Iosuae officium scriptoris iniungitur, ut tam actus quam peritia futuris in posterum commendetur. In vestimento et in femore scriptum habet *Rex regum et Dominus dominantium* Christus ipse, ut sine scriptura nequeat apparere perfectum Omnipotentis regium ornamentum.

℄ Defuncti docere non desinunt, qui sacrae scientiae libros scribunt. Plus Paulus scribendo sacras epistolas Ecclesiae profuit fabricandae quam gentibus et Iudaeis evangelizando sermone. Nempe per libros cotidie continuat comprehensor, quod olim in terra positus inchoavit viator; sicque verificatur de doctoribus libros scribentibus sermo propheticus Danielis 12: qui ad iustitiam erudiunt multos, quasi stellae in perpetuas aeternitates.

℄ Porro polychronitudinem antiquorum, prius quam Deus originalem mundum cataclysmo dilueret, adscribendam miraculo, non naturae catholici decrevere doctores, ut Deus ipse tantum eis vitae concederet, quantum reperiendis et in libris scribendis scientiis conveniret: inter quas astronomiae miranda diversitas, ut experimentaliter visui subderetur, sexcentorum annorum periodum secundum Iosephum requirebat.

℄ Verumtamen non abnuunt, quin terrae nascentia illius temporis primitivi utilius alimentum praestarent mortalibus quam moderni, quo dabatur non solum hilarior corporis euexia sed et diuturnior florens aetas; ad quam non modicum

Richard de Bury

Jeremiah, with ink in the book. Christ bids His beloved disciple John, *What thou seest write in a book*. So the office of writer is enjoined on Isaiah and on Joshua, that the act and skill of writing may be commended to future generations. Christ Himself has written on His vesture and on His thigh *King of Kings and Lord of Lords*, so that without writing the royal ornaments of the Omnipotent cannot be made perfect.

℩ Being dead they cease not to teach, who write books of sacred learning. Paul did more for building up the fabric of the Church by writing his holy epistles, than by preaching by word of mouth to Jews and Gentiles. He who has attained the prize continues daily by books what he long ago began while a sojourner upon the earth; and thus is fulfilled in doctors who write books the saying of the prophet: *They that turn many to righteousness shall be as the stars for ever and ever.*

℩ Moreover, it has been determined by the doctors of the Church that the longevity of the ancients, before God destroyed the original world by the Deluge, is to be ascribed to a miracle and not to nature; as though God granted to them such length of days as was required for finding out the sciences and writing them in books; amongst which the wonderful variety of astronomy required, according to Josephus, a period of six hundred years, to submit it to ocular observation.

℩ Nor, indeed, do they deny that the fruits of the earth in that primitive age afforded a more nutritious aliment to men than in our modern times, and thus they had not only a livelier haleness of body, but also a lengthened period of vigour; to which it contributed not a little that they lived

contulit, quod virtuti vivebant omnimode, resecato super-
fluo voluptatis. Igitur quisquis Dei munere scientia est
dotatus iuxta consilium spiritus sancti, Ecclesiastici 38:
sapientiam scribe in tempore vacuitatis; ut et praemium cum
beatis et spatium in praesenti augeatur aetatis.

℃ Caeterum, si ad mundi principes divertamus sermonem,
imperatores egregios invenimus non solum artis scribendi
peritia floruisse, sed et ipsius operi plurimum indulsisse.
Iulius Caesar, primus omnium et tempore et virtute, Com-
mentarios reliquit tam belli Gallici quam civilis a semetipso
conscriptos; item de Analogia duos libros, et Anticatones
totidem, et poema quod inscribitur Iter, et opuscula alia
multa fecit.

℃ Tam Iulius quam Augustus cautelas scribendi litteram
pro littera adinvenit, ut quae scriberent occultarent. Nam
Iulius quartam litteram proposuit loco primae, et sic deinceps alphabetum expendit; Augustus vero secunda pro prima,
et pro secunda tertia, et ita deinceps usus fuit. Hic in
Mutinensi bello, in maxima mole rerum, cotidie et legisse
et scripsisse traditur ac etiam declamasse. Tiberius lyricum
carmen scripsit, et poemata quaedam Graeca. Claudius similiter, tam Graeci quam Latini sermonis peritus, varios libros
fecit. Sed prae his et aliis Titus in scribendi peritia floruit,
qui cuiuscunque volebat litteram imitabatur facillime, unde
se profitebatur falsarium maximum, si libuisset, fieri po-
tuisse. Haec omnia Suetonius, De vita duodecim Caesarum,
annotavit.

according to virtue and denied themselves all luxurious delights. Whoever therefore is by the good gift of God endowed with the gift of science, let him, according to the counsel of the Holy Spirit, write wisdom in his time of leisure (Eccli. 38), that his reward may be with the blessed and his days may be lengthened in this present world.

⁋ Further, if we turn our discourse to the princes of the world, we find that famous emperors not only attained excellent skill in the art of writing, but indulged greatly in its practice. Julius Caesar, the first and greatest of them all, has left us Commentaries on the Gallic and the Civil Wars written by himself; he wrote also two books *De Analogia*, and two books of *Anticatones*, and a poem called *Iter*, and many other works.

⁋ Julius and Augustus devised means of writing one letter for another, and so concealing what they wrote. For Julius put the fourth letter for the first, and so on through the alphabet; while Augustus used the second for the first, the third for the second, and so throughout. He is said in the greatest difficulties of affairs during the Mutinensian War to have read and written and even declaimed every day. Tiberius wrote a lyric poem and some Greek verses. Claudius likewise was skilled in both Greek and Latin, and wrote several books. But Titus was skilled above all men in the art of writing, and easily imitated any hand he chose; so that he used to say that if he had wished it he might have become a most skilful forger. All these things are noted by Suetonius in his Lives of the XII Caesars.

CAPITULUM XVII

De debita honestate circa librorum custodiam adhibenda

NON solum Deo praestamus obsequium novorum librorum praeparando volumina, sed sacratae pietatis exercemus officium, si eosdem nunc illaese tractemus, nunc locis idoneis redditos illibatae custodiae commendemus; ut gaudeant puritate, dum habentur in manibus, et quiescant secure, dum in suis cubilibus reconduntur. Nimirum post vestes et vascula corpori dedicata dominico, sacri libri merentur a clericis honestius contrectari, quibus totiens irrogatur iniuria, quotiens eos praesumit attingere manus foeda. Quamobrem exhortari studentes super negligentiis variis reputamus expediens, quae vitari faciliter semper possent et mirabiliter libris nocent.

℄ In primis quidem circa claudenda et aperienda volumina sit matura modestia, ut nec praecipiti festinatione solvantur, nec inspectione finita sine clausura debita dimittantur. Longe namque diligentius librum quam calceum convenit conservari.

℄ Est enim gens scholarium perperam educata communiter et, nisi maiorum regulis refraenetur, infinitis infantiis insolescit. Aguntur petulantia, praesumptione tumescunt; de

CHAPTER XVII

Of showing due Propriety in the Custody of Books

WE are not only rendering service to God in preparing volumes of new books, but also exercising an office of sacred piety when we treat books carefully, and again when we restore them to their proper places and commend them to inviolable custody; that they may rejoice in purity while we have them in our hands, and rest securely when they are put back in their repositories. And surely next to the vestments and vessels dedicated to the Lord's body, holy books deserve to be rightly treated by the clergy, to which great injury is done so often as they are touched by unclean hands. Wherefore we deem it expedient to warn our students of various negligences, which might always be easily avoided and do wonderful harm to books.

❡ In the first place as to the opening and closing of books, let there be due moderation, that they be not unclasped in precipitate haste, nor when we have finished our inspection be put away without being duly closed. For it behoves us to guard a book much more carefully than a boot.

❡ But the race of scholars is commonly badly brought up, and unless they are bridled in by the rules of their elders they indulge in infinite puerilities. They behave with petulance, and are puffed up with presumption, judging of everything

singulis iudicant tanquam certi, cum sint in omnibus inexperti.

℀ Videbis fortassis iuvenem cervicosum, studio segniter residentem, et dum hiberno tempore hiems alget, nasus irriguus frigore comprimente distillat, nec prius se dignatur emunctorio tergere, quam subiectum librum madefecerit turpi rore; cui utinam loco codicis corium subderetur sutoris! Unguem habet fimo fetente refertum, gagati simillimum, quo placentis materiae signat locum. Paleas dispertitur innumeras, quas diversis in locis collocat evidenter, ut festuca reducat quod memoria non retentat. Hae paleae, quia nec venter libri digerit nec quisquam eas extrahit, primo quidem librum a solita iunctura distendunt, et tandem negligenter oblivioni commissae putrescunt.

℀ Fructus et caseum super librum expansum non veretur comedere, atque scyphum hinc inde dissolute transferre; et quia non habet eleemosynarium praeparatum, in libris dimittit reliquias fragmentorum. Garrulitate continua sociis oblatrare non desinit, et dum multitudinem rationum adducit a sensu physico vacuarum, librum in gremio subexpansum humectat aspergine salivarum. Quid plura? statim duplicatis cubitis reclinatur in codicem et per breve studium soporem invitat prolixum, ac reparandis rugis limbos replicat foliorum, ad libri non modicum detrimentum.

℀ Iam imber abiit et recessit et flores apparuerunt in terra nostra. Tunc scholaris quem describimus, librorum neglector potius quam inspector, viola, primula atque rosa necnon et

Richard de Bury

as if they were certain, though they are altogether inexperienced.

℃ You may happen to see some headstrong youth lazily lounging over his studies, and when the winter's frost is sharp, his nose running from the nipping cold drips down, nor does he think of wiping it with his pocket-handkerchief until he has bedewed the book before him with the ugly moisture. Would that he had before him no book, but a cobbler's apron! His nails are stuffed with fetid filth as black as jet, with which he marks any passage that pleases him. He distributes a multitude of straws, which he inserts to stick out in different places, so that the halm may remind him of what his memory cannot retain. These straws, because the book has no stomach to digest them, and no one takes them out, first distend the book from its wonted closing, and at length, being carelessly abandoned to oblivion, go to decay.

℃ He does not fear to eat fruit or cheese over an open book, or carelessly to carry a cup to and from his mouth; and because he has no wallet at hand he drops into books the fragments that are left. Continually chattering, he is never weary of disputing with his companions, and while he alleges a crowd of senseless arguments, he wets the book lying half open in his lap with sputtering showers. Aye, and then hastily folding his arms he leans forward on the book, and by a brief spell of study invites a prolonged nap; and then, by way of mending the wrinkles, he folds back the margin of the leaves, to the no small injury of the book.

℃ Now the rain is over and gone, and the flowers have appeared in our land. Then the scholar we are speaking of, a neglecter rather than an inspector of books, will stuff his

quadrifolio farciet librum suum. Tunc manus aquosas et scatentes sudore volvendis voluminibus applicabit. Tunc pulverulentis undique chirothecis in candidam membranam impinget et indice veteri pelle vestito venabitur paginam lineatim. Tunc ad pulicis mordentis aculeum sacer liber abicitur, qui tamen vix clauditur infra mensem, sed sic pulveribus introiectis tumescit quod claudentis instantiae non obedit.

¶ Sunt autem specialiter coercendi a contrectatione librorum iuvenes impudentes, qui cum litterarum figuras effigiare didicerint, mox pulcherrimorum voluminum, si copia concedatur, incipiunt fieri glossatores incongrui et ubi largiorem marginem circa textum perspexerint, monstruosis apparitant alphabetis; vel aliud frivolum qualecunque quod imaginationi occurrit celerius, incastigatus calamus protinus exarare praesumit. Ibi Latinista, ibi sophista, ibi quilibet scriba indoctus aptitudinem pennae probat, quod formosissimis codicibus quo ad usum et pretium creberrime vidimus obfuisse.

¶ Sunt iterum fures quidam libros enormiter detruncantes, qui pro epistolarum chartulis schedulas laterales abscindunt, littera sola salva; vel finalia folia, quae ad libri custodiam dimittuntur, ad varios abusus assumunt; quod genus sacrilegii sub interminatione anathematis prohiberi deberet.

¶ Convenit autem prorsus scholarium honestati ut, quotiens ad studium a refectione reditur, praecedat omnino lotio lectionem, nec digitus sagimine delibutus aut folia prius volvat, aut signacula libri solvat. Puerulus lacrimosus capitalium litterarum non admiretur imagines, ne manu fluida

volume with violets, and primroses, with roses and quatrefoil. Then he will use his wet and perspiring hands to turn over the volumes; then he will thump the white vellum with gloves covered with all kinds of dust, and with his finger clad in long-used leather will hunt line by line through the page; then at the sting of the biting flea the sacred book is flung aside, and is hardly shut for another month, until it is so full of the dust that has found its way within, that it resists the effort to close it.

℄ But the handling of books is specially to be forbidden to those shameless youths, who as soon as they have learned to form the shapes of letters, straightway, if they have the opportunity, become unhappy commentators, and wherever they find an extra margin about the text, furnish it with monstrous alphabets, or if any other frivolity strikes their fancy, at once their pen begins to write it. There the Latinist and sophister and every unlearned writer tries the fitness of his pen, a practice that we have frequently seen injuring the usefulness and value of the most beautiful books.

℄ Again, there is a class of thieves shamefully mutilating books, who cut away the margins from the sides to use as material for letters, leaving only the text, or employ the leaves from the ends, inserted for the protection of the book, for various uses and abuses—a kind of sacrilege which should be prohibited by the threat of anathema.

℄ Again, it is part of the decency of scholars that whenever they return from meals to their study, washing should invariably precede reading, and that no grease-stained finger should unfasten the clasps, or turn the leaves of a book. Nor let a crying child admire the pictures in the capital letters, lest he

polluat pergamenum; tangit enim illico quicquid videt. Porro laici, qui librum aeque respiciunt resupine transversum sicut serie naturali expansum, omni librorum communione penitus sunt indigni.

℃ Hoc etiam clericus disponat, ut olens ab ollis lixa cinereus librorum lilia non contingat illotus, sed qui ingreditur sine macula pretiosis codicibus ministrabit. Conferret autem plurimum tam libris quam scholaribus manuum honestarum munditia, si non essent scabies et pustulae characteres clericales.

℃ Librorum defectibus, quoties advertuntur, est otius occurrendum; quoniam nihil grandescit citius quam scissura, et fractura, quae ad tempus negligitur, reparabitur postea cum usura.

℃ De librorum armariis mundissime fabricandis, ubi ab omni laesione salventur securi, Moyses mitissimus nos informat, Deuteron. 31°: Tollite, inquit, librum istum et ponite illum in latere arcae foederis Domini Dei vestri. O locus idoneus et bibliothecae conveniens, quae de lignis sethim imputribilibus facta fuit auroque per totum interius et exterius circumtecta! Sed omnem inhonestatis negligentiam circa libros tractandos suo Salvator exclusit exemplo, sicut legitur Lucae 4°. Cum enim scripturam propheticam de se scriptam in libro tradito perlegisset, non prius librum ministro restituit, quam eundem suis sacratissimis manibus plicuisset. Quo facto studentes docentur clarissime circa librorum custodiam quantumcunque minima negligi non debere.

Richard de Bury

soil the parchment with wet fingers: for a child instantly touches whatever he sees. Moreover, the laity, who look at a book turned upside down just as if it were open in the right way, are utterly unworthy of any communion with books.

℀ Let the clerk take care also that the smutty scullion reeking from his stewpots does not touch the lily leaves of books, all unwashed, but he who walketh without blemish shall minister to the precious volumes. And, again, the cleanliness of decent hands would be of great benefit to books as well as scholars, if it were not that the itch and pimples are characteristic of the clergy.

℀ Whenever defects are noticed in books they should be promptly repaired, since nothing spreads more quickly than a tear, and a rent which is neglected at the time will have to be repaired afterwards with usury.

℀ Moses, the gentlest of men, teaches us to make bookcases most neatly, wherein they may be protected from any injury: *Take*, he says, *this book of the law, and put it in the side of the ark of the covenant of the Lord your God.* O fitting place and appropriate for a library, which was made of imperishable shittim-wood, and was all covered within and without with gold! But the Saviour also has warned us by His example against all unbecoming carelessness in the handling of books, as we read in S. Luke. For when He had read the scriptural prophecy of Himself in the book that was delivered to Him, He did not give it again to the minister until He had closed it with His own most sacred hands. By which students are most clearly taught that in the care of books the merest trifles ought not to be neglected.

Quod tantam librorum collegimus copiam ad communem profectum scholarium et non solum ad propriam voluptatem

NIHIL iniquius in humanis perpenditur quam quod ea quae geruntur iustissime malignorum obloquiis pervertuntur, et inde quis reportat infamiam criminis, unde magis meruit spem honoris. Oculo simplici perpetrantur quam plurima, nec sinistra dextrae se commiscet, nullo fermento massa corrumpitur, neque ex lino vestis lanaque contexitur. Perversorum tamen praestigiis opus pium mendaciter transformatur in monstrum. Haec est nimirum peccatricis naturae reprobanda conditio, quod non solum in factis moraliter dubiis pro peiore parte sententiat, immo frequenter illa, quae speciem boni habent, nequitiosa subversione depravat.

℄ Quamvis enim amor librorum in clerico ex obiecti natura praeferat honestatem, miro tamen modo obnoxios nos effecit iudiciis plurimorum, quorum admirationibus obtrectati, nunc de curiositate superflua, nunc de cupiditate in illa dumtaxat materia, nunc de vanitatis apparentia, nunc de

CHAPTER XVIII

Showeth that we have collected so great Store of Books for the common Benefit of Scholars and not only for our own Pleasure

NOTHING in human affairs is more unjust than that those things which are most righteously done, should be perverted by the slanders of malicious men, and that one should bear the reproach of sin where he has rather deserved the hope of honour. Many things are done with singleness of eye, the right hand knoweth not what the left hand doth, the lump is uncorrupted by leaven, nor is the garment woven of wool and linen; and yet by the trickery of perverse men a pious work is mendaciously transformed into some monstrous act. Certes, such is the unhappy condition of sinful nature, that not merely in acts that are morally doubtful it adopts the worse conclusion; but often it depraves by iniquitous subversion those which have the appearance of rectitude.

ℂ For although the love of books in a clerk from the nature of its object bears the aspect of goodness, yet, wonderful to say, it has rendered us obnoxious to the censures of many, by whose astonishment we were disparaged and censured, now for excess of curiosity, now for greed, in that matter at least, now for the exhibition of vanity, now for

voluptatis intemperantia circa litteras notabamur, quorum revera vituperiis non plus quam caniculorum latratibus movebamur, illius solius testimonio contentati, ad quem renes et corda pertinet perscrutari.

(Cum enim voluntatis secretae finalis intentio homines lateat unicoque Deo pateat, cordium inspectori, perniciosae temeritatis merentur redargui, qui humanis actibus, quorum fontale non vident principium, epigramma tam faciliter superscribunt sinistrum. Finis enim se habet in operabilibus, sicut principia in speculativis vel suppositiones in mathematicis, teste Aristotele, 7° Ethicorum. Quapropter, sicut ex principiorum evidentia conclusionis veritas declaratur, ita plerumque in agibilibus ex honesti finis intentione bonitas moralis in opere sigillatur, ubi alias opus ipsum iudicari deberet indifferens quo ad mores.

(Nos autem ab olim in praecordiis mentis nostrae propositum gessimus radicatum, quatenus opportunis temporibus exspectatis divinitus aulam quamdam in reverenda universitate Oxoniensi, omnium liberalium artium nutrice praecipua, in perpetuam eleemosynam fundaremus, necessariisque redditibus dotaremus; quam numerosis scholaribus occupatam, nostrorum librorum iocalibus ditaremus, ut ipsi libri et singuli eorundem communes fierent, quantum ad usum et studium, non solum scholaribus aulae tactae, sed per eos omnibus universitatis praedictae studentibus in aeternum, secundum formam et modum, quem sequens capitulum declarabit. Quapropter sincerus amor studii zelusque orthodoxae fidei ad aedificationem ecclesiae confirmandae

intemperance of delight in literature; though indeed we were no more disturbed by their vituperation than by the barking of so many dogs, satisfied with the testimony of Him to whom it appertaineth to try the hearts and reins.

℆ For as the aim and purpose of our inmost will is inscrutable to men and is seen of God alone, the searcher of hearts, they deserve to be rebuked for their pernicious temerity, who so eagerly set a mark of condemnation upon human acts, the ultimate springs of which they cannot see. For the final end in matters of conduct holds the same position as first principles in speculative science or axioms in mathematics, as the chief of philosophers, Aristotle, points out in the seventh book of the Ethics. And therefore, just as the truth of our conclusions depends upon the correctness of our premises, so in matters of action the stamp of moral rectitude is given by the honesty of aim and purpose, in cases where the act itself would otherwise be held to be morally indifferent.

℆ Now we have long cherished in our heart of hearts the fixed resolve, when Providence should grant a favourable opportunity, to found in perpetual charity a Hall in the reverend university of Oxford, the chief nursing mother of all liberal arts, and to endow it with the necessary revenues, for the maintenance of a number of scholars; and moreover to enrich the Hall with the treasures of our books, that all and every of them should be in common as regards their use and study, not only to the scholars of the said Hall, but by their means to all the students of the before-named university for ever, in the form and manner which the following chapter shall declare. Wherefore the sincere love of study and zeal for the strengthening of the orthodox faith to the edifying of the

pepererunt in nobis sollicitudinem hanc stupendam num-
micolis, ut collectos codices undecunque venales neglectis
sumptibus emeremus, et qui venumdari non debebant,
transcribi honestius faceremus.

℄ Cum enim delectationes hominum ex dispositione
caelestium corporum, cui mixtorum complexio frequenter
obedit, diversimode distinguantur; ut hi in architectura, illi
in agricultura, hi in venationibus, illi in navigationibus, hi in
bellis, illi in ludis eligant conversari; cecidit circa libros nostrae Mercurialis species voluptatis honestae, quam ex rectae
rationis arbitrio, cuius nulla sidera dominantur imperio, in
honorem ordinavimus maiestatis supremae ut, unde mens
nostra tranquillitatem reperit requiei, inde devotissimus cre-
sceret cultus Dei.

℄ Quamobrem desinant obtrectantes, sicut caeci de colo-
ribus iudicare; vespertiliones de luminibus disceptare non
audeant, atque trabes gestantes in oculis propriis alienas
festucas eruere non praesumant. Cessent commentis satiricis
sugillare quae nesciunt et occulta discutere, quae humanis
experientiis non patescunt; qui nos fortassis affectu com-
mendassent benevolo, si ferarum venatui, alearum lusui,
dominarum applausui vacassemus.

Richard de Bury

Church have begotten in us that solicitude so marvellous to the lovers of pelf, of collecting books wherever they were to be purchased, regardless of expense, and of having those that could not be bought fairly transcribed.

℄ For as the favourite occupations of men are variously distinguished according to the disposition of the heavenly bodies, which frequently control our natural composition, so that some men choose to devote themselves to architecture, others to agriculture, others to hunting, others to navigation, others to war, others to games, we have under the aspect of Mercury entertained a blameless pleasure in books, which under the rule of right reason, over which no stars are dominant, we have ordered to the glory of the Supreme Being, that where our minds found tranquillity and peace, thence also might spring a most devout service of God.

℄ Therefore let our detractors cease, who are as blind men judging of colours; let not bats venture to speak of light; and let not those who carry beams in their own eyes presume to pull the mote out of their brother's eye. Let them cease to jeer with satirical taunts at things of which they are ignorant, and to discuss hidden things that are not revealed to the eyes of men; who perchance would have praised and commended us, if we had spent our time in hunting, dice-playing, or courting the smiles of ladies.

CAPITULUM XIX

De modo communicandi studentibus omnibus libros nostros

DIFFICILE semper fuit sic homines limitare legibus honestatis, quin astutia successorum terminos niteretur praecedentium transilire et statutas infringere regulas insolentia libertatis. Quamobrem de prudentum consilio certum modum praefiximus, per quem ad utilitatem studentium librorum nostrorum communicationem et usum volumus devenire.

❡ In primis enim libros omnes et singulos, de quibus catalogum fecimus specialem, concedimus et donamus intuitu caritatis communitati scholarium in aula ·N· Oxoniensi degentium, in perpetuam eleemosynam pro anima nostra et parentum nostrorum necnon pro animabus illustrissimi regis Angliae Edwardi tertii post conquestum ac devotissimae dominae reginae Philippae consortis eiusdem, ut iidem libri omnibus et singulis universitatis dictae villae scholaribus et magistris tam regularibus quam saecularibus commodentur pro tempore ad profectum et usum studendi, iuxta modum quem immediate subiungimus, qui est talis.

❡ Quinque de scholaribus in aula praefata commorantibus assignentur per eiusdem aulae magistrum, quibus omnium librorum custodia deputetur, de quibus quinque personis

CHAPTER XIX

Of the Manner of lending all our Books to Students

IT has ever been difficult so to restrain men by the laws of rectitude, that the astuteness of successors might not strive to transgress the bounds of their predecessors, and to infringe established rules in insolence of licence. Accordingly, with the advice of prudent men, we have prescribed the manner in which we desire that the communication and use of our books should be permitted for the benefit of students.

❡ *Imprimis,* we give and grant all and singular the books, of which we have made a special catalogue, in consideration of affection, to the community of scholars living in . . . N . . . Hall at Oxford, as a perpetual gift, for our soul and the souls of our parents, and also for the soul of the most illustrious King Edward the Third from the Conquest, and of the most pious Queen Philippa, his consort: to the intent that the same books may be lent from time to time to all and singular the scholars and masters of the said place, as well regular as secular, for the advancement and use of study, in the manner immediately following, that is to say:

❡ Five of the scholars sojourning in the Hall aforesaid shall be appointed by the Master thereof, who shall have the charge of all the books, of which five persons three and not

tres et nullatenus pauciores librum vel libros ad inspectionem et usum dumtaxat studii valeant commodare; ad copiandum vero vel transcribendum nullum librum volumus extra saepta domus concedi.

℃ Igitur cum scholaris quicunque saecularis vel religiosus, quos in praesenti favore ad paria iudicamus, librum aliquem commodandum petiverit, considerent diligenter custodes an librum talem habuerint duplicatum; et si sic, commodent ei librum cautione recepta, quae librum traditum in valore transcendat iudicio eorundem, fiatque statim tam de cautione quam de libro commodato memorialis scriptura, continens nomina personarum quae librum tradunt et illius qui recipit, cum die et anno Domini quo continget fieri commodatum.

℃ Si vero custodes invenerint, quod ille liber qui petitur duplicatus non fuerit, talem librum nullatenus commodent cuicunque, nisi fuerit de comitiva scholarium dictae aulae, nisi forte ad inspectionem et infra saepta domus vel aulae praedictae, sed non ad ulterius deferendum.

℃ Scholari vero cuilibet praedictae aulae liber quicunque per tres de praedictis custodibus valeat commodari, nomine tamen suo cum die quo librum recipit prius annotato. Nec tamen ipse possit librum sibi traditum alteri commodare, nisi de assensu trium de custodibus supradictis, et tunc deleto nomine primi nomen secundi cum tempore traditionis scribatur.

℃ Ad haec omnia observandum custodes singuli fidem praestent, quando eis custodia huiusmodi deputatur. Recipientes autem librum vel libros ibidem iurabunt quod eum

Richard de Bury

fewer may lend any book or books for inspection and study; but for copying or transcribing we direct that no book shall be allowed outside the walls of the house.

❡ Therefore, when any scholar secular or religious, whom for this purpose we regard with equal favour, shall seek to borrow any book, let the keepers diligently consider if they have a duplicate of the said book, and if so, let them lend him the book, taking such pledge as in their judgment exceeds the value of the book delivered, and let a record be made forthwith of the pledge and of the book lent, containing the names of the persons delivering the book and of the person who receives it, together with the day and year when the loan is made.

❡ But if the keepers find that the book asked for is not in duplicate, they shall not lend such book to anyone whomsoever, unless he shall belong to the community of scholars of the said Hall, unless perhaps for inspection within the walls of the aforesaid house or Hall, but not to be carried beyond it.

❡ But to any of the scholars of the said Hall, any book may be lent by three of the aforesaid keepers, after first recording, however, his name, with the day on which he receives the book. Nevertheless, the borrower may not lend the book entrusted to him to another, except with the permission of three of the aforesaid keepers, and then the name of the first borrower being erased, the name of the second with the time of delivery is to be recorded.

❡ Each keeper shall take an oath to observe all these regulations when they enter upon the charge of the books. And the recipients of any book or books shall thereupon swear that

vel eos ad alium usum nisi ad inspectionem et studium nullatenus applicabunt, quodque illum et illos extra villam Oxoniensem cum suburbio nec deferent nec deferri permittent.

⁋ Singulis autem annis computum reddent praedicti custodes magistro domus et duobus quos secum duxerit de suis scholaribus assumendos, vel si eidem non vacaverit, tres deputet inspectores alios a custodibus, qui librorum catalogum perlegentes videant quod omnes habeant vel in voluminibus propriis vel saltem per cautiones praesentes. Ad hunc autem computum persolvendum tempus credimus opportunum a kalendis Iulii usque ad festum sequens translationis gloriosi martyris sancti Thomae.

⁋ Hoc autem omnino adicimus quod quilibet, cui liber aliquis fuerit commodatus, semel in anno librum praesentet custodibus et suam si voluerit videat cautionem. Porro si contingat fortuito per mortem, furtum, fraudem vel incuriam librum perdi, ille qui perdidit vel eiusdem procurator seu etiam executor pretium libri solvat et eiusdem recipiat cautionem. Quod si qualitercunque custodibus ipsis lucrum evenerit, in nihil aliud quam in librorum reparationem et subsidium convertatur.

they will not use the book or books for any other purpose but that of inspection or study, and that they will not take or permit to be taken it or them beyond the town and suburbs of Oxford.

℄ Moreover, every year the aforesaid keepers shall render an account to the Master of the House and two of his scholars whom he shall associate with himself, or if he shall not be at leisure, he shall appoint three inspectors, other than the keepers, who shall peruse the catalogue of books, and see that they have them all, either in the volumes themselves or at least as represented by deposits. And the more fitting season for rendering this account we believe to be from the First of July until the festival of the Translation of the Glorious Martyr S. Thomas next following.

℄ We add this further provision, that anyone to whom a book has been lent, shall once a year exhibit it to the keepers, and shall, if he wishes it, see his pledge. Moreover, if it chances that a book is lost by death, theft, fraud, or carelessness, he who has lost it or his representative or executor shall pay the value of the book and receive back his deposit. But if in any wise any profit shall accrue to the keepers, it shall not be applied to any purpose but the repair and maintenance of the books.

Exhortatio scholarium ad rependendum pro nobis suffragia debitae pietatis

TEMPUS iam efflagitat terminare tractatum, quem de amore librorum compegimus, in quo contemporaneorum nostrorum admirationibus de eo quod tantum libros dileximus rationem reddere nisi sumus. Verum quia vix datur aliquid operari mortalibus, quod nullius respergatur pulvere vanitatis, studiosum amorem, quem ita diuturnum ad libros habuimus, iustificare penitus non audemus, quin fuerit forsan nobis quandoque occasio alicuius negligentiae venialis, quamvis amoris materia sit honesta et intentio regulata. Si namque cum omnia fecerimus, servos nos inutiles dicere teneamur; si Iob sanctissimus sua opera omnia verebatur; si iuxta Isaiam quasi pannus menstruatae omnes sunt iustitiae nostrae; quis se de perfectione cuiuscunque virtutis praesumet iactare, quin ex aliqua circumstantia valeat reprehendi, quae forsitan a seipso non poterit deprehendi? Bonum enim ex integris causis, malum autem omnifarie: sicut Dionysius, De divinis nominibus, nos informat.

℃ Quamobrem in nostrarum iniquitatum remedium, quibus nos omnium Creatorem crebrius offendisse cognosci-

CHAPTER XX

An Exhortation to Scholars to requite us by pious Prayers

TIME now clamours for us to terminate this treatise which we have composed concerning the love of books; in which we have endeavoured to give the astonishment of our contemporaries the reason why we have loved books so greatly. But because it is hardly granted to mortals to accomplish aught that is not rolled in the dust of vanity, we do not venture entirely to justify the zealous love which we have so long had for books, or to deny that it may perchance sometimes have been the occasion of some venial negligence, albeit the object of our love is honourable and our intention upright. For if when we have done everything, we are bound to call ourselves unprofitable servants; if the most holy Job was afraid of all his works; if according to Isaiah all our righteousness is as filthy rags, who shall presume to boast himself of the perfection of any virtue, or deny that from some circumstance a thing may deserve to be reprehended, which in itself perchance was not reprehensible? For good springs from one selfsame source, but evil arises in many ways, as Dionysius informs us in his book on Divine Names.

℘ Wherefore to make amends for our iniquities, by which we acknowledge ourselves to have frequently offended the Creator of all things, in asking the assistance of their prayers,

mus, orationum suffragia petituri, studentes nostros futuros
dignum duximus exhortari, quatenus sic tam nobis quam
aliis eorundem futuris benefactoribus fiant grati, quod beneficiorum nostrorum providentiam spiritalibus recompensent
retributionibus. Vivamus in eorum memoriis funerati, qui
in nostris vixerunt benevolentiis nondum nati nostrisque
nunc vivunt beneficiis sustentati.

ℂ Clementiam Redemptoris implorent instantiis indefessis, quatenus negligentiis nostris parcat, peccatorum nostrorum reatibus pius iudex indulgeat, lapsus nostrae fragi-
litatis pallio pietatis operiat et offensas, quas et pudet et pae-
nitet commisisse, divina benignitate remittat. Conservet in
nobis ad sufficiens spatium paenitendi suarum munera gra-
tiarum, fidei firmitatem, spei sublimitatem et ad omnes homines latissimam caritatem. Flectat superbum arbitrium ad cul-
parum suarum lamentum, ut deploret transactas elationes
vanissimas et retractet indignationes amarissimas ac delectationes insanissimas detestetur. Vigeat sua virtus in nobis,
cum nostra defecerit, et qui nostrum ingressum sacro bapti-
smate consecravit gratuito, nostrum progressum ad statum
apostolicum sublimavit immerito, nostrum dignetur egres-
sum sacramentis idoneis communire.

ℂ Laxetur a nostro spiritu amor carnis, evanescat penitus
metus mortis, desideret dissolvi et esse cum Christo, et in
terris solo corpore constituti cogitatione et aviditate in
aeterna patria conversemur. Pater misericordiarum et Deus
totius consolationis filio prodigo de siliquis reverenti beni-
gnus occurrat, drachmam denuo repertam recipiat et in the-

Richard de Bury

we have thought fit to exhort our future students to show their gratitude as well to us as to their other benefactors in time to come by requiting our forethought for their benefit by spiritual retribution. Let us live when dead in their memories, who have lived in our benevolence before they were born, and live now sustained by our beneficence.

℄ Let them implore the mercy of the Redeemer with unwearied prayer, that the pious Judge may excuse our negligences, may pardon the wickedness of our sins, may cover the lapses of our feebleness with the cloak of piety, and remit by His divine goodness the offences of which we are ashamed and penitent. That He may preserve to us for a due season of repentance the gifts of His good grace, steadfastness of faith, loftiness of hope, and the widest charity to all men. That He may turn our haughty will to lament its faults, that it may deplore its past most vain elations, may retract its most bitter indignations, and detest its most insane delectations. That His virtue may abound in us, when our own is found wanting, and that He who freely consecrated our beginning by the sacrament of baptism, and advanced our progress to the seat of the Apostles without any desert of ours, may deign to fortify our outgoing by the fitting sacraments.

℄ That we may be delivered from the lust of the flesh, that the fear of death may utterly vanish and our spirit may desire to be dissolved and be with Christ, and existing upon earth in body only, in thought and longing our conversation may be in Heaven. That the Father of mercies and the God of all consolation may graciously come to meet the prodigal returning from the husks; that He may receive the piece of silver that has been found again and transmit it by his holy angels

sauros aeternos per angelos sanctos transmittat. Castiget vultu terrifico exitus nostri hora spiritus tenebrarum, ne latens in limine portae mortis Leviathan, serpens vetus, insidias improvisas calcaneo nostro paret.

℄ Cum vero ad terrendum tribunal fuerimus advocati, ut cuncta quae corpore gessimus attestante conscientia referamus, consideret humanitas iuncta Deo effusi sui sancti sanguinis pretium et advertat divinitas humanata carnalis naturae figmentum, ut ibi transeat fragilitas impunita ubi clemens pietas cernitur infinita, et ibi respiret spiritus miseri ubi exstat proprium iudicis misereri. Amplius refugium spei nostrae post Deum virginem et reginam Theotokon benedictam nostri semper studentes salutationibus satagant frequentare devotis, ut qui per nostra facinora replicata meruimus iudicem invenire turbatum, per ipsius suffragia semper grata mereamur eundem reperire placatum. Deprimat pia manus brachium aequilibre, quo nostra tam parva quam pauca merita pensabuntur ne, quod absit, praeponderet gravitas criminum et nos damnandos deiciat in abyssum.

℄ Clarissimum meritis confessorem Cuthbertum, cuius gregem indigni pascendum suscepimus, omni cultu studeant venerari devote, rogantes assidue, ut suum licet indignum vicarium precibus excusare dignetur et quem successorem admisit in terris, procuret effici consessorem in caelis. Puris denique tam mentis quam corporis precibus rogent Deum, ut spiritum ad imaginem Trinitatis creatum post praesentis

into His eternal treasury. That He may rebuke with His ter-
rible countenance, at the hour of our departure, the spirits of
darkness, lest Leviathan, that old serpent, lying hid at the
gate of death, should spread unforeseen snares for our feet.

ℂ But [that] when we shall be summoned to the awful judgment-seat to give an account on the testimony of conscience
of all things we have done in the body, the God-Man may
consider the price of the holy blood that He has shed, and
that the Incarnate Deity may note the frame of our carnal
nature, that our weakness may pass unpunished where infinite loving-kindness is to be found, and that the soul of the
wretched sinner may breathe again where the peculiar office
of the Judge is to show mercy. And further let our students
be always diligent in invoking the refuge of our hope after
God, the Virgin Mother of God and Blessed Queen of
Heaven, that we who for our manifold sins and wickednesses
have deserved the anger of the Judge, by the aid of her ever-
acceptable supplications may merit His forgiveness; that her
pious hand may depress the scale of the balance in which our
small and few good deeds shall be weighed, lest the heaviness
of our sins preponderate and cast us down to the bottomless
pit of perdition.

℃ Moreover, let them ever venerate with due observance
the most deserving Confessor Cuthbert, the care of whose
flock we have unworthily undertaken, ever devoutly praying
that he may deign to excuse by his prayers his all-unworthy
vicar, and may procure him whom he hath admitted as his
successor upon earth to be made his assessor in heaven. Finally, let them pray God with holy prayers as well of body as
of soul, that He will restore the spirit created in the image

The Philobiblon of

miseriae incolatum ad suum reducat primordiale prototypum ac eiusdem concedat perpetuum fruibilis faciei conspectum: Amen.

℆ Explicit Philobiblon domini Ricardi de Aungervile, cognominati de Bury, quondam episcopi Dunelmensis. Completus est autem tractatus iste in manerio nostro de Aukeland xxiiij° die Ianuarii anno Domini millesimo trecentesimo quadragesimo quarto, aetatis nostrae quinquagesimo octavo praecise completo, pontificatus vero nostri anno undecimo finiente. Ad laudem Dei feliciter et Amen.

Richard de Bury

of the Trinity, after its sojourn in this miserable world, to its primordial prototype, and grant to it for ever to enjoy the sight of His countenance: through our Lord Jesus Christ. Amen.

℘ The end of the Philobiblon of Master Richard de Aungervile, surnamed de Bury, late Bishop of Durham. This treatise was finished in our manor-house of Auckland on the 24th day of January in the year of our Lord one thousand three hundred and forty-four, the fifty-eighth year of our age being exactly completed and the eleventh year of our pontificate drawing to an end; to the glory of God. Amen.

NOTES

p. 6. consilium] The προαίρεσις of Aristotle. The reference to Aristotle, as Inglis has remarked, is not very happy.

p. 8. It is possible that 'in inculto' would be a better reading here (line 13) as West suggested. M.

p. 10. assub] This word, which has been found unintelligible by the editors, is derived from the translations of Aristotle made from the Arabic, in which it means a falling star. Cf. Roger Bacon, *Op. Maj.* iii. 1, 'impressiones inflammatae in aere ex vaporibus ignitis in similitudinem stellarum, quae vocantur Arabice Assub'; and Vincent of Beauvais, *Spec. Nat.* ii. 84; iv. 72 ('De Asub, id est stella cadente'); see also Jourdain, *Traductions d'Aristote*, pp. 367, 414. I have even found the word used in poetry: see *Anonymi chronicon rhythmicum Austriacum*, printed in Pertz, *Scriptt.* xxv. p. 364. The word occurs in the *Promptorium Parvulorum* and the *Catholicon Anglicum*, as the rendering of 'sterre-slyme', the star-jelly supposed to be deposited by falling stars: see Way's note, *P.P.*, p. 474.

p. 12. Philobiblon] This is de Bury's word, though some of the editors have altered it to Philobiblion without sufficient authority. The phrase 'de amore librorum' probably represents nearly enough what he intended it to mean.

p. 16. Cratonis] The name occurs also in c. xiii. p. 126, where it is clearly the true reading. Here the sense would rather require *Catonis*, as more worthy to be coupled with Plato: cf. S. Augustine, *De Civ. Dei*, ii. 7; 'quid docuerit Plato vel censuerit Cato.' The Crato of the Golden Legend, ed. Graesse, p. 56, and Vincent of Beauvais, *Spec. hist.* xi. 39, or the fictitious Crato of the Pseudo-Boethius (s. 182 note) seems too obscure for this distinction. But the phrase *Cratonis cathedra* is perhaps conclusive; and very possibly de Bury thought they were the same person. Crato is mentioned in several liturgical hymns: cf. *York Missal*, ii. 212; Daniel, *Thesaur. Hymnol.* i. 93.

p. 18. Almagesti] The Astronomy, or Μεγάλη Σύνταξις, was probably so called to distinguish it from the Μαθηματικὴ Σύνταξις, or

Notes

Mathematics of Ptolemy. It was preserved and communicated to Europe by the Arabs, and the name Almagest is formed of the Arabic article and the Greek μεγίστη.

p. 20. sensus communis] See Roger Bacon's account of *Scientia perspectiva, Op. Maj.*, pars. v, for the part played in perception by 'imaginatio et sensus communis' (p. 192). John de Garlandia says in his *Dictionarius*: 'In cerebro sub craneo tres sunt cellulae. Prima est ymaginaria, secunda rationalis, tertia memorialis', ed. Scheler, p. 22.

p. 20. pannis] There may be some reference to the distribution of robes, which was expected in medieval times from an incepting master at the Universities: cf. Maxwell Lyte, *Hist. Univ. Oxford*, 215; Anstey, *Mun. Acad., passim.*

p. 24. In line 5 the alternative reading of 'utimur' might be preferred. M.

p. 26. sapientissimus] No doubt Solomon.

p. 26. librorum asseres (line 8)]. See *Notes & Queries*, vol. 174, p. 45. M.

p. 26. I have amended 'veritatis' to 'veritati' as do West, Nelson, and Altamura. M.

p. 30. Sol hominum Salomon] This phrase occurs in Walter Map, *De Nugis Curialium*, iv. 3.

p. 34. quadrivialium] The Trivium included Grammar, Dialectic, and Rhetoric—the introductory arts; the Quadrivium, the four sciences —'quatuor pennas'—of Music, Arithmetic, Geometry, and Astronomy.

p. 36. In line 10 I would prefer to read 'antonomastice'. M.

p. 38. figurae Pythag.] The letter Y as emblematic of the broad and narrow paths of vice and virtue.

p. 38. In line 20 I would follow West and read 'vallatus angustiis', i.e. 'fenced in on every side'. M.

p. 38. legendus liber] The claim to the *privilegium clericale*, or benefit of clergy, was established by the reading of a verse from the Bible by the prisoner. From *Piers Plowman*, xv. 127, it seems already to have been usual to set one particular verse.

p. 40. The sense demands an exclamation point after 'librorum' and a full stop after 'Roma', which I have supplied. M.

Notes

p. 42. bestia bipedalis] This sufficiently contemptuous reference to the fair sex was accentuated by some scribe, who added the words *scilicet mulier*, which the editors have printed in the text. We must remember that the Bishop is referring to the *focariae*, whose association with the clergy was forbidden by a long series of ecclesiastical prohibitions *ne clerici in sacris ordinibus constituti focarias habeant*.

p. 42. furraturas] Perhaps the word here means furs, but see Ducange under the various forms of the word: in this passage I notice the forms *farraturas, folraturas, ferraturas*, and *foderaturas*. Originally it does not seem to have meant any particular stuff, but stuffing or lining of any sort.

p. 44. Theophrasti] This does not refer to the *Characters*, as Cocheris supposes, but to a book against marriage attributed to him by St. Jerome, who quotes it at some length, *Adv. Jovinian*. i. 28: 'fertur aureolus Theophrasti liber de nuptiis, in quo quaerit an vir sapiens ducat uxorem.' John of Salisbury, *Policrat*. viii. 11, quotes the passage.

p. 44. Valerii] This refers not to Valerius Maximus, as Cocheris says, but to the *Valerius ad Rufinum de uxore non ducenda*, which was one of the most popular of medieval books, and seems even to have been printed as St. Jerome's. It is claimed by Walter Map as his own, and incorporated in the *De Nugis Curialium*, iv. 3, where he explains that he wrote it to a love-sick friend: 'me, qui Walterus sum, Valerium vocans, ipsum, qui Johannes est et rufus, Rufinum.' It must not be confounded with the poem *Golias de conjuge non ducenda*, which was, perhaps, also written by Map: see Wright's edition of his *Poems*, p. 77. There is some confusion in Wright's references to the *Valerius*, and also in the notices in Warton, ed. Hazlitt, i. 250, ii. 353. Cf. Chaucer in the Wife of Bath's prologue.

p. 44. In the last line the reading 'in lacrimis, vel cum', suggested by West and Nelson, seems to make better sense. M.

p. 48. Martialis Coci] Cocus or Coquus appears to have been long regarded as a cognomen of Martial, and in the Middle Ages he was constantly referred to as Martialis Cocus, or merely as Cocus, e.g. by John of Salisbury. The quotation is from Martial, *Epigrammata*, i. 38.

p. 48. Carmentis latruncula fuit Cadmi] Cf. note on p. 86.

p. 52. horas canonicas] The *horae canonicae* are due to St. Benedict, who

Notes

divided the twenty-four hours into eight periods of three hours, marked by as many acts of devotion.

p. 52. I have preferred the reading 'intervallis captatis', and suppressed the semi-colon after 'canonicas'. M.

p. 52. In line 12 I prefer the reading 'cum activa' to 'actione', as do West and Nelson. M.

p. 54. *Liber Bacchus respicitur*] This appears to be the first verse of a piece of rhyming doggerel. The repetition of the verbal play in 'Liber pater—Liber patrum' might suggest that the lines were scribbled in the margin by a copyist or reader and then found their way into the text. [The passage is here printed as verse. M.]

p. 60. Praedicatorum] The order of *Fratres Praedicantes* was founded by St. Dominic, who obtained the Papal sanction from Honorius III in 1216, on condition of adopting the Rule of St. Augustine. He prescribed other ordinances in his *Constitutiones*, where in the Prologue, c. 5, we find the words here referred to: 'Ordo noster specialiter ob praedicationem et animarum salutem ab initio noscitur institutus fuisse, et studium nostrum ad hoc debet principaliter intendere ut proximorum animabus possimus utiles esse.' Holstenius, *Codex Regularum*, iv. 10.

p. 60. Hiberas naenias] The phrase, which has puzzled the editors, comes from St. Jerome's preface to the Pentateuch: 'Quod multi ignorantes, apocryphorum deliramenta sectantur et Hiberas naenias libris authenticis praeferunt.' It is a favourite phrase with Jerome, and is usually explained to refer to the errors of certain heretics in Spain.

p. 62. anthropospatos] The word occurs in this form in Petrus Comestor, *Hist. Schol.*, in Gen. c. xxxi, who explains it: 'scilicet humana propassio, quando attribuitur Deo quod hominis est.'

p. 66. acervum Mercurii] Probably a reference to Proverbs xxvi. 8, but the meaning in the context is not clear. M.

p. 70. In line 16 *Socratis* is probably right. See Nelson, op. cit., p. 123, citing West. M.

p. 72. 'endelechia' is the better reading. M.

p. 72. Zenonis] De Bury has confounded Zeno the Stoic, who died of old age, with Zeno of Elea, of whom the story mentioned in the

Notes

text is told. But the confusion is not peculiar to de Bury: cf. Hauréau, *Philosophie Scol.*, ii. 56.

p. 74. secundo flammis] The first time being, of course, when Hercules, poisoned by the shirt of Nessus, ascended a pile of wood, and ordered it to be set on fire.

p. 74. Ionithus] According to Methodius, a fourth son of Noah, who was supposed to have invented astronomy.

p. 74. liber Logostilios] Inglis supposed this to refer to the lost *Logistoricus* of Varro. Cocheris has made hopeless confusion throughout the passage and confesses his inability to understand this phrase, which he proposes to explain as *Logos Tales* (*sic*) 'c'est à dire le traité de Thalès'. But the reference is clearly to the lost treatise of the quasi-mythical Hermes Trismegistus, extant only in the Latin translation of Apuleius, which was entitled Λόγος τέλειος, or as St. Augustine renders it, *Verbum Perfectum*: *Adv. quinque haereses*, c. viii. The title was written as one word in medieval times, e.g. Jo. Sarisb. *De Septem Septenis*, c. vii.

p. 78. Gades] This word, originally from the Punic word *gadir*, a boundary, is familiar in classical Latin as the name of a Phoenician colony on the site of the modern Cadiz.

p. 84. florenos] The first gold florins were issued at Florence in 1252. In 1343 Edward III issued a gold florin to be current at 6*s*. It is an extremely scarce coin, only two specimens being known, which were found together in the Tyne; it was replaced by a noble of the value of 6*s*. 8*d*. in 1344: see Kenyon, *Gold Coins of England*, pp. 14, 15. The continental florins were extensively used in international intercourse.

p. 84. panfletos] This appears to be the earliest instance yet noticed of this word, which is apparently the origin of our 'pamphlet'. It is not in Ducange: but see Mr. Skeat's account of the word in his *Dictionary*.

p. 84. pigmentaria potio] *Pigmentum* or piment was a mixture of wine, honey, and spices, much affected in medieval times.

p. 86. geuzahar] This word has been treated by the editors and translators as a proper name, though in that case the order of the words would be obviously wrong. It is a Perso-Arabic astronomical term meaning dragon, and refers to the relation between the equator and

Notes

the ecliptic, their points of intersection, or *nodes*, being respectively called the head and tail of the dragon. The word was written genzahar or geuzahar, with the common confusion of *n* and *u* in medieval manuscripts.

p. 86. virgo Carmenta] Cadmus the Phoenician is supposed to have introduced the alphabet into Greece, whence it was carried into Italy by Evander, the Arcadian. His mother Carmenta (more usually Carmentis) accompanied him, and she is said to have turned the Greek into Roman characters.

p. 88. generalia studia] *Studium generale* was a medieval term for a university, and is said by Mr. Maxwell Lyte to be of English origin: *Hist. Univ. Oxford*, p. 5. But Denifle shows that it was first used of Vercelli; *Univ. des M.*, pp. 2 ff.

p. 90. With West and Nelson I would prefer 'devirginatum' for 'denigratum' in line 11. M.

p. 90. eorum armaria] One of the chief complaints made against the mendicant orders by Abp. Fitzralph, at Avignon in 1357, was that they monopolized books.

p. 92. Minorum] The *Fratres Minores* were founded by St. Francis in 1210 and were a mendicant order.

p. 94. paedagogos] The schoolmasters of the fourteenth century were much looked down upon; the degree of master of grammar was the lowest at the universities, requiring only a three years' course, instead of the seven needed for the study of the trivium and quadrivium. The degree was conferred by the delivery of a rod and birch, after which the incepting master proceeded to flog a boy publicly: see Bass Mullinger, *Univ. Cam.*, p. 344; Maxwell Lyte, *Hist. Univ. Oxf.*, p. 235.

p. 98. Phocas] One of the favourite grammatical textbooks of the Middle Ages: see Keil, *Gramm. Lat.* v. 410.

p. 100. De Vetula] This poem, in three books of wretched hexameters, was regarded in medieval times as the genuine work of Ovid. It is cited, for instance, by Bacon, Burley, Bradwardine, and Holkot, though the last-named observes: 'An sit liber Ovidii, Deus novit.'

p. 102. Ambitione siquidem] The passage beginning with these words and ending with the words 'vix faucibus humectatis', preceded by

the passage beginning 'Vncinis pomorum' (c. vi. p. 64)—which words, however, are altered to 'pomis et potu'—to 'perniciem animarum', and the passage (p. 66) 'Quemadmodum psittacus' to 'prophetae magistra', appear, though in a very corrupt form, in a curious memorandum in the Oxford Chancellor's and Proctors' book, under the year 1358. The memorandum is directed against the *cerei doctores*, that is, persons who secured a degree by influence, and it is noted that such doctors were always of the mendicant orders.

p. 104. Perihermenias] The *De Interpretatione* of Aristotle, usually called in the Middle Ages by the name here given.

p. 104. papalis provisio] One of the abuses of the Church in the Middle Ages was the practice of obtaining from the Pope the promise of a bishopric or some other ecclesiastical dignity on the next vacancy. The Statute of Provisors was directed against the practice in 1350, and was followed shortly afterwards by the first Statute of *Praemunire*. De Bury was himself provided to the See of Durham. See the Introduction.

p. 110. oculis lynceis] This phrase, which is used by Aristotle (e.g. *De Generat. et Corrupt.* i. 10) and is not uncommon in classical Latin, originally referred to Lynceus, the Argonaut, who was famed for the keenness of his vision. But it was then transferred to the lynx, and gave rise to the fable that it could see through a wall.

p. 110. Pandectam] The term Pandects from the Greek Πανδέκται was applied to encyclopedic works, and the term is used by Justinian in referring to the digest of Roman law made by his orders from the writings of the Roman jurists. In medieval times it was also applied to the Bible.

p. 110. Tegni] The writings of Galen were known in the Middle Ages through the Arabian physicians, and the title of his Τέχνη Ἰατρική, the best known of his works, was corrupted into *Tegni* or *Tegne*.

p. 110. Avicenna Canonem] Avicenna or Ibn-Sina, the famous Arabian philosopher and physician of the eleventh century, drew largely from the writings of the Greeks.

p. 110. Almagesti] See note on p. 18.

p. 110. Parthenium] A Greek poet, of whom a single line has come down to us in consequence of its adoption by Virgil into the *Georgics* (i. 437). He was Virgil's tutor in Greek. De Bury probably owed

Notes

his knowledge of him either to Macrobius (v. 17) or Aulus Gellius (xiii. 26).

p. 112. Theotokos] Nestorius, the Bishop of Constantinople, refused to apply the name Θεοτόκος, 'the Mother of God', to the Virgin Mary, and this heresy led to his deposition and to the separation of the Eastern and Western churches.

p. 112. Cyrillus] A great part of the life of St. Cyril, the Bishop of Alexandria, was devoted to a vehement and unscrupulous contest with Nestorius, whose deposition he finally effected at the Council of Ephesus in 431.

p. 114. Clemens quintus] At the Council of Vienne in 1312, Raymond Lully obtained from the Council a decree for the establishment of professorships of Greek, Hebrew, Arabic, and Chaldee in Rome, Paris, Oxford, Bologna, and Salamanca, at the expense of the Pope and the prelates.

p. 114. grammaticam] These grammars have unfortunately not been preserved: it need not be assumed from the phrase *providere curavimus* that de Bury wrote them himself. It is more likely that he did not.

p. 116. amor hereos] Despite Thomas's doubts, this is probably the correct reading. It may be compared with the phrase '. . . the loveres maladye of hereos. . .' in Chaucer's *Knight's Tale* (1374) where it is equated with the Greek *Ἔρως*. M.

p. 118. scorpio in theriaca] The *De Pomo*, a treatise on the immortality of the soul, was falsely attributed to Aristotle, being really translated from the Hebrew by Manfred, son of the emperor Frederick II. The quotation occurs in Holkot, *Super Sap.*, f. 154c.

p. 118. In line 15 'synderesim' is probably right. M.

p. 122. In line 8 Nelson suggests 'diasyntaxim': West proposes 'diasynthesim'. Altamura retains 'diasyntheticam'. M.

p. 126. Elefuga] A barbarous name for what we call the *pons asinorum*, which is explained by Roger Bacon, *Op. Tert.* ii. 21: 'Quinta propositio geometriae Euclidis dicitur Elefuga, id est fuga miserorum'.

p. 126. Filius inconstantiae] This passage, and particularly the name Crato, have been an insoluble puzzle to the editors. But I believe

189

Notes

that the source is the *De disciplina scholarium*, which was long attributed to Boethius. The writer says (c. iii) of the *filius inconstantiae*: 'Cratonis studiis tutius inhiabat, cuius semicirculi capacitas multis formidabat quaestionibus', so that at length the unhappy listener exclaims: 'Miserum me esse hominem! utinam humanitatem exuere possem et asinitatem induere!'

p. 126. With West and Nelson I read 'eveniet, necesse est', in line 24. M.

p. 128. *Turbat acumen*] Before books were paged the usual method of citing was to give two or three words, as here, to indicate the reference more exactly.

p. 128. in Ennio] Referring to the story told in Donatus's life of Vergil, c. xviii: 'Cum is aliquando Ennium in manu haberet, rogareturque quidnam faceret, respondit se aurum colligere de stercore Ennii.'

p. 138. *Nulla libris*] The lines are from the *Entheticus*, or introductory verses to the *Policraticon* of John of Salisbury, 269–272, 281, 282.

p. 140. In line 6 I have preferred to start a new sentence with 'Spes', matching those already beginning with 'Fides' & 'Caritas'. M.

p. 140. In line 20 I have followed West and Nelson in preferring the reading 'salubriter' in place of 'similiter'. M.

p. 148. In line 6 the reading 'tacitum', alluding to the silent scribe, would seem to make better sense: cf. Mynors: Cassiodorus *Institutiones*, p. 75. M.

p. 150. In the last line 'energia' must be wrong and 'euexia' [εὐεξία], as suggested by West and Nelson, has been substituted. M.

p. 156. emunctorio] This word, which is found in the dictionaries only in the sense of 'snuffers', is here obviously a pocket-handkerchief. [Thomas may be right, but the invention of this useful article is usually attributed to the reign of Richard II. M.]

p. 156. In line 10 I have followed West and Nelson in reading 'evident*er*'. M.

p. 156. eleemosynarium] The alms-bag, which 'in those days answered the purpose of what we call a pocket': Maitland, *Dark Ages*, p. 425. In this sense the feminine form was generally used (see Ducange, s.v.) and hence perhaps the reading *sacculum*.

Notes

p. 158. Latinista, ibi sophista] The students of the early colleges at Oxford were enjoined to use Latin in ordinary conversation, and might therefore be called *Latinistae*. In the third year of his residence the student of the liberal arts was allowed to become a 'sophister', and to take part in logical disputations. See Maxwell Lyte, *Hist. Univ. Oxford*, pp. 86, 205.

p. 158. lotio lectionem] Forks, of course, were not yet invented. The bishop may have had in his mind the maxim of the Schola Salernitana:

> 'Lotio post mensam tibi confert munera bina;
> Mundificat palmas et lumina reddit acuta.'

p. 168. .N.] The best manuscripts read .N., which probably stands for *Nomen* and signifies that some name was intended to be filled in. The ed. pr. omits it, but the Spires and Oxford editors print *nostra*, of which Hearne approves: Leland, *Collectt.*, iii. 385, vi. 299. On the question raised by the reading of the text, see the Introduction.

p. 170. cautione recepta] The practice of taking a pledge or bond on lending manuscripts was extremely common throughout medieval times.

p. 170. In line 17 the addition after inspectionem of 'et usum' (by Thomas) seems unnecessary; the book is to be examined within the walls of the college. M.

p. 172. West and Nelson prefer the reading 'Iunii' in line 12. The feast of St. Thomas is on 7 July, only six days after 1 July, but surely a week would be enough to carry out the check proposed here? M.

p. 180. Explicit Philobiblon] For the questions arising in connexion with the concluding note, which is not found in any of the printed texts, see the Introduction. From the phrase *praecise completo* it would appear that the book was finished on the Bishop's birthday.